THE
SOURTOE
COCKTAIL
CLUB

Other Books by Ron Franscell

Fiction

Angel Fire (1998)
The Deadline (1999)
The Obituary (2003)

Nonfiction

The Darkest Night (2008)
Crime Buff's Guide to Outlaw Texas (2010)
Delivered from Evil (2011)
Crime Buff's Guide to the Outlaw Rockies (2011)

THE SOURTOE COCKTAIL CLUB

The Yukon Odyssey of a Father and Son in Search of a Mummified Human Toe . . . and Everything Else

Ron Franscell

Guilford, Connecticut

Text design: Sheryl P. Kober
Layout: Joanna Beyer
Project editor: Ellen Urban

Library of Congress Cataloging-in-Publication Data

Franscell, Ron, 1957-
  The sourtoe cocktail club : the Yukon odyssey of a father and son in search of a mummified human toe– and everything else / Ron Franscell.
    p. cm.
  ISBN 978-0-7627-7156-1 (pbk.)
  1. Franscell, Ron, 1957- 2. Fathers and sons. I. Title.
  PS3556.R35189Z46 2011
  813'.54–dc23
  [B]
                                        2011024332

Printed in the United States of America

10 9 8 7 6 5 4 3 2 1

TO MY SON

CONTENTS

Halfway to Yesterday

Half of life is fucking up. The other half is dealing with it.
—HENRY ROLLINS

I don't really remember when I started dreaming about the Toe, except that it was sometime after I died and sometime before I began traveling in time.

It wasn't a proper death, of course, but my life stopped in every way when my twenty-year marriage imploded. Our undoing wasn't infidelity, money, or abuse; we had simply and sadly stopped believing in each other. We had evolved into strangers who slept together. And that's all I will say about that.

At the end, a few weeks before Christmas when there was no point in pretending for the children that we still loved each other, she asked me to leave. Since we had been running a small-town newspaper together, I suddenly had no job, no home, and no place to go. But I went. One frosty December day, I kissed my son and daughter good-bye and hit the road.

A few miles outside of the northern plains town where we lived, I pulled off the icy road and puked out my soul into the dirty snow. From that moment on, I was no longer a husband, a father, a friend, a neighbor. I belonged to nobody and no place. I was my own ghost.

I crash-landed in a $24-a-night fleabag on Colfax Avenue in Denver called the Bugs Bunny Motel and spent a frigid Christmas morning in the back booth of a cheerless IHOP, where I called my mother and cried for a long time. When my cash ran out, a friend—a sweet, single mom suffering through her own divorce—gave me a proper bed that thankfully wasn't stained and cratered by a thousand reckless fucks.

Eventually, my ghost took refuge on the road. I got a job at the *Denver Post,* driving more than a thousand miles a week, writing about the ethereal, timeless West—whatever or wherever that is. I bought a house up in the mountains, away from the city, but I was seldom there. I escaped the malignant undertow of my depression by driving around it, desperately seeking blue highways, working damn near every waking hour, eating countless bags of chocolate mini-doughnuts that routinely rode on my empty passenger seat, and always sleeping on the side of hotel beds farthest from the phone.

I drove more than 80,000 miles that first year, more than a lot of long-haul truckers. I often didn't know where I was going. No matter. I had lost almost everything in my life except my abiding faith that I could find a good story anywhere. I stayed just ahead of the black dog.

So I chased the ghost of Route 66, spent a few days with the subzero guests in an Arizona cryonics lab, found the scattered survivors of a Montana abortionist's thriving postwar baby trade, prayed in a sweat lodge with two tubby Crow Indian "warriors" where Custer died for our sins, got a sunburn in the safest spot in America, cavorted with naked freaks in the Nevada desert, and walked away unwounded from a white separatist militia compound in Idaho. I met visionaries, vagabonds, and vagrants. And, oh, I fell into a war on the other side of the world, too.

It turns out there's a brittle line between being completely free and being completely lost.

I was haunted by distance—both physical and emotional—so the pull of a long, straight road was mighty. Too many long, lonely, seemingly endless highways disappeared into the distance, beckoning me. I was addicted to the siren song of humming tires. If home is not just a house, but the place where I belong, I spent that year—or maybe even the decade since—not entirely sure where my home is, so any road might lead me there.

Destination and way.

Dysphoria and escape.

Ah, but the road occasionally led me back to Matt, who was only thirteen. I would rent a motel room for a few days at a time in the town where I no longer lived and watch my son play basketball, run a race, or just see a movie with him. He was beautiful to watch, a natural athlete whose mind always seemed one or two beats ahead of the action. Afterward, we often went to his favorite little Mexican place in town, where we talked about the games the way fathers and sons do, and every night I'd drop him off at his mother's house. My house, once.

I began to wonder, *What if I never came back?*

In happier times, Matt was our livewire. He was smart and athletic, practical sometimes, adventurous always.

One Thanksgiving long before the divorce, when we were still a family like other families, we went around the table and answered the question: What are you thankful for? I started, saying I was thankful for my family, for being together, for the time we had, and other patriarchal oratory. My wife was thankful for similar things. My daughter, maybe eight at the time, added her lengthy list of friends and possessions.

Then came four-year-old Matt. He was still thinking, but soon it dawned on him, this thing he was most thankful for in his so-far short life.

"Handles," he said.

Once, in junior high, he was invited to a friend's backyard party. For inexplicable reasons, the girls ended up climbing a tree while the preteen boys played grab-ass on the grass. But Matt broke away and wandered beneath the tree. He talked for a while to a pretty blond girl sitting on a limb. Then, in front of God, her giggling Munchkin posse, and his astonished buddies, he asked her to go steady.

To the girls, he instantly became a stud horse among colts. And the colts? Well, somebody had to spread the legend.

There was another time when we stopped at a spa in a small Wyoming town on a warm spring Saturday, snatching a little quality time in the amniotic waters. I'd been here as a child with my own family on rare, idyllic weekends when my stepfather had geared down enough to have fun. Time got all tangled up.

Matt, then six, was perched ten feet up on the high-diving platform . . . and almost thirty years back in my memory. The little guy wasn't much past Page One in the lessons of life. And the lesson this weekend was that the high-dive always looks lower from the shallow end.

So deceived, Matt decided to jump—but only if I'd tread water below, just in case. It is the same deal I'd made with my own stepfather, on the very same high-dive, three decades before. Satisfied I'd hold up my end of the bargain, Matt scrambled out of the pool and headed toward the platform in that stiff little run-walk kids do when the lifeguard hollers, "Don't run!" He spidered up the ladder and onto the flat square that must have seemed to him, at this moment, at least a mile above the green water.

From below, I coaxed him farther onto the jumping plank, and I heard my stepfather coaching me from the past.

"It's okay," he said. "Move out to the edge. Don't worry. You'll be okay. I'm right here. That's it, son."

And when I looked up, I saw a skinny little kid who looked like my son, but not him, standing on the platform, clutching the side rail. Brave enough to be standing there, not brave enough to jump, stuck between his stepdad and endless blue sky.

"Don't be afraid," the father says. "Just come out to the edge and jump feet first. That's all. It won't hurt. I'm right here for you."

And the son edged out a little closer to the edge of the plank, which suddenly looked to him as if it would buckle under the weight of a six-year-old.

"That's right. A little farther now. You're doing great, son. Easy now. See, I'm right here."

The little boy, so brave moments before, permitted himself a whimper and pondered whether it'd be wiser to leap or to step aside for the next diver. By now, a few swimmers were engrossed enough in the drama to watch furtively, not certain if they'd witness a triumph or a train wreck.

And Mom sat on the deck nearby, rendered superficially stoic behind her sunglasses, pretending not to be nervous. At this distance, you couldn't see she was biting her lip.

"The water's deep enough, you won't hit anything," the dad says in the tone a father reserves for the most genuine of moments with his son.

"After you do it, you'll want to do it again. That's the way it was for me. Honest."

Little feet edged nervously to the brink of the wet plank. In less time than it takes for a father to see himself in his son's eyes, the boy jumped. He didn't dare breathe or open his eyes, though it took only a second . . . or was it thirty years? . . . to splash down.

As the son paddled up through the effervescence of his own plunge into the unknown, he found his dad's hand reaching out to him under the water, true to his word.

"Great job, son!" my stepfather told me. "Ready to go again?"

And I jumped many times after that, and sometimes my dad was there, just in case.

"Great job, son!" I told Matt as we dog-paddled to the side of the deep water. "Ready to go again?"

"Will you be here?" he asked.

Always.

———•———

In the year after the split, Matt sprung a slow leak.

Where my soul had busted out in one spectacular hemorrhage, his was seeping out through hidden cracks. In a few years, he'd be as empty as I had become, but back then, I just didn't see it. I only saw him growing taller, his shoulders turning sinewy and brown, his voice changing. He was becoming a man, but part of me hoped he was not becoming his father, or his father's father.

My worst dreams were coming true. I was the estranged son of an estranged son, and I feared my son would grow up estranged, too. To my horror, my disjunctive family tree was sprouting a new branch, and it was higher than I could reach.

My daughter Ashley was on the verge of college, of becoming her own woman. The divorce gut-punched her, too, although she had more tools to repair herself, more hope for the next day, and the next. Nonetheless, I was no wiser about relieving her pain than my own.

But Matt needed a daily father more than ever as he navigated the perilous passage between child and man, between need and independence. I saw him often, but not every day. And for a long time, I could barely hold myself together, much less be a strong father to a boy who needed one. Or at least needed me to teach him how not to need me.

I convinced myself Matt needed me more than ever, but really, I needed him more than ever. And I wanted desperately to be needed. In fact, I couldn't see him oozing away because I wasn't really thinking about him. I was thinking about me.

Oh god, I'd give anything to go back in time and do it again until I got it right. But that's one place the road never goes. There's no going back.

We are all time-traveling on a one-way street.

———•———

I kept love at arm's length after that. No, in fact, I ran from it. It was the only exercise I got.

Women drifted through my suddenly single life, some more seriously than others, but none stayed. Or maybe I didn't stay. Most of our good-byes were rather vague, undefined. I just ran away from too many things, and no place was too far to run.

Oh, I wished I could love recklessly. I longed to fall deeply, madly, mindlessly in love with many of the women who opened their hearts to me, but something was broken in me. I don't know what it was. I'd never died before.

What I wanted most in my life since my divorce—to belong to a family again, to rediscover my place in the world—required emotional risks I was unwilling to take. Yeah, I leapt at the chance to cover a war in the Middle East, peered into the growling maw of a category 3 hurricane for a story, interviewed killers, and spent a sleepless, frigid night alone at a remote murder scene where two of my childhood friends met ghastly fates—but risking a committed relationship, or, more specifically, another painful ending? I didn't have the balls.

One day, I got an e-mail from a woman named Mary who had recognized my byline in the *Post*. She cheerfully laid out our history: Twenty-five years before, I was a twenty-year-old college kid working as a waiter in a fancy local nightspot in my hometown, and she was a teenybopper busgirl, barely out of junior high, with a feverish crush on me—but I didn't know it. Fact is, I didn't remember her or even know she existed. But we came from the same small town, and the fragile connection was enough to arrange to meet for dinner at a Cajun restaurant in Denver to talk about old times that only she recalled.

Mary had grown up to be a thirtysomething high school English teacher. That night, she wore a printed skirt with red roses and a white blouse. I don't know why I remember that. Over wine and étouffée, we talked about football, her cat and my dog, her teaching and my newspapering, how our paths had crossed at least twice before (unknown to me), books she had read and books I had written, and how she cared for her mother who had advanced Alzheimer's. Mary was good company.

Then suddenly, she leaned across the table and kissed me. It caught me off guard. I'd certainly been kissed before, but never by an English teacher.

"Where'd that come from?" I asked her.

"I've waited a long time to see what it would be like."

Patience is a strange virtue.

After dinner, we left the restaurant and walked the streets of Denver's LoDo District, maybe all of them. We stopped at a cheesecake bistro for dessert on the way, but mostly we just walked and talked about everything and nothing.

Somewhere around two a.m., we found ourselves back at the Cajun place's parking lot, where our cars were the only ones left. I kissed her good-night and watched her drive away before I began the hour-long trip back to my hermitage in the mountains.

And for the first time in a long, long while, the road seemed too long and my sanctuary was just an empty house.

That summer after my wife and I split forever, my son Matt came to Colorado for his first long visit. I was deliriously happy. I gave him his own room in my snug hundred-year-old Victorian in the Rockies because I wanted him to feel as if it were his home, too.

For dinner, we often barbecued on the back deck or walked to the local pizza joint where we fantasized about its legendary fourteen-pound pie that was free if two people could eat it in one sitting. We literally didn't have the guts for it.

And we did father-and-son stuff: fishing, hiking, ball games, four-wheeling on old mine roads, even panning for gold in the stream near my house. I wanted him to stay forever. I wanted to make plans for his growing up with me. I wanted back all the time I had already lost with him . . . but I knew he had to go back to his mother's home.

The last few nights of that first visit, I slept fitfully. *What if he never came back?* I dreamed up plans for the next visit, and the next, and the next, dangling the promise of adventure like a shiny lure. Since the road had become my sanctuary, maybe a road trip, just the two of us. Not Disneyland or Tombstone. Someplace mythical. Someplace beyond our grasp. Someplace we needn't share with every other father and son.

One night after Matt had gone to bed, I came across a trivial item in the darkest recesses of the Internet. The next morning, I fidgeted until he got up so I could tell him about this place way, way up north in the Yukon . . . *Yeah, a saloon in a town called Dawson, where they pour a special drink with a mummified human toe in it . . . yeah, a dead toe . . . and it has to touch your lips . . . yeah, your lips . . . a real corpse toe. They call it the Sourtoe Cocktail. Funny, huh?*

Four thousand freakin' miles, one way. So not too many people do it. No kidding. Wouldn't it be cool if . . .

Maybe because Matt was a teenage boy, the idea of a severed human toe in a glass of booze had double appeal. He was intrigued, and I promised to take him someday when he was old enough to walk into a bar with his old man. We laughed, then went fishing. A day or so later, he was gone and I cried alone in the dark of my old house.

But when he visited again at Thanksgiving, he casually mentioned the Toe over dinner. And again when he came for spring break. And again the next summer. The Toe became our adventure-to-be, a dream unlived, an imaginary journey we both embraced but never took. It was a fantasy too big, too far, too deep, too long, or just too damn surreal.

On second thought, maybe it was just safer to imagine a dead toe touching your lips than to actually do it.

———•———

A few years later, I left Colorado for a newspaper job in Texas. Mary, who'd become my closest friend, helped me pack up the Victorian and rode with me on the thousand-mile trip to Beaumont, an industrial bayou city on the muggy, buggy Gulf Coast, where the air tasted like a bad penny and more rain would fall in a weekend than Colorado would get in a whole year.

We stuffed my worldly possessions into a storage shed and Mary flew back to Denver, to her own home, to her job, to her life. If I had asked her to stay, she would have stayed. But I didn't ask, mostly because deep down I feared dying twice. I understood the consequences. I might never see her again.

That first night alone in a shabby local motel, aching and tired, I pondered every roadman's choice: It's not just the things you carry, but also the things you leave behind.

Before summer, I found a claustrophobic apartment where I slept fitfully on increasingly hot, humid nights. I grew accustomed to the prickle of sweat in the dark. I worked long hours and most weekends to avoid the place. Sometimes, when I couldn't sleep, I'd call Mary on the phone and talk about nothing. Mary wasn't the sort to make ultimatums, but we both knew the window of opportunity was closing. She spoke plainly about her wish to be closer to me, but despite my loneliness, I still pushed back.

"Isn't this all a little hasty?" I asked her.

"Maybe you haven't been thinking about it, but I have. A lot. I've known for a long time who I want to be with."

"You can't walk away from your career like that."

"I'm a teacher. I can work anywhere."

"You'd hate it here. The humidity, the bugs. It stinks. It's a long way from your family."

"You're there."

"But I can't promise I'll ever be the man you want me to be."

"You already are."

"I don't want to be married again. Ever."

"I know."

"I like my freedom. I don't want to be held down. I like being able to do what I want to do, when I want to do it."

"I know that, too."

"I can't change."

"I'm glad."

"I can hear it now, the first sign of trouble; you'd blame me for ruining your life."

"I'm a big girl. It'd be my choice. It's my life."

That night, I'd spent all my inane arguments, and I'd had my fill of being alone. And it had been a long, long time since anyone—including myself—believed in me the way Mary did. It felt a little like . . . well, like a distant memory.

"Okay, it's your choice," I told her. "I tried to be honest. If you want to come here, I won't say no . . . and I gotta admit, it'd be nice to see you again. Honest. I've missed you."

The next day, she put her house up for sale.

Five years after the Toe began floating through my deadened dreams, Matt embarked on his own road. He drove himself to his freshman year at college in Lincoln, Nebraska, ten long hours from his mother's home in Wyoming. He'd never driven so far alone before, and in myriad ways, he wasn't entirely sure where he was going. So I told him to call me from the road if he got bored or tired or just wanted to talk.

Matt called three times that long day. The last time, about sundown and still a couple hours from Lincoln, he sounded exhausted. So we just talked, mostly about nothing.

"This is a big thing you're doing," I told him. "Excited?"

"Not really."

"Nervous?"

"A little."

"Nebraska's a good school. You'll meet a lot of cool people."

"Yeah."

"Some of them will be girls."

"Yeah, maybe."

"You don't like girls?"

"They're okay."

"Thought any more about a major?"

"Nah. That's what college is for."

And so it went: I told him how I loved him, how I wanted him to succeed, how he'd grow confident, how he'd meet lots of girls, how I couldn't believe he'd grown so fast to be a man . . .

He grunted. I meant it all, but mostly I wanted to keep him on the phone, to know he was awake. Alive.

During a lull in my one-sided conversation, he finally spoke a single meaty sentence.

"I've been thinking all day," Matt said, "about the Sourtoe Cocktail."

I was speechless. By god, he'd had the dreams, too. And in a moment no longer than it takes to awake from a long nightmare, I knew we'd go.

And what if we never came back?

Lighting Out

It's hard to make a comeback when you haven't been anywhere.
—WRITTEN IN THE DUST ON THE BACK OF A BUS
IN CHEYENNE, WYOMING

I almost slept through the very first morning of my rebirth.

I had planned an early escape. I wanted to be on the road in time to avoid the rush hour in Dallas, five hours away, and maybe get as far as Kansas before the day was over.

The first leg of my trip is solo. I will pick up Matt in Wyoming, fifteen hundred miles away, where he spends his summers working for his mom's new live-in boyfriend on a construction crew. (I hate going there. Nobody seems to understand the agony of being forced to see what once was mine—a workbench, a picture on the wall, an easy chair, a bed, a woman—converted to another lover's use.)

But all night, I just skidded across the slippery surface of slumber, obsessively peeping at the green glow of the clock radio on the nightstand . . . *One-thirty . . . two-oh-seven . . . two-forty . . . three-ten . . .* until I finally shoved its smug little beaming face to the wall.

Without my hearing aids I can't hear for squat, but I was inexplicably aware of distant whistles blaring as night trains made empty crossings every half-hour in the muggy darkness, and an insomniac dog barked at shadows across the drainage canal out back. I heard the incessant tick-tick-ticking of the brass ball chain against the globe on the unbalanced ceiling fan, and the rasping of bugs in the trees, and the rhythmic whisper of blood against my gimpy eardrums, and the soughing of my own breath. Other than that, I couldn't hear anything.

Irritated, I slip out of bed and pour myself one glass of Panamanian rum to douse whatever fires still burned, and another to numb myself. It burns as it goes down, and I feel the prickle of sudden sweat on my skin as I lay back on the lukewarm sheets in the dark. The rum settles my mind, softens the sleeplessness, makes me think of another long journey, of another father and another son, of a plum-colored night far away, of broken angels and the howlers on the morning side . . .

I sleep. I must have dreamed, too. When I finally roll out of bed after ten in the morning, Mary pours me a cup of strong coffee and tells me I was talking in my sleep.

"What did I say?"

"You didn't make any sense," she says. "You were looking for something."

"What was it?"

"A shovel key."

"What the hell is a shovel key?"

"I don't know," she says. "It was your dream, sweetie. I was just eavesdropping. I didn't even know shovels had keys."

I'm pretty sure they don't. I Google it anyway.

I don't believe dream-stories are anything more than a brain's way of making sense out of haphazard electrical sparks popping across randomly firing synapses—albeit sometimes with serendipitous results. I don't remember last night's dream about the cryptic shovel key, but I suddenly realize I've forgotten to pack something for our plunge into the North American wilderness, where we planned to camp.

An hour later, I am still rummaging in my own garage, ripping through moving boxes never unpacked, sweaty and pissy. The Subaru is outside, already loaded with enough gear for a three-week, ten-thousand-mile adventure to the Arctic and back. And I can't find my camp shovel.

For ten months, I'd cached the stuff we'd need—toiletries, sleeping bags, canned goods, my many-pocketed war jacket, bug dope, guidebooks, GPS, underwear, tools, sunscreen, digital voice recorder, maps, favorite CDs, cameras, batteries, first-aid supplies, hatchet, and other necessaries. Then a stray dream wanders through my rummy brain about a nonexistent shovel key and I realize that somehow my camp shovel never made the list.

I've already wasted this muggy June morning, good driving time on a long journey toward my son, looking for it. My mild pique has turned to obsession. Sure, I could pick one up for five bucks at the war surplus store on my way out of town, or in a hundred burgs I'll pass on the way, but right now, at this very moment, I want *my* freaking shovel!

I can't find it anywhere. Maybe it didn't survive the divorce either.

Shovel-less, I close the garage, and, in a huff, make sure all the Subaru's tie-downs are tight. It's after noon and I am already hours late for the road. A sluggish breeze as hot and pungent as dog's breath rolls off Beaumont's refineries and chemical plants and roils the few driveway redbuds that survived the last hurricane. Thirty years ago, college girls here couldn't wear nylon stockings outdoors because mysterious chemicals in the polluted air literally melted them off their legs.

I open all four of the Subaru's doors to drain off the boiling air inside. Before I get in, I kiss Mary good-bye and call Matt on his cell phone. He's at a job site, carrying concrete forms for his mom's boyfriend.

"I'm about to hit the road," I tell him. "I should be there in a few days. Crack of dawn Tuesday. You packed?"

"Mostly. I don't need that much."

"Well, don't forget your passport. And a coat. And money. And please have everything ready. I don't want to fart around there."

"Relax, dude. I got it all. I'll be ready."

"One more thing . . ."

"Yeah?"

"Could you get your hands on a camp shovel?"

"Why do we need a shovel?"

I really don't have an answer. Or a shovel. Or a shovel key, whatever the hell that is. All I have is a dream I can't remember, and it would sound silly—or insane—to explain it.

"I don't know," I say. "We'll be camping out. Just in case, I guess. A little shovel can't hurt, can it?"

———— • ————

Not yet on the road, barely to the end of my own driveway, Sydney pipes up.

Sydney is my new GPS, a gift from Mary, who apparently feared I'd lose the road somewhere in the Yukon wilderness and never find my way back to her. Sydney, bless her silicon heart, is Mary's surrogate. Her cool, controlled, kinda sexy Australian voice eases me, as if I had a passenger riding shotgun, keeping watch on the map. She's good company on the road. She finds her answers in the stars. And she cares most about where I am, a little about where I am going, and not at all about where I've been.

"Please drive the highlighted route," Sydney advises, and I do, but I know this way by heart. It's just nice that Sydney—and the stars—agree.

The road speaks to me, too. Not in a voice, but in the rhythms of white lines, bridges, distant towns with their water towers and team pride spelled out in white rocks on nearby bluffs, the far-off virga rains that never touch the ground, passing cars, sunsets and sunrises, the road-killed birds who always seem to die with one wing in the air, mile markers, radio stations that come and go, the mysterious white buckets that proliferate in the barrow pits, the trill of meadowlarks through the open window, the seams in the asphalt keeping time . . . Old roads are like old friends, familiar and undemanding.

Most of these first thousand miles are familiar to me. I've traveled these same highways before: Texas 51 to Conroe, I-45 to Dallas, I-35 to Salina, I-70 to Denver, I-25 to . . . well, places that were once my home.

Road food is part of the charm of a great adventure, but not the adventure itself. Let the supercilious Anthony Bourdain mug his way through poached rice-field rats and crunchy whole fried sparrows in Burma or smoked cow's lung in Colombia. Give me a late porterhouse, chicken toes, and a loaded baked potato at Two Frogs Grill in Ardmore, Oklahoma. An early frozen custard and a steak burger at Freddy's in Salina, Kansas. Some takeout chicken for the cooler from the historic Al's Chickenette in Hays. A package of six preservative-stoked chocolate mini-doughnuts and a pop from a c-store in Russell, boyhood home of Bob Dole. A bag of teriyaki beef jerky from a mom-and-pop in Kanorado, which perches lightly on the Kansas-Colorado line . . . comfort foods that will, in time, kill me all over again.

It's not that I lack an adventurous gut. I'll eat anything once. I've dined on bushmeat (monkey) in Southeast Asia, grilled pigeons in Cairo, broasted grasshoppers and earthworm pie in Wyoming (on a dare) and rattlesnake kebabs in Texas. I've choked down durian, a pungent Malaysian fruit that stinks worse than a dead man's feet and has thus been banned on Bangkok buses. I once ordered spotted dick without even knowing what it was. Criminy, bull testicles just don't seem that exotic anymore.

No, I prefer to eat like the natives wherever I go, especially overseas, but there's always an air of anticipation and even a curious formality at those meals, requiring focus and thought. On the American road between Here and There, I prefer the informality and efficiency of, well, eating like the natives. The chances are pretty good that infinitely more indigenous Midwesterners will be eating Aunt Fannie's meat loaf, green beans, and peach cobbler tonight, not free-range kung pao chicken or stewed bats. It's even getting hard to find good squid jerky in Cedar Rapids.

Besides, there's always something else unexpected and peculiar on the road: swarms of swirling fireflies in Oklahoma pastures, the green-glowing carpet of young shoots in a Kansas field, an Impressionist summer sunset refracted through a thousand bug corpses kamikaze'd against a pixelated windshield, the one-armed toll-taker whose "good" hand was missing all its digits. I wonder, *What possesses a one-armed, fingerless human to choose a career in grasping?*

I pass the exit to Vesper, Kansas. I make note of this town's lyrical name for a future story, maybe set in West Texas—Vesper, Texas—about the blues, about fathers and sons, about sunsets and prayers, about looking backward, hoping to find where you lost the road. Another story for someday. God, I already have too many stories for someday, and I only type with two fingers.

But I write it down anyway in the little notebook I carry most of the time. You just never know.

———————

Too many people are geographic idiots.

Most Americans couldn't identify the State of Iowa on an unlabeled map, much less Iraq. The average American's geographical proficiency consists of giving directions straight to Hell for anyone who says Joe Sixpack is a geography retard. Just don't ask him to draw a map.

I'll admit that my notion of geography—roads, distances, borders, topography, distinct cultures, and such—is so twentieth-century. In our virtual world—and only there—Manhattan is infinitely closer to Berlin, Germany, than to Toad Suck, Arkansas (a real place, by the way).

In the old days, how humans were arranged physically in time and space was important to our self-knowledge and world-view, but the Internet is a separate, infinite, alien world where there are no boundaries, no mile markers, no horizon. Scale is nonexistent, at least in our picture-book brains, and distance is not a measure of space but of dissimilarity. In this artificial land-scape, great settlements are built from data, and we can perceive with only two senses—sight and hearing. Borders and roads are immaterial, maybe fictional. And we are safely ensconced behind our fortress walls of glass, plastic, and circuit boards, breathing our safe, familiar air. We are Palahniuk's chickenshit peak-boosters, time-travelers who can't get dirty.

Maybe if "there" is a vague concept, then so is "here." Can we truly appreciate home without knowing something about the world beyond? Worse, if we wander away from the place where we belong, can we find our way back without knowing where the sun sets, how the stars align, or even where the road goes?

Who am I fooling here? It is precisely the unknown that makes me want to go, as much as it is the unknown that makes others want to stay. It is the possibility of stumbling upon some-thing amazingly unexpected that drives me. A true traveler yearns for an extraordinary surprise, the gift of different light.

I prefer dust and dead ends and maps that can never be refolded right. I want to smell, taste, and feel a place, to absorb it.

I want to stand in places where great people have stood . . . and where nobody has ever stood before. I want to feel the grinding road-weariness of a great adventure, not lament the stiffness in my clicking finger.

I have a bit of the tumbleweed in me, and I love any wind that blows.

———•———

The road sign isn't much, but looking across the flat plains of eastern Colorado from the highway, the Genoa Wonder Tower looks like a popular place. The parking lot is full, and I can see a woman in a red dress on the widow's walk, her skirt fluttering in the afternoon breeze.

Seduced, I exit and follow the signs to the Tower, of which I'd heard tales but never stopped.

I get out of the car and almost immediately sidestep a pile of dog shit. A similar-sized lump of chump starts to take shape in my gut when I look around. Somebody has propped up crude dummies in the Tower's windows. Somebody has parked rows of junked cars sunken into the prairie-dirt parking lot to lure curious travelers who can't stand to be left out of the party. Somebody suckered me in.

Somebody is Jerry Chubbuck. This local character (with his wife Esther's help) has run the place for more than forty years. He's the beaming seventy-something mug waiting at the door.

"I don't fool easy," I say, a little abashed, "but you got me."

"Well, you're here now," Jerry says. "Might as well have a good time."

Inside, Jerry plays a game of "guess what" with me. If I can identify ten oddball items from his vast collection of artifacts—many of them twice-dumped junk, liberated from abandoned garbage dumps—he'll give me back my dollar admission. I'm stumped right off the bat by the camel nose bells. Unless one is intimately familiar with obscure crap like old-fashioned razor-blade sharpeners, dinosaur turds, walrus penises, or rooster eye-glasses, it's best to just pay the buck and start the tour.

The cockeyed Tower is simultaneously an anal-retentive's worst nightmare and a pack rat's unsurpassed orgasm. Every square inch of its twenty-two rooms is a weird discovery waiting to happen, a jubilee of rubbish. Mutants and monsters in mayonnaise jars. The world's worst diorama of Wild Bill Hickok's last card game. A collection of art so bad a blind man wouldn't hang it. More rust than a battalion of forgotten Tin Woodmen.

And talk about clinking, clanking, clattering collections of caliginous junk: A sharp-eyed visitor might spy the advertisement for a Roy Rogers Restaurant tacked up by Roy Rogers himself, or a nineteenth-century old sidewalk brick from Hutchinson, Kansas, warning pedestrians not to spit on the sidewalk. And it's hard to miss the two hundred and fifty dented milk cans, twenty thousand authentic arrowheads and Indian tools, and fifty thousand old bottles and jars. The Tower just might be the Louvre of empty glassware.

But, damn, the Talking Indian Mummy is gone. I'd heard about this artifact and I was perversely fascinated by him, or the promise of him. Long ago, Jerry had wired the musty old guy with a tinny radio speaker just to twit gawkers who might lean a little too close. It seems some Indian tribe wanted their dead guy back, so the feds came and got him. He will talk no more forever.

In fact, Genoa, Colorado, is a trifling prairie village of 187 souls, give or take, that could comfortably sit in the parking lot at Mile High Stadium (aka Invesco Field) 100 miles up the road in Denver. But it doesn't.

Instead, it has existed for the past 120 years on an unusual bump in the high plains. Not a huge bump, mind you, but enough of a bump that Genoa (pronounced *jen-OH-uh*) can claim fairly confidently to be the highest point on a straight (and generously wide) line between New York City and Denver.

Surprisingly, Genoa—at 5,607 feet above sea level—is 327 feet higher than Denver, the Mile High City. But a few more miles beyond Denver, the Rockies begin their abrupt ascent to more than 14,000 feet, so discretion being the better part of valor, Genoa doesn't claim to be anything more than a modestly high flatland town eighty miles from the Kansas border.

Ah, but it isn't Genoa's geography that is enigmatic.

In the early years of the last century, a quirky Kansas railroader named Charley Gregory often passed this wide spot on the highway that would someday be called U.S. 24, one of the original federal highways (which included Route 66), and slithered from Pontiac, Michigan, to Grand Junction, Colorado.

Route 24 was commissioned only ten years after Pancho Villa's brigands attacked a small town in neighboring New Mexico, and during Prohibition, it was a popular route for bootleggers. So the West it penetrated was still wild enough, still mythical enough in 1926 to frighten or entice potential travelers. On this slender, 1,540-mile river of concrete, macadam, and white paint, every traveler was an explorer.

And explorers needed food, water, a place to bed down, a place to pee. Charley imagined that this nearly invisible bump on Colorado's inexorably flat eastern plains would be perfect for a "one stop"—a roadside oasis where travelers could find a meal, a tank of ethyl, a lumpy bed, postcards, a map drawn in the dust, a bus, a dark parking lot for backseat sex, a shot of rotgut, and anything else a high-plains wanderer might need, such as, oh, a rattlesnake pit, a prairie dog town, and a fellow standing in a six-story tower shouting through a megaphone at passing cars. You know, the usual roadside attraction.

Gregory was one of those eccentric dreamers descended from colorful folks. His great-great-great-grandfather Bry Gregory was an enormous man, a Revolutionary War veteran who called himself Old Cuss, and, according to a family history, provoked his own end.

"A thunderstorm arose and lightning struck close to his house," the unknown historian wrote. "Old Bry went to the door, raised his arm in defiance of the Almighty, ripped out a big oath, cursed God and called on Him to 'Try Old Cuss a pop.' The words had hardly left the old man's lips when lightning struck him and he fell into the yard. His shoes were torn from his feet and the old man struck dead in a moment of time.

"It is needless to add that this dreadful end had a very sobering effect on others who might have been inclined to trifle with the Almighty."

Thirty years after the Almighty separated Bry Gregory from his shoes and his mortal coil, Charley was born. The year was 1876, when Custer died for our sins, Bailey joined Barnum in the circus business, Wyatt Earp and Bat Masterson became cops in Dodge City, the James Gang was routed in Northfield, Minnesota, and Colorado became the thirty-eighth state.

Ah, but more importantly to the story of Charley Gregory, 1876 is also the year that a grumpy European embryologist named Karl Ernst von Baer died at age eighty-four, shortly after he declared that all new and significant ideas must survive three stages: first, being rejected as piffle; second, being rejected as anti-God; and third, finally being celebrated as absolutely true—most especially by the people who bitched the most about it in the first place.

You see, Charley was a dreamer. He imagined things nobody else could imagine or understand. He was destined for great things.

You might not know it if you'd passed him on the street. Charley grew up a pudgy kid in western Kansas. He married his prairie sweetheart, Ethel Mae, moved to Goodland, where he took work as a tinner in the Rock Island Railroad and worked his way up to engineer in the waning days of the Wild West, when trains were still being robbed by outlaws known as Butch, Black Jack, and Flat Nose. And very quickly, the first of his six children was born.

He also suffered in the most ordinary way. Charley was only twenty-five years old when one of his children, a daughter named Mae after her mother, died of cholera shortly after her first birthday. No family historian ever recorded the depth of Charley's grief over his daughter's premature death. Maybe he died a little, too. All that's known is that he continued to drive his trains, wherever they would go, as far as anyone could see and beyond. He had certainly been loosened from his moorings, and the rails of the open West were the only place he could defy gravity.

Charley and Ethel Mae's oldest son, Verle, grew up to be a stout young man. He enlisted in the U.S. Marines in the first days of World War I and was much decorated as a Corps wrestler. But Verle died young, too. He wasn't yet thirty when he died on a veterans hospital operating table.

That's when Charley began to trifle with the Almighty. In his secret shop, he began to tinker with a "perpetual motion machine" that would generate a strange "Power" without any more fuel than irrepressible, never-ending movement. Who knew better than Charley the restorative power of motion? In stillness, the traveler knew, was nothingness.

He showed his peculiar device to a few friends, even pondered selling stock. One of Charley's more mechanically minded pals later said the machine would have revolutionized power generation if properly engineered, but the "Power" it generated in Charley's dark little shop was uncontrollable and dangerous.

Charley knew it. He junked his curious contraption, telling a friend it was "too dangerous to become publicly known."

Then in 1926, when Ethel Mae was only forty-seven years old, she died after a long sickness, too, and Charley buried her beside their little daughter in the Goodland cemetery. This time, the trains weren't enough. Charley's frayed tether snapped.

So Charley Gregory, wizard of perpetual motion, trifler of the Almighty and defyer of gravity, left everything and lit out for Colorado, to an unusual bump he knew in the grand empty plains, where he had an idea that he might help fellow travelers, other drifters, anybody who might stop.

But Charley wasn't content to build your typical café / service station / bus stop / saloon / museum / truck stop / dance hall / motor court / gift shop / rattlesnake pit. No, he also shaved a few inches off the highest spot on a straight line between New York City and Denver and erected the one and only Genoa World's Wonder View Tower on the new U.S. Route 24—one of the world's lesser wonders, to be sure, but still, one of the rare locales in the expansive American West where, on a clear day (he claimed), one might see parts of six different states.

Six stories above the prairie floor, Charley swore it was possible to see Colorado (of course), Kansas (only eighty miles), Nebraska (indistinguishable from Kansas), and the distant mountains of Wyoming, South Dakota, and New Mexico.

Some customers were dubious, since those peaks were more than two hundred miles distant, so Charley reportedly invited experts from the U.S. Geological Survey and the esteemed cartoonist Robert Ripley of *Believe It or Not* fame to substantiate his farsightedness, so to speak.

Without getting into finer technical details about atmospheric refraction, Pythagorean math, and the frequency of sucker births, Ripley drew a cartoon about the Tower and the USGS installed a government marker confirming the Tower's observation deck to be exactly 5,751 feet. Naturally, Charley soon posted a sign that said CONFIRMED BY RIPLEY!,[1] and that seemed to satisfy folks they were getting an authentic glimpse of six states for the price of admission—a nickel.

Even today, the Wonder Tower's steps are neither for the fainthearted nor the big-butted. In some places, the passageway is only seventeen inches wide as the climber ascends toward the lowest layer of outer space that lies somewhere under the rainbow, where Charley wasn't in Kansas anymore but he could still see it. If he could also see parts of five other states, well, that was just good for business.

Through his spyglass on the sixth floor, Charley could discern the license plates of cars rumbling down old U.S. 24, and when they'd pass the Wonder Tower, a mellifluous voice from the heavens—Charley on a megaphone—would thunder, "Hey, Buckeye State, slow down and have a soda pop!" or "Pull in here, Missourah, and I'll show you a one-eyed pig!"

Charley, the prairie wizard who came to be known as the P. T. Barnum of Colorado, gathered stones from every state and a few territories to build his merry outpost, and added rooms like a mad Pueblo Indian architect for years. He collected Indian artifacts, guns, and stuffed freaks like two-headed calves and eight-footed pigs for his roadside museum, and remodeled the interior into imitation caverns.

When a hard-luck Indian woman started waiting tables in his greasy spoon, huckster Charley gave her a new name—Princess Raven Wing—a fairy-tale history, and a paintbrush that she used to create a thousand pictographs on the rock walls before she disappeared back into obscurity, maybe on the same late-night bus that had brought her.

---

1. Believe it or not, the archives at Ripley's Believe It or Not, now an international conglomerate that profits nicely from people's incredulity, still contain Robert Ripley's cartoon about Charley Gregory's World's Wonder View Tower, published on January 23, 1933. There's no evidence Charley's claims were "confirmed" at all, just repeated—but because Ripley's illustrated trivia was widely accepted as fact, Charley and his Tower were both legitimized and made famous in one fell swoop.

And the people came to see the wizard. Each was seeking something. Not atonement, courage, or family, but a sip of water, a tank of gas, or the redemptive blessing of seeing Eden's snakes caged. Oh, and an alleged glimpse of six states.

Nothing lasts forever. During the winter of 1943, Charley froze his foot and infection set in. Doctors told him to slow down and give it a chance to heal, but Charley put his faith only in perpetual motion. Gangrene set in. Doctors amputated one of Charley's legs to forestall the infection, but it was too little, too late. A few days after the big Fourth of July party at the Tower in 1943, Charley died. He was only sixty-six.

The perpetual-motion machine known as Charley Gregory had stopped. If ever a wiz there was, suddenly there wasn't.

He had already dug his own grave down in a copse of scrub cedar a couple hundred yards from the Tower, but the state wouldn't allow such a makeshift burial. So his son escorted Charley's body on the Rocket—what the locals called the Rock Island line—back to Goodland, where he was buried in a bureaucratically acceptable grave beside his beloved wife and child.

It's hard to know where Charley belonged. Maybe he didn't know himself. At any rate, Charley was past caring.

Despite the prosperity of the postwar boom in road trips, Charley's magnificent tower fell on hard times that got even harder when Interstate 70 bypassed it. Over the years, the café closed, the motel tumbled down, the service station quit pumping gas, the buses stopped coming, and long-haul truckers stuck to the superslab. New owners came and tired owners went until all that remained was the Tower, still keeping watch over six states even when nobody was looking.

Like Charley, U.S. 24 is just a ghost today. Along much of its length, this fossil road is haunted by the ghosts of mom-and-pop filling stations, diners, tourist courts, lunch counters, and watering holes where travelers cooled their overstimulated radiators and filled canvas water bags for the continuing journey. Once-vigorous outposts of American entrepreneurial spirit and pre-franchise novelty, their tumbledown husks stand mutely along the abandoned way, ceilings open to the sky. In places like Genoa, amid the broken glass, rusty cans, strewn car parts, bottle caps, and old mattresses flensed of their ticking, only field mice make a living off old Route 24 now.

But the Genoa Wonder Tower still exists. It has outlasted quirky visionary Charley Gregory and the road itself. It remains a splendid roadside freak show, even by the larger-than-life, neon-splashed standards of Route 66. I mean, where else can you go to see *six* states and *three* two-headed calves *and* an albino rattlesnake for a buck?

———•———

As I climb the absurdly catawampus ladder that leads to the Tower's topmost floor, I say a little prayer for myself. I'm too old to be risking my life just to determine if it's genuinely possible to see six states from a brilliantly eccentric man's badland belfry, and too young to die at a cheesy roadside attraction. However, it's comforting to know there's at least one unused grave on the premises.

And let's be frank: The absurdly ballyhooed suggestion of seeing six states is not as thrilling as it might have been in the Jazz Age or even the Depression, before we could Google down on any square foot of the Earth from satellites in space, complete with digitized borders, GPS coordinates, and the occasional nude sunbather who thought only God could see.

To be honest, the Tower's view on a good day like today is merely whelming, neither under- nor over-. Standing with Jerry Chubbuck's makeshift mannequins in the upper-level winds of the Colorado plains, I can see an arguably crowded Colorado parking lot (but not the pile of dog shit by my car) right below me, and what I presume to be Kansas on the eastern horizon. After that, it gets a little fuzzy. No Black Hills, no Tetons, no Sangre de Cristos. No sparkling spires of distant cities, no grand lakes or rivers, no state lines painted across the landscape. Just endless prairie to the east, north, and south, and the thin blue line of the Rockies to the west.

Was it worth a dollar's admission just to stand here and wonder why it was so important anyway? Is it better to *see* far or to *go* far? How would life be different if I could genuinely spy six states from the top of a decaying tower built by a beautiful oddball who believed it was more dangerous to trifle with perpetual motion than the Almighty? Would my life have been better or worse if I had just sped past? Is there a Coke machine downstairs?

Yeah, I suppose it was worth a buck; the two-headed calves and the dinosaur turds were just a charming bonus. And in the existential tug-of-war between knowing and not knowing, I tend to think knowing is better, even if the thing I know is meaningless. But who knows what we need to know?

I don't know a lot of stuff—how to make love stay, exactly how harmony works, whether you are more likely to be killed by a flying champagne cork or a poisonous spider—so I often feel the urge to change the subject.

But sometimes, I just know. And because I stopped at the Genoa Wonder Tower, I know these things:

People laugh at dreamers, but nobody remembers scoffers. If you want to be immortal, dream.

Like the Talking Indian Mummy, the dreamer Charley Gregory found his way home, which isn't always where you live. Princess Raven Wing probably never did, but sometimes it's more romantic to be a wandering ghost.

And no matter where I go, some dog is gonna shit where I'll step in it.

I gotta go now. It's the shank end of the afternoon, hours before moonrise, and the road waits. Miles to go, and all that. I sidestep the pile of dog shit again and get back in the car.

As I roll out of the dusty lot, back to the less-traveled junction with I-70, I call Matt on the cell phone, but it goes straight to voice mail. I don't know why I called. I don't know what to say. I don't know why I feel lonely.

But this trip is just beginning, so I don't even know everything I don't know yet.

————•————

Late on my second long day of driving, just a few hours past the rust-black hole of the Wonder Tower, I cross the invisible boundary between the place I have always considered home and the outside world: the Wyoming state line.

No matter what marvelous places I've been, or how long it's been since I've actually lived in Wyoming, I am always strangely comforted to cross this threshold. It is home . . . *heartearth*. It is not just a matter of place, but of belonging. Some journeys take you farther from where you come from, but closer to where you belong. This journey, in some small way, is to find my way back to where I belong.

In Cheyenne, I meet my friend, David, for dinner at an Applebee's out on Dell Range Boulevard. Over burgers and fries, we talk about journeys of many kinds.

David tells me how his mother recently remarked about a mysterious moment in his life "when we lost you." He didn't ask what she meant, but being, on balance, a good kid for his forty-five years, it bothered him. He had never felt lost. He'd never even felt mildly astray. What did it mean to be *lost,* and how could he not have noticed? Had he secretly fallen from grace? Had he strayed from his parents' plans for him? Had he curled himself into an imperceptible shell that even he couldn't see? Had the child just become a man?

I was an unintentional lost boy, too.

My mother and stepfather would say they lost me when I quit college at the United States Naval Academy at Annapolis (and its "free" college education) to become a newspaperman instead of a naval officer. Of course, I didn't know I was lost to them at that moment, but I had certainly wandered beyond their grasp, diverged from their path.

My mother's disapproval simmered like a low-grade fever in her. One day while I was still a college kid, I made the mistake of revealing a dream. I told her that, someday, I wanted to run my own small-town newspaper.

She harrumphed. My own mother harrumphed.

"Why set yourself up for disappointment?" she asked curtly.

Eventually, I put myself through civilian college in Wyoming, got my journalism degree. I never once considered that disappointment is why my mom and stepdad seldom called or wrote to me for many years after that, and didn't attend my wedding a month after I graduated from journalism school.

If my mother had dreams of her own, she never spoke of them. I suspect she once dreamed fantastic dreams, especially when she first loved. But when the baggage of disappointment weighed her down, she shed her uncarryable, useless dreams. Being a mother, she would rather her son live a dreamless life than to be freighted with disappointment. So in a perverse way, she was trying to protect me.

Her plan didn't work in either case. I became a newspaperman, and I have been hurt. Even now, I dream a lot, but I still drag my failures around behind me like an old leather bag I just can't seem to throw out.

Thank God for handles.

***

The road between Cheyenne and Casper—Wyoming's two biggest towns—is 170 miles long, unless there's a headwind. Then it's much longer.

You pass only five smaller towns—fewer than ten thousand people if every man, woman, and child in all five towns gathered for a box social in the same place—in the three-hour drive through these wind-scraped badlands. Out here, the intermittent ranch houses, plunked down randomly in the middle of nowhere, tend to be farther apart than New York City and Poughkeepsie. And this is one of Wyoming's more-populous corridors.

You see more snow fences, pronghorn antelope, and broken-down windmills than cars. You also pass a few mobile homes with old tires on their roofs, as if vulcanized rubber were a talisman (or simply a weight) against the ceaseless, intense prairie gales. Billboards are sparse because the wind, which might blow sixty miles an hour on a casual day, would yank them out by the roots.

It's summer now, thankfully. The worst snowstorms blow in from the Arctic north in April, often around Easter, and when they do, this stretch of road is the first to close, mostly because it is so desolate and treacherous that a snow-blinded driver can easily disappear in the horizontal wet plaster of a whiteout and not be found until the thaw.

Civilization did the best it could against the forces of nature in this part of the world. Sometimes civilization simply went elsewhere.

Between the tiny, sandblasted town of Chugwater and the slightly larger sandblasted town of Wheatland, the wind funnels through a gap in the Laramie Mountains and slices incessantly across I-25 like a hurricane passing through a soda straw. The highway department has erected bright orange wind socks on the roadside as a warning. In literally hundreds of trips along this stretch, I have never—not once—seen them drooping flaccid.

This day is no different. The swollen wind socks protrude indecently. And there, tits-up in the barrow pit, is a thirty-foot Airstream trailer, its gleaming silver shell crumpled when it was literally ripped from its hitch and bowled over by a gale-force gust.

A Nebraska fella—I can tell by the license plate on his cherry-red Ford F350, the bright red 'Husker ball cap on his head, and the red-lettered OKLAHOMA SUCKS T-shirt stretched across his prodigious belly—stands with his shell-shocked wife on the oily shoulder, their backs to the growling wind, which is still running full out.

I pull over and get out of my Subaru. The wind is blowing so hard that it's difficult to open the door, and when I do, I get a face full of Wyoming grit.

"Everybody okay?" I ask as I walk up.

"Yeah," the guy says in a loose Midwestern drawl that's nearly drowned out by the squall. "Looks badder than it is. But the vacation is all fucked up."

"Carl . . . ," his wife cautions. She's holding a tissue in her shaking hand and looks as if she's about to burst into tears at any second, but for the moment, it takes all her energy and balance just to keep from being swept off the edge of the Earth by the next big gust.

"Pardon my French," Carl says.

Carl isn't a young man. His rumpled reddish neck suggests he's an angry farmer. He wears a clunky old hearing aid behind his right ear and old-fashioned horn-rimmed Buddy Holly glasses. His faded jeans with a chew ring on the back pocket sag perilously because he has no ass to help his belt hold them up. He takes off his 'Husker cap and wipes a big, weathered hand across the clammy, fallow field of his scalp.

His agitated wife glances at him, then back at the wrecked trailer, then back at him, like a puppy looking for some sign of what to do next. Carl just splurts a syrupy glob of tobacco that's blown another yard east by the ill wind.

"Can I call somebody for you?" I ask them.

"Already called on the wife's cell. Wrecker's comin'," Carl says, the muscles in his jowls grinding. "Goddamned Wyoming wind . . ."

"Carl . . ."

"Saw 'er startin' to shimmy a hunnerd yards back," Carl says. "Didn't think the damn wind was bad enough to tip 'er, though. Headin' up to Yellowstone country. Big vacation. Just me and the wife. A whole week. Self-contained, the whole nine yards. Don't need to hook up to nobody or nuthin'. Only had 'er a couple years, but this here was the big trip, goddammit."

"Carl . . ."

"Axle looks okay," Carl says. "Maybe if I can get 'er back on 'er wheels . . ."

Carl's just talking. Maybe the axle is fine, but the business end of Carl's Airstream looks like an enormous wad of aluminum foil tossed in the bar ditch. Back home, I have no doubt, Carl would have thrown a chain on the upended trailer and rolled her right, but she looks totaled from where I stand. Then again, I'm neither an insurance agent nor a farmer.

"Wheatland's just up ahead," I tell them. "If you need anything, a ride, some water . . ."

"Thanks, we best wait here. We're okay. 'Fraid this is as far as we go, unless we get blowed back to Grand Island first. Can't do nuthin' now but wait. Thanks for stoppin', but there's no need for you to waste your time here."

I worry another car won't pass for a while, so I give Carl my cell-phone number. But I won't hear from Carl ever again. Not because this stretch of road is a notorious dead zone, but because Carl's the kind of proud, self-reliant Midwesterner who wouldn't call for help if his wife—or, worse, his Cornhusker tickets—spontaneously combusted.

I guess I can understand how a man with a thirty-foot, self-contained Airstream trailer, even a busted one in the ditch, might feel like he doesn't need anything or anybody else.

Airstreams have the power to make a man believe he can separate himself from the outside world, reflecting the harmful rays of sunlight, pain, and expectation. A man doesn't need anything but a five-ton rolling silver bullet with fifty-four-gallon water tank, a forty-thousand-Btu furnace, a six-and-a-half-foot ceiling, a built-in beer cooler, a king-size master suite (and other hidden beds for people you'll never see), a praline-colored interior, and a foot-and-a-half hitch-ball height. Hell, if you could grow your own food and pump your own natural gas, you might never have to look another human in the face . . . well, until you needed sex, more beer, or the satellite dish stopped working.

But no man is an island. Not even in Grand Island.

Or so they say.

Who am I kidding?

I am haunted by Airstream trailers.

———

When my marriage first started to dissipate, I decamped to Phoenix, where we owned a vacation townhouse. We called it a "separation," but it was really just a confused, headlong, angry getaway.

In happier times, we'd brought the kids here every March for spring-training baseball, and spent most of our days in the warmth of field-level seats and creamy sunblock we smeared on each other.

Now, to me, the townhouse was a little like a waiting room in a morgue, where I was suspended between worlds.

I spent those days in a languid depression, sleeping late and often, staring at the ceiling, pretending to write my next great novel, microwaving hot dogs for dinner, marking down the number of oranges I picked in the stamp-sized backyard, and keeping a thorny, uninhibited bougainvillea at bay on the rare days when pruning didn't seem like too much work.

Through my eyes, the world was like an old TV screen going bad, going gray from the edges. I tried not to imagine the coming catastrophe, but I could think of nothing else. Any effort to avert it seemed as fruitless as trying to slow down a sunset.

One day, I rolled out of bed late and drove to California. It wasn't as impulsive as it sounds. The California line is only two hours from Phoenix on Interstate 10. But I took the long way, some back roads through dusty snowbird burgs like Surprise, Forepaugh, and Salome, because I was in the early stages of a fantasy about retiring to an Airstream trailer somewhere in the desert, among the saguaros and snakes, maybe with a one-legged Mexican housekeeper-whore named Consuelo, supporting myself by raising a herd of scorpions to be entombed in acrylic paperweights for tourists, as far from civilization as the dirt roads would take me.

Fantasies require more concentration than simple escapes.

Late in the afternoon, I crossed the Colorado River into California and grabbed a greasy burger at a roadside diner in Blythe, a small farm town on the border, then turned around. I came, I saw, I ate badly . . . therefore I was. And at that moment, that's all. I just was.

On the way home to Phoenix, a hot, fat sun tailgated me. It flashed in my rearview mirror and reflected off the shiny rear windows of the cars ahead. It wouldn't let me turn down the air conditioner. I'm sure if I'd dialed the radio away from the classic rock station, it would have had a flare or something. I was pissed off and I wasn't going to win this game of chicken, so I just wouldn't play.

I took the next exit, somewhere west of Quartzsite. After a mile or so, some dusty tire marks curled out of the desert onto the blacktop from the faintest whisper of a happenstance dirt road. It called to me. I locked in the four-wheel drive and followed it.

The thermometer in my truck said it was 110. Blistering. Maybe it was 110, but the damn truck was overheating; although the sun would set soon, it would plunge temperatures to merely feverish. I had crossed a few arroyos and crested a couple of skeletonized ridges when a glint of sun off a large pile of pale stones caught my eye on the other side of an impassable wash, no more than a quarter-mile away. It looked like a cairn. I decided to walk.

The heat was suffocating and sharp, and sweat was sudden. As I walked, keeping one eye out for rattlesnakes and one for scorpions, I began to rethink the Airstream idea. I reckoned I could be a reclusive scorpion rancher in a far less rigorous landscape.

I arrived at the cairn sopping and damn near prostrated, but it wasn't a cairn at all. It was a stone fireplace hearth, built by hand from desert rocks and a salvaged car hood, into which someone had inserted a rusty pipe to carry the smoke up and away. Nearby, an empty folding chair sat beside a rough-hewn and weathered table no bigger than a lamp stand. I felt as if I'd walked into someone's parlor, and I realized that a ring of stones encircled every clump of greasewood near the camp, as if the mysterious resident had tried to give order to wildness.

Beside the hearth, a white cross made of PVC pipe threw a long shadow in a kaleidoscopic sunset's protracted light. And near

that, someone had sunk a salvaged highway marker, on which he
had scrawled:

BUILT BY
GYULA SZECSI
"JULIUS"
A GOOD MAN
FRIEND TO ALL
BORN JULY 1934
DIED MARCH 4, 1999
ON THIS SPOT
PLEASE DON'T
DESTROY

Gyula hadn't been dead more than a month. Who was he?
What had brought him to ground in this ultimately final spot?
What about him had inspired someone to make this shrine to
him in a caustic desert? He was only sixty-four . . . had his end
been unnatural?

The heat was getting to me. I felt a little light-headed, and
the sand under my feet was turning to gritty liquid. The sun had
beaten me, and we were both rapidly sinking. I wanted a few
more minutes there, but dark was coming, and I had to find my
way back to the highway. I'm not much for praying, but I said a
little prayer anyway, then left.

Later that night, far away in the twinkling, air-conditioned,
irrigated, electrified, and chlorinated blue bosom of Phoenix,
I scoured the Internet for Gyula's obituary in the local papers,
from Quartzsite to Salome to Blythe. I found nothing.

No, that's not entirely true. I found something, but not his
obituary.

A few years before, a young man had posted a beseeching
note on a bulletin board, seeking any stray bit of information

about his father, a Czech immigrant named Gyula Szecsi, who'd abandoned his wife and kids in California in 1971. The poster left an e-mail address, but it had long since been abandoned, disconnected like an old phone.

The next day, I called the coroner's office in the county where Gyula had died, and they knew little more than the name on his driver's license. An itinerant friend told them how he'd lived and died. The old desert rat was found stone dead by another old desert rat, a friend. Besides his stale corpse, his feeble van had contained some old prospecting tools, moldering food, a few letters, and a small vial containing a few flakes of gold. His heart had simply given out.

Nothing more.

Gyula had been a dreamer like Charley Gregory, although maybe his dream proved too big. He was buried in a pauper's grave. His van and its contents were sold for a few hundred dollars to pay the expense of digging his hole. Nobody came to the burying.

I wept. For Gyula, still lonely and cold in his unmarked grave. For his son, who never knew his father. Maybe for myself, because I was also alone, and the only life I knew was slipping out of my grasp, too. Maybe I could see myself sitting in a rickety wooden chair outside my Airstream in the desert someday, wondering whatever became of my kids and my wife, wishing for more time to find whatever treasure I had missed, trying to slow down the sunset.

Maybe.

But one inescapable fact remained: I was likely the only person in the world who knew this son was seeking a dead father. I felt a great burden to find him, whatever the cost. It became my reason to keep getting up in the morning. For weeks, I phoned any Szecsi whose name could be found in the Internet white pages, e-mailed dozens of people who might have had the frailest connection. I left my name with dozens more, marking my trail in the hope that if I could not find this son, he could find me.

Suddenly, I had a purpose.

After a couple of fruitless months, I surrendered and returned to the lesser tasks cluttering my life, such as nurturing my melancholy the way I'd nurtured the bougainvillea, and microwaving hot dogs. I was unable to splice the broken wire between this father and son. I thought about buying a headstone for old Gyula, but like everything else, I failed at that, too.

The world was bigger than I was.

I had driven this road to its end.

———•———

The separation failed, as they always do.

Oh, I went back to my wife and kids in Wyoming briefly, but the marriage was no more healed than I was. We made plans to break for good after the New Year, but trying to survive the holidays with plastic smiles was a sham. My wife asked me to leave a few weeks before Christmas, and I did.

I called Matt and Ashley on the phone, but it was always hard to talk about anything important. I'd always start to cry. I was a crookedy cowboy barely keeping one leg on each side and my head in the middle of the rank bull called Sanity that could pitch me at any second.

More than a year after I'd found Gyula Szecsi's *memento mori* in a desert sunset, my divorce was all but final. That gray, cold winter—without my kids, without a job, without a home, without any of the things that had defined me as a father, husband, or newspaperman—I was lost. And I wasn't sure any road led back to familiar country.

Then one frigid morning, I opened my e-mail to find a note from James Szecsi. He'd eventually learned of his father's death from the people at Social Security, and had gotten my name and e-mail address from a county employee in Quartzsite who'd actually written them down.

"She told me that you had given her my name and that I had been on the Internet looking for my father," the son, now an army recruiter, wrote. "I am sending you this to say thank you for trying to help. Thank you for trying."

I sent him photos of his father's hearth, and the rings of stone around the desert garden his father had tended, since God had taken leave of this place. I told him I was sorry the news he sought was not good, but it was *something,* and the mystery of Gyula's life was maybe solved. I knew what it was like to chase a father's ghost. And although I didn't know it at the time, our separate stories would soon get all tangled up.

I searched for profound words about fathers and sons, how knowing is better than not knowing, and how someone admired his father enough to erect a small memorial in the desert. I told him a deputy had found a minuscule amount of gold in the van, in case he wanted to ask authorities about it.

Within a few days, I got a reply.

"It's okay," James wrote. "I didn't think much of him."

One must choose his roads without regret. I'll never know James or Gyula Szecsi's hearts, whether they regretted the roads they'd chosen, or the roads chosen for them. I only know their separate journeys would have been meaningless if they had always been facing backward.

Orpheus looked back, and you know what happened to him.

Maybe I am Orpheus.

———•———

Before dawn the next day, I roll up to the curb outside Matt's house. My window is open to the morning. It's early June in Wyoming, so the air before sunrise is indifferent, unmoved.

My son. He is why I came. He is why we're going in search of a dead human toe. I am happy.

The front yard hasn't changed much in seven years, except the spruce tree we planted is a little bigger, and the carpenter's truck in the driveway isn't mine. The old backboard by the garage is gone, too, but it was past its prime anyway.

I pour three cold fingers of hundred-mile, c-store cappuccino in the gutter as I get out, and French vanilla mixes with the runoff from a neighbor's sprinkler on a long-ass journey to the Gulf of Mexico. Just as I start up the faux-flagstone walk toward the front door, the double-garage door begins to roll up, revealing Matt's athletic silhouette as soft yellow light spills out onto the concrete drive.

"You awake?" I ask with a good-morning hug. He's taller than me, and his body is hard.

"Barely."

Matt's nineteen, so he's mildly allergic to morning. He probably slept in his best skater-metal traveling gear: a Pantera T-shirt, baggy shorts, a black toboggan skullcap that doesn't come near to containing his wicked cool shag, black Nikes, and earbuds dangling around his neck. At his feet are two fat soft-side bags, a laptop case, and a ballistic-nylon CD cache big enough to contain the complete works of every heavy-metal band that ever banged a head (plus, I would learn soon enough, every episode of every season of the TV show *Scrubs*). We shoehorn it all into the back of the Subaru and jam the door closed.

But there's one more thing.

"The shovel?" I ask.

"What?"

"Did you find a camp shovel?"

"C'mon, do we really need it?"

"I don't know. What would it hurt? I guess I'd rather have one and not need it than to need one and not have it. Humor me."

Matt swears under his breath and goes back in the garage, where he raises enough racket to wake the neighbors as he scrabbles through a tangle of garden tools. Against all odds, he comes up with a cheap, OD green entrenching tool.

"Here you go, shovel boy," my son says.

He wedges it into a crevice in the Subaru's bed and mounts up in the passenger seat beside me.

The sun is almost up, and I am as content as I've been in two thousand dawns.

And it has nothing to do with the shovel.

So you're thinking this is how and where it all starts, and you'd be mostly right. This particular journey with my son to the edge of the Earth—to sip a peculiar cocktail containing a mummified human toe—began as the sun rose on a June morning, but before I reveal to you what happened, there's something else you should know.

Sideways Dreaming

He had always loved his children but he had never before realized how much he loved them and how bad it was that he did not live with them.
—From *Islands in the Stream* by Ernest Hemingway

Mi *Padre* is the hero of all his stories, although he always tells them with a great show of modesty.

His few admitted missteps are almost always the inadvertent sins of a gallant, well-meaning knight that turn sour despite the best motivations. Six or seven marriages, a federal prison stretch, lost parents, lost children, lost time . . . all, to him, an unfortunate series of events sparked by the best and noblest of intentions.

It was late when Thom met me at Tocumen International Airport in Panama, where he has lived off and on for more than two decades. I hadn't seen him in many years, and he looked older than that last time, back in Idaho around the time my marriage was falling apart. But so did I, and he was trimmer.

We stowed my bags in his new white Mercedes and drove to a restaurant on the Miraflores locks in the Canal Zone, where the back patio snugged up against the locks and the mammoth ships that lumbered past, close enough to imagine a whiff of the seamen's cigarette smoke and man-sweat.

The place was packed. It was past eight p.m., the dinner hour in Panama, and the Canal-side patio was filled with diners, but Thom sweet-talked the hostess and she seated us at a small two-top out there.

It was also the Saturday night before a big election, and since national law forbade liquor sales on an election weekend, we drank sweet tea. So without the benefit of something stronger, we buttered our bread, watched the ships passing in the night, and talked about why I had come: to explore some issues between fathers and sons. Mine and his.

You see, I descend from a long line of accidental bastards. My great-grandfather, a buggy-whip salesman named Thomas Elbert Blodgett, farmed out his five children after his wife—their mother—died in the great influenza epidemic of 1918, and they were never truly reunited.

One of his sons, my grandfather, Thomas William Blodgett, or T.W., was a sometime sailor, sometime politician, sometime impresario, sometime taxi driver who left a wife and two children alone when he ran off with another woman. After the divorce was final, their mother sent Thom—then six years old—and his sister to live with separate foster families, who raised them to adulthood. In a deliberate snub to his estranged father, Thom took the name of his foster parents: Lane. But a new name didn't change his inherited restlessness; less than a year after marrying my mother, not long after she'd announced she was pregnant, Thom surrendered to his nomadic birthright, left her, and never looked back.

That night under Panama's sanguine skies, with a parent I never needed and who never needed me, two passing ships watching other passing ships, without liquid lubrication, the spirits of five men sat around our table for two: Thomas Elbert, T.W., Thom, me, and Matt.

Four generations who had walked away from the next ... and one who could end the streak.

———•———

Over sea bass and paella, we talked about loving and losing . . . and leaving. We talked about our impatience with disappointment. We talked about wanderlust. We talked about women. We talked about my girlfriend Mary back in Texas and how I feared the thought of commitment.

After six wives in fifty years, Thom now has a young Panamanian lover, Ledys. He's seventy-one, she's in her twenties. She keeps the books for his real-estate development business and lives in his villa at Playa Venao, on Panama's remote western coast. He was proud of his prowess with Ledys, and the fact that he was more active than men half his age, with scuba, surfing, and sailing.

When I asked if he planned to marry her, he claimed they were already married in the eyes of the Panamanian culture, but he's unlikely to ever make it official. Nevertheless, he'd adjusted his will to take care of her if and when he dies . . . but he couldn't imagine dying, so it was just a kind of formality.

He also promised that I would meet other young women here, even making a subtle pitch for me to be open to possible relationships. "You like to travel a lot," he said once, "and that's an excellent reason to have a Panamanian wife. They really know how to travel."

The possibility of a twenty-something woman becoming my stepmother? It was really the least of the surrealities between us at this moment.

Mi Padre's prodigious libido comes from a strange place. For many years, he said, he only wanted to be wanted. He married my mother because she was the first one who ever chose him;

nobody had ever chosen him, not his father and mother or any-one else. He only wanted to be chosen.

So he tells his story: My pregnant mother left him, just packed up one day and moved while he was at work. She filed for divorce, and he was prevented from seeing her anymore by her father. He claims he came to the hospital where I was born and saw me through the nursery's glass window, then walked out of the hospital and my life.

He says my mother made the grievous error of marrying a boy, not a man. When she'd had enough of him, he didn't care to fight for what he was losing. He merely moved on to avoid soil-ing the life of his newborn son, and he says he never made any attempt to contact me because of a promise he claims he made to my protective grandfather.

A flawed hero swept along by events out of his control, whose promises are more important than blood, and whose weaknesses make you want to hug him. That's how he tells it.

And here's how I tell it: Thom Lane walked away from my mother while she carried me inside her, maybe because she told him to walk away. She married Joe Franscell before I was two, before the curse of memory. She might have left it at that. Some do. But for reasons only she knows, she decided to tell me about Thom Lane when I was eight.

It was an efficient, workmanlike communication on the ratty front-room sofa, she at one end, I at the other. I still wonder why she didn't sit closer.

"Joe is not your real father," she said in my memory-movie.

I am empty of words. I am, after all, eight. The first bombshell of my life has just been dropped. Direct hit.

"Your father is a man named Thom Lane," she continued. "He was my husband, but he left before you were born. He's your father. I don't know where he is now and it doesn't matter. He didn't love you."

This is the part of the scene where my throat suddenly aches every time I see this movie.

"Any questions?"

Questions? I was fucking eight years old.

I could do only what eight-year-olds do: I wept. I hurt and didn't know why. Something deep down in the heart of the heart of my little heart tumbled from its precarious perch, was swept away in a torrent of confused blood and tears, and never found. He was never mentioned again in that house. From that day forward, Thom Lane's presence in my life was his absence.

After he abandoned her, my mother had erased Thom Lane from her life, wiped the whole sordid scene clean of his fingerprints. When she was finished destroying all his pictures, letters, jewelry, clothing, and everything else, there was just me. The only thing she couldn't get rid of.

But my grandmother had salvaged their discarded wedding album from the trash. Nothing else. She hid it until the summer before I graduated from journalism school, when she gave it to me. I opened the album and a little music box played the wedding march. That day, for the first time, I saw a photograph of my old man.

He was me. Or I was him. The real me and the photographic him were about the same age—twenty—and the resemblance was uncanny. Thom Lane in his white tuxedo and 1955 flattop, his charming grin so vaguely familiar. And my mother, so young, so pretty, so happy, so white, so . . . seventeen. These pictures obsessed me, as if I were looking into a mirror in a different room.

The guest book was signed by almost one hundred family and friends. Except for my mom's parents, none of the names were familiar to me.

But there was something else: a newspaper clipping.

It was my mother's wedding announcement. Until then, all I'd ever known about Thom Lane was that he'd married and abandoned my mom, and never loved me. But before my eyes, he was developing like an old Polaroid snapshot, a little bit at a time. I learned that his father Clarence ran an appliance repair shop and his mother worked for the Automobile Club of Southern California. Thom had graduated from Phineas Banning High School in Wilmington, California, in June 1953, had won the American Legion Award, been student body vice president, and a four-year varsity letterman in tennis and gymnastics. And he'd just come home from a two-year hitch in the U.S. Army Airborne.

His best man had been a high school friend named Leo Carrillo, not the actor who played the Cisco Kid's sidekick Pancho on TV, but his nephew.

My mother, the story noted in the last paragraph, had graduated from Banning five months before the wedding and was a member of the yearbook staff. Her gown of Chantilly lace and white tulle with lace sleeves and white satin bows likely went out in the trash with everything else a year later.

Although the man remained an elusive shadow, he was coming into focus.

Finally, I had questions.

—— • ——

"Do you ever wonder if you are capable of truly loving someone," I asked him thirty years later on the banks of the Panama Canal, a fair question because I had so often asked it of myself, "or do you ever feel that something is broken inside you?"

With his fork, Thom winnowed the rice on his plate, searching for an answer in it.

"Yeah, I wonder sometimes," he said, not looking up. "But I am comfortable with what passes for love, which might be love itself. I just don't know for sure. Maybe nobody does."

"Which would please you more: to love someone desperately, or to be loved desperately?"

"Neither," Thom said. "It would be to love myself first."

Another ship passes.

"I don't feel lovable," I confessed to the man who never loved me, "and for a long time I've mistrusted it when people say they love me—mostly because I could never be sure."

"Have you ever said it and not meant it?"

I winnowed my rice.

"I don't think so. I mean, I never lied. But maybe later it turned out I was wrong. I was just feeling . . . I dunno . . ."

". . . What passes for love?"

Yeah, that.

———•———

Before the Internet, finding someone who might prefer not to be found was infinitely harder.

My search for Thom Lane began soon after my grandmother gave me that wedding album. I started calling as many Thomas, Tom, or T. Lanes in Southern California as a cub reporter on a $194-a-week salary (before taxes) could afford. I wrote letters to government agencies for tax, military, land, and death information. I even called the Screen Actors Guild to get contact information for the late Cisco Kid, actor Duncan Renaldo, whose widow gave me a number for the late Leo Carrillo's widow, who had lost track of her nephew years before. All dead ends.

I kept it all a secret from my mother. My obsession with finding Thom Lane could only hurt her and Joe, the man I had always called "Dad." I wasn't seeking a new father, only a lost one, but I knew they wouldn't understand.

Years passed without luck. I set my curiosity aside many times to focus on my new wife, new jobs in new towns. Present and future were simply more important than past.

Then my daughter Ashley was born. My wife and I took jobs at the paper in Santa Fe, finally making good money, moving up. Life was good then. We were extraordinarily happy and almost complete. Just one missing piece haunted me . . .

I called my grandmother. A mostly fruitless conversation ended with a vague memory that some relative of Thom's mother's second husband had worked in the same factory as my late grandfather. She couldn't remember their names—except that she knew they were similar. Two brothers, cousins maybe, but with slightly different last names. But, she recalled, they'd all come to the wedding.

While she was still on the phone, I dragged out my mother's wedding album and scanned the names on the guest list. In the middle of the second column were two, one after the other, as if they'd arrived together: Mr. and Mrs. Anton Langstraat . . . and Mr. and Mrs. Ernest Longstreet.

"Yes," my grandmother said. "Oh, yes, that's them. Tony and Ernie. Your other grandma Genie married Ernie. I remember now. Last I heard, Tony—they called him Tony—still lived in Garden Grove or some such, but that was a long, long time ago."

As soon as we hung up, an operator gave me a number for an Anton Langstraat in Garden Grove. As I dialed, I decided to tell him I was an old army buddy looking for Thom Lane, because I couldn't risk that a protective relative might slam the door on a son seeking his long-lost father. These people were from different times.

A man answered. Very quickly, we established that, yes, he was sort of Thom's step-uncle, but, no, he didn't know where Thom had gotten to. But, yes, Thom's mother Genie and his brother Ernie were living in Oregon and, yes, he was sure they'd know where he was. *Here's the number . . .*

I set it aside for a couple days. I wasn't sure how a grown man introduces himself to his grandmother. And, again, I couldn't risk that she'd put loyalty to her son ahead of any mistakes he might have made in his life—including me. But mostly, I knew this bell could not be unrung.

One night, I shut myself in a back bedroom and dialed the number. A sweet little voice answered.

"Forgive me for calling so late," I said. "I'm looking for a Thom Lane. We were in the army together. Are you his mother?"

"Yes, I am."

"Oh, good. Is he—"

"Still alive? Oh yes, but I haven't seen him in a long time."

"Do you know here he is? An address or phone?"

"Panama. The country. He lives on his boat down there somewhere. I don't have a phone number, but I have an address if you'll wait a minute . . ."

I must have smiled there in the dark. I'd already waited much, much longer than a minute.

"Here it is," she said, then slowly read a long international postal address to me.

"Thank you, ma'am," I said, "This is perfect. I'm really grateful for your help."

I started to hang up, but my unwitting grandmother wasn't finished.

"How did you find us?" she asked.

I was caught flat-footed. I hadn't fabricated an elaborate-enough lie.

"Oh . . . well . . . a long story." I stalled. "I ran into his ex-wife's mom . . . somewhere . . . a while back."

"Which wife?"

"Donna. His first. Well, I think his first."

Her sweet little voice turned urgent.

"Oh my, did she say anything about Ronnie? My Lord, I have always wondered about that little boy. We lost him. I think about him all the time. Do you know anything?"

Okay, I didn't see that coming.

I confessed my lie. She cried. And that's how I met my "other" grandmother.

Some hellos are harder than any good-byes.

In the spring of 1985, I struggled with what to say in a letter—my first communication—to Thom Lane. I wanted to explain who I'd become, that I loved my family very much, how curiosity about my history and his face had led me here, and that our account had long ago been settled. And I wanted to say there had been times in my life when I'd felt abandoned by him and others. At those times, I sought out the affections of many people around me, some who soothed me and some of whom I hurt when I didn't need them anymore.

Ah, genetics.

What I *didn't* want to say was that his leaving meant nothing. It meant something.

Thom responded in a long letter. He'd gone to Panama to get rich for a third time, having lost two previous fortunes for reasons unexplained. In a Central American country where politics, business, and revolution mixed as naturally as rum and Coca-Cola, he knew a savvy *yanqui* could make a killing. He said he'd thought about me from the day he'd last seen me in the hospital nursery, and apologized for doing nothing about it for almost twenty-nine years. He blamed his immaturity for breaking my mother's heart. And he referred vaguely to resentment he felt toward his own natural father, discordant feelings with which he had made his peace, just as he had made peace with the notion of a long-lost son. He signed off, "Take care, and thanks for making the effort."

Many letters followed over the next couple of years, fat with sea-stories and drama. At various times, he painted himself as a treasure-seeker hunting a Caribbean pirate's gold, a competitive sailor, an attorney with erstwhile ties to the U.S. military in Panama, a ship broker, a sailing instructor, the organizer of a hemispheric fund-raiser for a paralyzed Panamanian boy, a freelance journalist, a travel agent . . . and the target of a nefarious, boat-stealing commandante of Panama's *Guardia Nacional*. His own mother mused that he might be running guns—or worse—for *narcotraficantes*, small-time dictators, or other global rogues.

Maybe all forsaken sons imagine their misbegotten, misguided, or mislaid fathers to be swashbucklers. They certainly never imagine them to be common shape-shifters.

———•———

Not long after my son Matt was born, I met his grandfather for the first time.

In 1987, during one of his trips stateside, Thom Lane and I shared a moment that should have happened thirty years before: We embraced. Then we sat down to a white-linen nouvelle lunch in the arboretum of a chichi Marin County, California, bistro where we had arranged our afternoon rendezvous, and talked past one another. Thom ordered Bordeaux or Burgundy or some such when I might have preferred one of the American piss-water beers our *GQ* waiter didn't serve, but he made a big deal out of this being his treat. So over microscopic pseudo-Gallic helpings of risotto and avocado and salmon and vinaigrette and prosciutto and a scattering of leaves I didn't recognize,

I showed him pictures of my baby boy, and he told some Panama stories. I told him about my mother, and he told me he'd once enrolled in one of those 1970s I'm-okay-so-why-aren't-you, self-actualization seminars, so he didn't feel guilty anymore. I told him about growing up reasonably happy in Wyoming, and he told more Panama stories.

Only after a dessert of crème brûlée and profiteroles, when it was time to go, did I say what I came to say.

"I don't need a father," I told the man whose blood flowed in my veins but who'd never given me anything but a fancy French lunch. "I've already got a good one who was always there when I needed him. Still is. The best you can hope for is that we can be friends."

He said he understood, but mostly he just seemed relieved.

I got stuck in rush-hour traffic and I cussed a blue streak. Not because the freeway was jammed but because I'd wasted my chance to ask why he'd run away and never looked back.

———•———

Twenty years later, I asked.

We rose at dawn the morning after our Canal supper to embark on our six-hour drive across Panama to Playa Venao. The rough-jointed Pan-American *autopista* pavement thrummed beneath us, tapping time in a *ticka-ticka-ticka* 110-kph tempo as we traveled deeper into the countryside.

Out here among the *pueblitos* and *espacios sin explorar* (open, unoccupied spaces) is the real Panama, where many people walk, ride rickety bikes, or, for longer trips, hitch rides with truckers or the vagabond buses known as *diablo rojo*, or red devils. They do whatever will earn a few dollars, whenever it comes along.

During Carnaval, *muñecas*, or mannequins, stand guard in the soft-scrabble yards of the often-colorful *diminutas* to ward off evil spirits. Witches are an issue for everyone here. Rather than file an American-style lawsuit for some imagined offense, rural Panamanians might visit a *bruja* to buy a spell against another person, and when things begin to go inexplicably "bad" for the subject of the curse, then he might pay another *bruja* to cast a spell of "protection," which will likely be a greater and more devastating "response" curse known as a *hechizo*.

And Thom pointed out little side roads that disappear into the green cumulus of jungle. They lead to "pushbuttons," clandestine motels designed specifically for lovers' trysts. These *cuartos frios*, or cold rooms, allow couples to park their cars in a small garage connected to a single room where they can exchange bodily fluids and even order room service, which is delivered through a no-see-um slot. When they leave, they pay through a similar slot, unseen by the clerk on the other side. A door opens on the other side of the garage and they exit by a different road than the one they entered. All in all, a rather civilized approach to infidelity.

Somewhere out there, amid the weathered *muñecas* and the *diablo rojo* and the *cuartos frios*, thousands of miles from where I started and thousands more from where I was going, I asked why he never looked back.

"I let other people make decisions for me," *Mi Padre* said.

"Doesn't seem like you," I said.

"I've grown up."

"So you want me to see you, as a young man, like some sort of pinball getting busted around? Weren't you making some of your own choices?"

"I was making choices, sure, but . . . one door closes and another opens."

"What choice was made for you?"

"Your mother's father told me to stay away, to give you a chance to grow up in a stable and secure family. I allowed him to make that choice for me. That makes me a wimp, I guess."

"Had you reached a point with my mom where it didn't matter if you stayed or left?"

"No. I was broken up," he said. "I didn't know why it was happening. She left. No warning. The apartment was empty and she was gone. I felt terrible. She was the first love of my life."

"The first to choose you."

"Yeah."

"So what broke your heart: the loss of a love . . . or being un-chosen?"

"I don't know. Both maybe. I just accepted it and moved on."

To illustrate, *Mi Padre* conjured an allegorical yellow box that apparently some people can see as green, even though we can all agree there is a little box in the room.

"I won't argue the point that you see a green box because when you say it's green, that's because that is the color you see on your side, and I can't see that side of it because I can only see my side of the box, which happens to be yellow. I accept the fact you see a green box. That's my way: Don't try to change the world."

"What's in the box?" I asked.

"I don't know. It doesn't matter. It's just a yellow box."

"No, it's green."

"Okay, green."

"But aren't you curious?"

"There's nothing in the box. I'm just using it to make a point."

"But you said you didn't know what was in the box."

"Forget the box."

"It just seems to me that if we're gonna argue about a box, we should find out what's in it."

"We're not arguing about the box. That was my point: I accept that you see it differently. I don't need you to agree with me. People see things differently."

"We're arguing now. About the box."

"Were you always like this?"

I smiled.

"See what you missed?"

———•———

Mi Padre calls his beach villa "Malibu," which, it surprises me to learn, is not a Spanish word, and nobody knows what it means anyway. But to Thom, it means freedom.

The moment I saw Malibu, I could no longer remember what I had expected it to be. Its secluded beach, the entire main floor that opened to the sea, the terraced grounds, the winding Mediterranean stairs, hip-bluesy-oldies beaming down from some distant satellite in the cobalt sky, the intimacy of the place—it all enchanted me.

My apartment was spacious, with tiled floors, its own bathroom, and a double bed. The indifferent Pacific breeze flowed constantly through the seaside screen door, through the rooms and out the bathroom window to the north.

Ledys was charming, and young. She was barely five-foot-two, not more than ninety pounds—and in my arms she felt like my own daughter Ashley when I hugged her. She waits on Thom hand and foot, eagerly.

Road-weary, I sunk into a hammock on the patio. I sipped a beer, and nodded off to the sound of the waves pounding harder under gray skies. The hypnotic surf was tinged white, roiled by a distant storm that would never reach us. My veins and the surf pulsed in my brain. On this side of the looking glass, water and blood are *la vida*, life. It is late October . . . springtime. The sky is turned upside down, and all the prayers and big band music are leaking out.

Before my siesta, I began to think that I might actually like living here on the brink of humanity, if there was such a place for me, where the clocks run backward . . .

I awoke to a supper of smoked pork chops, boiled potatoes, and sauerkraut, with a Chilean Malbec. Afterward, we poured glasses of smooth Panamanian rum known as Abuelo ("Grandfather"), and retired to an expansive patio overlooking the Pacific surf.

I took the bottle.

After dark, the giant *sapos* came out of the dark. Bullfrogs as big as a child's head squat on the patios and pathways, snatching fat jungle bugs from the air as Thom keeps selling his notion, like the born pitchman he is, that he's as transparent, upbeat, and honest as any man. I wondered whom he was trying to convince—the *sapos?*

At one moment, he talks about deal-making with the Cali drug cartel in the old days, but explains it as merely ill-advised adventuring. The next, he explains complicated land deals that hint at bribery of public officials, but expresses moral discomfort about slipping $5 to a *transito,* a local traffic cop who caught him speeding. He explained it all as accepted in this culture, as therefore not a serious sin in Heaven or on Earth, which, of course, are upside down here.

I poured another glass of Grandfather.

Thom did a couple years in federal prison for his role in an offshore drug deal. The innocent story *Mi Padre* tells me varies significantly from the court papers. He says he only introduced some friends in a real estate deal; federal prosecutors say he helped to smuggle more than $100 million in cocaine into the United States over a two-year period. If he was innocent of bogus charges, why plead guilty and do time?

I pour another glass of Grandfather.

That night, Thom talked about estrangement with other children, half- or stepsisters of mine. He admitted some bad choices and wrong decisions, but he has made little or no effort at rapprochement. Another son visits a couple times a year, but it's been years since he's seen his daughter and stepdaughter from two earlier marriages.

The one intolerable thing that could mark my relationship with my own children—to be disconnected from them, or unloved—is not as big an issue for *Mi Padre*.

But Thom is terribly happy here in the tropics, for many reasons. Among the things he freely admits: His home is his sanctuary. It embodies his dreams, or what substitutes for dreams. He lives beside his beloved sea. He sleeps with a beautiful young woman. He maintains a quality of life that suits him . . . for less than $20,000 U.S. dollars a year, including gardeners, a small cadre of *los trabajadores* (gardeners and handymen who double as waiters at his lavish parties), housekeepers, travel, and so much more.

Among the things he might not admit, but which must be powerful: He is somebody to whom people turn for help and show enormous respect, a *patron* in the truest sense. For someone who admits to wanting nothing more than being wanted by someone—even if he claims he has outgrown it at seventy-one—it must satisfy him immensely that almost everyone within an eighty-kilometer radius knows him and seeks him out for advice, sometimes on momentous decisions. He is proud to tell how the provincial governor, the local colonel of the national police, various *alcaldes*, bankers, and other important men commonly spend a weekend with him, enjoying the accommodations of the apartment I now occupied.

Thom points out many spots in the hills and along the beach where he dreams of building homes or hotels or *pueblitos*. It occurs to me that his dreams often don't become realities, but I also wonder if that's so bad. Even an unrealized dream comforts the dreamer. And how sad it would be to imagine a future that is nothing more than the past.

He also starts here with a clean slate. Whatever mistakes, missteps, or misgivings might have followed him in the

States, they seem to have not cleared Panamanian Customs when he arrived. He is free to be the man he wishes people to believe he is. For reasons spoken and unspoken, Thom is utterly comfortable here, and I believe him when he says he will die here.

How nice it would be to start again. God, how nice.

Another glass of Grandfather softens the night.

———•———

Before bed, we beheaded a boa constrictor that curled in the breezeway outside my apartment door. It frightened Ledys, so we fetched a machete and decapitated the snake, although it would not have harmed us. I thought later it might have been wiser to fling it alive back into the jungle to feed on the local vermin. He was only three feet long, although I was already certain he'd be much bigger in later retellings.

We killed like champions . . . then the snake-slayers trudged off to bed. Thom warned me that the howler monkeys in the jungle would likely wake me in the morning.

A little drunk, I turned off the lights, stripped bare, and lay on the bed. It felt good to be naked, the sea air on my damp skin.

Naked in Panama. In more ways than one.

Malibu.

———•———

The howlers didn't wake me.

I might have slept all morning except for Grandfather, who grouched and farted behind my eyeballs, the son of a bitch. He was more fun the night before. I wormed to the edge of the bed and felt around for my watch: six-forty a.m. Panama time. The sun was up and the tropical air was already clingy.

The first day of the rest of my life had begun . . . and I was hungover. I rinsed my mouth at the bathroom sink, stepped back into the cargo shorts that lay on the floor exactly where I'd stepped out of them the night before, and went out to the beach for a long walk.

That's where I met Shirley, the first of three angels sent to visit me. I first saw her in the distance, too far for my rum-soaked eyes to discern any detail. In the distance, I could only make out the denim blue of her sun shawl, the fray of her Panama hat, her pale-lime tank suit. But closer, I could see her legs were tan and supple, and her skin was soft where her shawl had slipped off her shoulder. Not over thirty, she was beautiful.

We were passing on the long, empty shore, walking in different directions. I spoke first.

"*Hola. Habla Inglés?*"

Her smile rose like the sun beneath her tattered brim.

"Yes," she said. "Good morning."

She said she was from Costa Rica and her name was Shirley because her mother liked Shirley Temple movies. She and her Swiss husband Yorick owned a farm nearby, but it was failing and they were trying to sell it, so far unsuccessfully. Until they did, they were separated from two of their three children, ages ten and twelve, who were living with her sister back in Costa Rica.

I turned to walk with her, back the way I'd come. I told her I was an American tourist visiting family, that I had children of my own, nothing more; I've always been a little uncomfortable revealing that I am a writer, as if it might be wiser to claim to be a piano player in a whorehouse. Ah, she'd already heard of the *patron* in the big house. So we walked along the beach together for a long time, talking about Shirley's kids, ending eventually where her husband had parked his car and played with their three-month-old boy in the shade of a green tarp.

Because she was beautiful, and because I knew Thom could help, I suggested she and Yorick come around and ask him for advice on how to sell the farm. Shirley hugged Yorick, and then hugged me, grateful for the audience with Thom, a little overwhelmed by the possibility she might soon see her children again after two months away.

"We have been away too long," Shirley said as she began to cry. "If you cannot hear your children cry, you are too far."

The next angel came at sunset on the opening day of bocce season.

We spent part of the day exploring the jungle and the rest drinking Panamanian beer at a beachside *jardin,* an open-air cantina where chickens ranged freely among the half-dozen tables out back, trying to stay one short hop away from the next blueplate special. The *jardin* catered to Venao's surfers, who needed little else beyond an occasional bowl of *sancocho,* some fried plantains, the usual spirits, cigarettes and potato chips, Coca-Cola in old-fashioned bottles, and someplace to smoke a joint where nobody would blow a gasket.

In late afternoon, we returned to Malibu, where we mixed that old fart Grandfather with orange juice, passion fruit, guava, and lime in a sweet cocktail Thom claims he invented and calls a Venao Sunset. We filled our indecently large tumblers and convened on the villa's regulation bocce court near the beach, where Ledys, Thom, and I played a round-robin, keeping score by sliding wooden balls across the wires of a big abacus-like scoreboard, talking trash and drinking while the sun plunged toward the sea.

Then Cynthia and Claudia arrived.

Cynthia is Thom's young Panamanian lawyer, and Claudia is Ledys's younger sister who often translates for him in business meetings and the occasional visit to the governor. They spend a night or two every week at Malibu in another apartment down the breezeway from mine. They were both beautiful and full of life, so I was immediately smitten, especially with Cynthia. She was smart, outgoing, and confident, and very good with her English, partly because she spent one year of college in Minnesota.

We all played bocce until dinner, which was a four-hour feast of meatballs, warm potato salad, fried plantains, wine, cake, and cappuccino. We ate and drank and talked mostly about men and women.

In less than three days, the rhythms of my speech were slipping into a Spanish cant, and foreign words had begun to take shape in my mind, to mean something. Words like *siempre* (always), *todo* (all), and *nada* (nothing) had begun popping into my head before their English equivalents.

Over coffee, I used the word *shit,* and asked Cynthia how to say it in Spanish. She demurred. The Spanish word for "shit" was too offensive for her to speak, although she admitted she is entirely comfortable with saying *shit* in English . . . and she used it several times that evening. Why? Because it was not her language. For her, naturally, Spanish was more intimate, English more detached.

Suddenly, I realized that it was true for me, too, on this side of the looking glass: I had no difficulty here speaking of Thom as *Mi Padre*, but I had not spoken the words in English—*my father.* My native language was too intimate on this point.

When everyone else had gone to bed, Cynthia and I walked on the beach under a starry sky. Barefoot in the sand with her back against my chest, she pointed out the faithful North Star at one end of the sky and the Three Marys of Orion's Belt above us, and Saturn riding high in the east . . . while I smelled her hair.

"Where is the Southern Cross?" I asked her.

"Waiting," she said. "It's not the time for it yet."

We sat in the dark and talked about stars and other people's love—or what passes for love. She said she was attracted to me, although she was conflicted about Harry, with whom she'd had a four-year relationship that was running on fumes. She was only twenty-nine, and she had kissed only him. There was more, but she was too proper to talk much about it. Oh, many men make passes at her, she said, and she resists, but she cannot wall herself off from the professional circumstances that put her in the company of these men.

"We have a saying here in Panama about sex," she told me. "Every man wants to be his woman's first, and every woman wants to be her man's last."

I couldn't lie. I was attracted to her, too, but I was already involved in a complicated love affair two thousand miles away. I fumbled for reasons that even a kiss would be wrong, although the very thought of it appealed to me. I was leaving in less than a week. And I was too old for her, although she argued vigorously that age was not important, and that she found men her age to be mostly uninteresting. Even a kiss, I told her, would not be correct, honest, or smart . . . even though I was seldom correct, honest, or smart about women. One bit of DNA I couldn't deny.

Cynthia accepted it.

"Life is complicated," she said.

We walked back to our separate apartments. Before I turned out the lights, I looked again at the pictures we'd taken at the bocce court. They made me smile.

Later, I dreamed Cynthia came to my apartment, where she stood outside the open dawn-side window and asked to sleep with me in my bed. In my dream, I told her my bed was too small for both of us, but that she could sleep there and I could sleep in one of the hammocks just outside my room.

I awoke . . . astonished.

Yes, life is complicated.

My third and last angel was a real angel.

A few days later, we wove the Mercedes down pocked roads to the village of Pedasi. The back roads are lined with barbed-wire fences whose milled posts have, miraculously, sprouted new growth. Post holes were dug in the fertile, moist earth, and posts cut from various woods like *macano* or *almacigo* were stuck in the ground. In time, they come back from the dead and require regular pruning.

In Pedasi, we hunted a sign painter whom Thom wishes to paint some signs for his realty business. The painter was not at his shop—a surf / fruit juice / bike rental / island tour emporium in a ramshackle roadside bungalow—so Thom asked people we saw on the street (each of whom he apparently knows), and each pointed to some new spot in the village where he wasn't.

When we ran out of spots for the sign-painting, surfboard-renting, fruit-juicing, bike-renting tour guide to be, we found him pumping gas into a friend's car at a service station / ristorante at the edge of town. Thom sealed a deal in a few minutes of back-slapping and joking in Spanish. Small towns are the same everywhere.

On the way home to Malibu, we stopped at a tiny *cementerio* beside the road to Mariabe, the tiny village where Thom's late wife Clara grew up. She died at age forty-nine from cervical cancer and is buried there in a magnificent white crypt.

Shortly after Clara was entombed, Thom promised to maintain the overgrown graveyard, which was low on the impoverished township's list of priorities. He even dreams of using local grandmothers and GPS to locate and identify the graves there, but wishes to avoid being seen as the gringo who comes and takes over. In time, he said, in time.

When we arrived, three of Thom's *trabajadores*—Roberto, Jose, and Diogenes—were whitewashing the *cementerio*'s walls and scything the weeds around the graves. Earlier, they had painted and swept the tiny chapel at the rear of the graveyard.

I wandered among the graves. Some are aboveground marble crypts with elaborate architectural touches or stone angels; others are simple, imperfect concrete crosses. Some had plastic flowers in all the rain-washed, sun-bleached colors of death; most did not. Some were marked with hand-painted lettering, others not marked at all. But all shared Mariabe in life and in death.

Propped against one weathered stone was a headless, legless plaster angel, long past her prime but still standing guard over the dead. Even angels break, I suppose. And in a place where dead fence posts come back to life, who'd risk throwing out a broken angel?

Like the angel, nearby Mariabe would have been a dismal little village except for hope. It consists of a handful of modestly kept traditional houses, the well-painted local *escuela,* and a Catholic church, whose front yard was, in fact, a playground festooned with swings, basketball and soccer goals, a slide, and other play equipment that Thom and his *trabajadores* had installed and kept in working order. Soon, he said, they would paint new lines on the paved combination soccer/basketball court.

Ah, but there's faith in the village's very name. Many, many years ago—legend has it—a little blind girl named Maria went swimming in the nearby river. At one point, she submerged, and when she popped her head out of the water, she could see again. The astounded villagers thanked God for the miracle and rechristened their village *Mariabe* ... "Maria sees."

They gave a name to what they could not explain.

Down a dirt road from the church is the home of Jacienta Jaen, Clara's recently widowed mother. The house was unlighted, the front door wide open, and Jacienta and her daughter Delia—the family *bruja*—were in the kitchen, stirring pots of boiling meat. Stooped, wrinkled, and rheumy-eyed, Jacienta sat with us in the dark, spartan front room. Thom offered to run an errand for her, any errand she might need, but she declined. We drove away, and I felt sad for her, for the whole town, even though they seem to be living the life they want, nothing more and nothing less. What right have I to pity Mariabe?

Back at Malibu that night, I poured a cup of Grandfather and walked on the beach, collecting a few stones and seeking treasure. I was leaving the next day and wasn't sure if this long trip had been worth it. My eyes were on the sand, but my mind was on Jacienta, Mariabe, lumber that comes back from the dead, and the broken plaster angel keeping vigil in the *cementerio*. I kept my head down, as if I would actually see something of value that had washed ashore. I didn't.

But I found something else.

Faith is a mysterious thing; I can't explain it any better than the villagers of Mariabe. What's the point of dreaming if you don't have faith?

I hope to find a priceless bauble on a beach.

I hope every dead fence post will blossom anew.

I hope there's a good place for broken angels.

And I hope my son will always call me Father and be the hero of all my stories.

Three angels came to me in Panama. They carried parables about regret, longing, and faith in things I couldn't fathom or slow down . . . time, sunsets, past, present, future. Together, they showed me the way back to the road I'd lost, a road that would take me to the top of the world.

"You must go to the Yukon," *Mi Padre* said when he hugged me on the departure curb at Tocumen International before I flew home. The way he said it, it sounded like the first line of a poem.

"You go and never look back, not once. There's nothing behind us. I know what you're looking for and it isn't back there. It's still out there."

On the Wind

If I make no complaint of the pain it is because knights-errant are not permitted to complain of any wound, even though their bowels be coming out through it.

—Don Quixote de la Mancha

Now, twenty-five miles deep into Montana, past Lodge Grass and the dry washes known as Half Way, Good Luck, and Sunday, the sun is up. Matt is slumped against the passenger window, asleep, although I can hear heavy-metal music buzzing like a mosquito in his earbuds—which is, in reality, no worse than the music playing in my head.

"Garryowen."

It happens every time. Up ahead is the patch of prairie known best as the Little Bighorn, where Lieutenant Colonel George Armstrong Custer made his last flamboyant blunder and entered history as the archetype of hubris. This lilting Irish drinking song has provided the soundtrack to countless Hollywood films about Custer's vainglorious death, sometimes even making it seem as if the cavalry's fifers were playing it as they rode to their deaths. C'mon, if you were trying to sneak up on a big camp of experienced warriors, would you be playing martial music? Only in Hollywood.

But damn if "Garryowen" isn't playing in my head as I zip through the heart of the Crow Indian reservation, which engulfs the battlefield.

As I cross the Little Bighorn River, the battleground humps up a few hundred yards to the north. I think about stopping, as I always have. I have friends here from older days, from other stories. To me, this is holy ground not because of Custer's debacle, nor because it is also holy ground to my Crow friends, but because great history happened here, and there are still ghosts. Roadside myths draw me in.

Somehow, my mind has always wanted to make the spaces where intriguing history has happened as large as the events themselves. Shouldn't great events play out on great stages? But the place where Custer and his troopers died at the Little Bighorn—like Dealey Plaza, Oklahoma City's Murrah Building, the OK Corral, Antietam's Bloody Lane, the Alamo, Ground Zero, and Ford's Theatre, to name a few—is extraordinarily compact. Random and lonely white markers dot the vast prairie at some distance in every direction, but the greatest number of them are clustered around Last Stand Hill, on a patch of land smaller than a city block.

And Custer didn't waste a lot of valuable historic time either. The annihilation of his Seventh Cavalry has reverberated across more than 130 years as one of the most memorable battles in American military history—yet it might have been over in as little as a half-hour. He barely had time to say, "My bad."

It makes me wonder: In the infinity of time and space, why do these comparatively inconsequential human events (which, more often than not, involve the spilling of blood) consume so much of our collective imagination's disk space? In our personal histories, do we also reserve extra pages for intimate blood-lettings—oh, say, like divorces—in the scrapbook of our memories?

At the height of America's indignation over Custer's annihilation by Sioux and Cheyenne forces on the blood-hot summer noon of June 25, 1876, some wanted to rename the Little Bighorn for Custer. Today, many Anglos shorten it to, simply, the Little Horn. Some Crows who still speak their language call it *aaush bud shu*, the Mean River, because it has swallowed so many of them. Whatever the name, it is sixty miles of chocolate-green water running through a historic, cultural, spiritual, social, economic, mythical landscape, as well as many contemporary Western issues.

In Crow tradition, an unobstructed river is the most sacred because it is the least troubled. Its movement is its own magic, real, but as mysterious as gravity or time. The Little Bighorn's water is simply snowmelt from the Big Horn Mountains or prairie rain, but its flow makes it holy. Believers among the Crow say the only way to capture the sacred current in a cup is to dip with it, not against it.

Time is a current in Crow country, too. The flow of Crow history has been turned here and there, the way a boulder or deadfall might change the course of a river. In the past hundred years, the tribe has faced many obstructions that challenge not only their spirituality but also their very existence.

As time and the river flow through the "rez," the Crow population erodes, more land is sold to outlanders, children leave, language falls into disuse, and the culture dwindles. In that, it's like other reservations.

Today, some Crows refuse to drink or even swim in the Little Bighorn because they consider it too dirty.

From the spot where Custer fell, a few hundred yards north of the river, the gentle plains unfurl for miles in every direction. But just outside the battlefield gates, in Crow Agency, souvenir shops ambush tourists, an empty casino lies waiting for new occupants and new gamblers, and other businesses have sprouted. Across the river to the south, in the outpost of Garryowen—yes, named for Custer's battle song—a convenience store, gas station, trading post, and museum promise free arrowheads and other Indian geegaws.

A more insidious threat is the slow decay of Crow culture. Ninety percent of the last generation spoke the Crow language; today, only about 35 percent of Crow children speak it. Like bloodlines and great rivers, the language is being diluted from the outside as kids scramble parts of both languages, or speak English exclusively.

A Crow friend, Marvin Dawes, once stood with me among the willows at the confluence of the Little Bighorn and the Bighorn, a spot on the very edge of the Crow world, a place of perpetuity. Dawes, now in his middle years, is the grandson of a respected chief, a father, and one of a handful of men entrusted to perpetuate Crow spiritual and cultural ways. He slips in and out of Crow when talking to friends he meets on the street or in the college hallways where he works.

"Our way is what makes the Crow people who we are," Dawes told me that day. "Without our beliefs we wouldn't be Crows. We would lose the true meaning of 'us.' We want to keep our beliefs, yet we have to get with today's trend to keep up with modern technology, education, and being part of a much larger community. Sometimes, it's hard to know what to keep and what to let go."

I wanted to ask him, Does anybody ever know what to keep and what to let go? But I didn't.

Here's another word: The all-purpose Crow word for river is *xaaxalaawa,* the one that moves all the time. As long as it moves, you can't step in the same river twice.

As long as I move . . .

I nudge Matt, who is sleeping against the passenger window. He opens one eye in a foggy, prairie-green, death-metal, dashboard dreamscape.

"Little Bighorn," is all I say.

He squints out the tinted glass toward the spectral specks on the distant hillside that mark the spots on the battlefield where Custer and his boys fell.

"Great," Matt says. "A park for killing Indians."

———•———

A little past noon, we cross the Musselshell River deep in the heart of the heart of Montana, where the landscape is buckskin tan and the sky is biggest. I've been here before, though it seems like another life.

"I fished this river a few years back," I tell Matt. "A couple good hidey-holes."

He tugs his earbuds free and scans the prairie to see what I am seeing in this river. He can't.

"Catch anything?"

"A couple smallmouth bass, I think, on an old crawdad fly I had. Nothing big. Put 'em back."

Back when I was roaming the American West for the *Denver Post,* I carried a fishing license from almost every state west of the 100th meridian. My fly rod and tackle were stowed in the back of my Jeep—Flattery was her name, because she got me everywhere. I knew the great rivers not from fishing magazines, but from books, and in my mind each one bore the name of the writer who'd introduced us.

I'd usually stop toward sunset, knowing I could drive in the dark, but I couldn't fish. My excursions were often planned in the space between the accelerator and the brake pedal, when I saw a tempting pool made transparent by the lowering light, rippled only by midges lighting on the surface.

That's how I came to know the Musselshell. I first stopped here in the spring of the annus horribilis, 2001, before everything changed. Before the sunsets started coming faster. Before I stopped fishing altogether.

"What brought you here?" Matt asks. "It's kinda the ass-end of nowhere."

"Coming from a story I don't remember and going to another story I don't remember," I say. "I was between towns. Just saw the river and stopped to fish, that's all. I did that a lot, you know, after . . ."

Even now, years beyond, I can't say *divorce* in front of my kids. As if it were something else not so final, not so legal, not so weak, not so faulty. Sometimes, like now, I just don't fill in the blank.

"Just stopped?"

"Yeah, just stopped. I'd always see these pools and I'd wonder if there were fish, and I just couldn't leave it at that. I had to know. I always figured I'd never come back this way again. Too many roads, you know? So I just stopped."

"Sweet."

Here, the Musselshell and U.S. 12 entwine with the long-abandoned tracks of the defunct Chicago, Milwaukee, St. Paul and Pacific Railroad—and its forebear, the Montana Railroad, locally known as The Jawbone because its promoters always talked bigger than its balance sheet—in a 292-mile braid of asphalt, forged steel, snowmelt, and the occasional knot of cottonwood.

Montana has more blue-ribbon fishing rivers than Minnesota has lakes, from Norman Maclean's Big Blackfoot to Tom McGuane's Yellowstone to Ivan Doig's Smith to Ernest Hemingway's Clark Fork. But after that first time on the Musselshell—which doesn't belong to any writer as far as I can tell—I sometimes detoured to U.S. 12 because almost nobody fishes the Musselshell except the people of nearly invisible burgs like Two Dot and Shawmut and Delphia. That's mostly because so much of this land is private, itinerant fishermen have a hard time finding a place to lay out a line.

Before there were roads, there were rivers. The shortest distance between two points might be a straight line, but water finds the easiest route. Explorers like Lewis and Clark knew this as they traversed this country in search of a distant sea. They followed the Musselshell River.

She rises in the Crazy Mountains, gathers herself below the tree line, trickles across wildflower meadows, cuts through deer trails and timber falls, warms her icy blood in the early-morning sun that paints the eastern slope of the Crazies. Sometimes in spring, warm air from the basin seeps up the canyons and cools over the cold water, congealing in a "Cheyenne fog" that drapes the boulders and the trails and the trees and the graceful shadows of brown trout just below the surface.

Down in the otherwise treeless flats and pleated badlands, she snakes slowly east and north, absorbing whatever intermittent tributaries with names like Haymaker and Ninemile have to offer. And, true to the habits of rivers and men, she chooses every easiest inch toward the Missouri, the Mississippi, and the Great Water.

I touch Matt's leg and point to the barbed-wire fence in the barrow pit.

"Red-winged blackbird," I say.

Matt says nothing, but I'm absorbed in the accordion folds of a life-imitates-art-imitating-life moment.

"That's just a cool coincidence. Just like that book, *Zen and the Art of Motorcycle Maintenance.* The guy and his son go on the road. On the first page, they see a red-winged blackbird . . ."

"Never read it," Matt says.

"It's a true story. There's a lot of philosophical crap, deep hoo-ha about romance and rationale, but this father went crazy once and had shock treatment, and he's worried his son might go crazy, too, so they get on a motorcycle and head across Montana to California."

"To see blackbirds?"

"No. Just to . . . I don't know. Make sure . . ."

"Of what?"

"You know, father-and-son stuff. That they didn't lose each other. That they shared one thing that nobody else shared. That . . . I don't know . . . that nothing could come between them."

I am shoveling smoke here. Worse, I am tangled up in those discordant accordion folds, not sure if I'm talking about the book or us.

"What happened in the end?"

"The guy comes to the conclusion that life is complicated, and that might be because we have confused what we are and what we do, and so there's this metaphysical—"

"No, Dad," Matt interrupts, "I mean with the guy and the kid."

"Oh. I think they come to a big cliff, nobody jumps, then they go back home and live happily ever after," I say. "Well, not exactly. I guess after the book came out, the kid grew up and got stabbed to death by a mugger."

Matt studies my face for the telltale twinkle in my eye or the slight lilt at the corner of my mouth that always gives my lame jokes away, but it was true.

"You serious?" he says. "That sucks."

We go for a long time without talking. Not even Sydney, the disembodied GPS girl, has anything to say on this long, straight highway. Matt watches the patchwork of pasture and prairie pass, and sips his Rockstar energy drink. I know he's thinking about dying now. Not the messiness of it, but more the abstraction of it. He is old enough to see through the delusion of immortality, young enough to still find romance in death.

Or maybe not.

Maybe that's one of the reasons a father and a son embark on a long journey together—to strike a balance between death and immortality.

Or maybe not, again.

"Is it deep?" Matt asks.

"The book?"

Matt rolls his eyes.

"The river."

"Not really. Wider than it is deep. And slow."

"I haven't really been fishing since that time we went to the creek in Colorado," he says.

God, I want to stop, right here, right now, and take my son to the river.

"If I had my gear, we'd go," I say. "Maybe in Canada . . ."

I am not a graceful fisherman, but I draw no distinctions between time and trout streams. Every excursion is more a place than a measure of a year, and every stream flows through days, through me. I know fishing is about patience, which, like hope, is really just another way of describing the passage of time. I am not as patient as I imagine great fishermen to be, but I am getting better . . . I just want to get better faster.

My grandfather Joe taught me to fish. He was my stepfather's father. For a long time I didn't know we weren't blood-related, and after that, it just didn't matter. Giuseppe Pietro Franscella voyaged alone from his small Italian village to Ellis Island when he was just seventeen. With twenty-five bucks in his pocket, he caught a train to San Francisco—where, in his zeal to be an American, he renamed himself Joseph Peter and shed the "a" in his surname as if it were all that shackled him to the Old Country. Forty-six years later, when my mother married his son, he was an ordinary Joe.

Long before I came along, Joe had been a big-time chef in Hollywood's rococo-swank Alexandria Hotel and the glamorous Ambassador, where he met silent movie stars like Valentino and Nazimova, a Russian actress with whom he was curiously taken.

My grandfather was the proto-Bourdain: profane, adventurous, street-smart, intensely honest, tough, and a good cook. He always claimed he could sleep anywhere, "like a badger," because, well, he must have respected badgers' toughness or sleep habits. After he retired, he often made breakfast for the visiting grand-children, and it might be silky oatmeal, French crepes—or eggs scrambled with calf brains. He could also cuss in several lan-guages. He was the first adult I ever heard say "fuck," but his favorite invective was "crap," whose "r" was chopped and diced by this cantankerous Italian chef until it unzipped more like *krrrep*. For a long time, I didn't even know *krrrep* was English.

He didn't just tell other people's stories. He lived his own stories, and they were good stories.

Joe was also a master fisherman. A hook-and-bait man, more intuitive than methodic. He taught me on the treacherous banks of the roiling ribbon of Big Pine Creek in California's Sierras, where he'd built a cabin with his three sons, one of whom would become my stepfather. Early on, he'd secretly hook a rainbow trout and then hand the rod to me. I might or might not realize there was a fish on the other end, mostly because my little fingers hadn't yet become sensitive to the faint twitching of the nylon line that would someday cause me to slam my brakes at nothing more than a glimpse of a promising trout stream.

Matt never knew Joe, except from my stories. My grandfa-ther died the year before my son was born. I'm pretty sure Matt never knew that when I took him fishing, I'd secretly hook a trout, then hand the rod to him. The faint twitching of the nylon line was somehow connected across time to Giuseppe Pietro Franscella.

"When's the last time you fished?" my son asks.

The derelict train tracks, leading nowhere, run along beside us.

"A long time ago. It was with you. That time in Colorado."

"Why did you stop?"

"You left."

We follow the wind, literally, to a quixotic land of giants.

U.S. 12 meanders west toward Helena, scrambling up and over the Rockies, and rolling down the other side to the Pacific Ocean, so Sydney advises us to abandon U.S. 12 and the Musselshell, to stair-step north on Route 191 toward Great Falls, through the Judith Basin, across the Judith River, in the shadow of the Judith Mountains, cut across Judith Basin County, right up the main street of Judith Gap.

(This Judith trend all started with a nameless river and a couple of lonely guys. More than a year after they began their expedition in 1804, strapping captains Meriwether Lewis and William Clark must have been feeling a little goatish. They found themselves literally in the center of what would someday become the State of Montana, on the banks of a "handsome river," with a soft bottom and fair banks. Clark, who explored farther up the river than Lewis, named the river for the girl he had left behind, his fiancée and thirteen-year-old cousin, Judith Hancock of Virginia. In time, Judith's name was slapped on pretty much every possible geographic feature in the area—a peak, a mountain range, a town, several streets, a recreation area, a county, and the whole damn basin.)

Judith Gap (Pop. 164) is a windblown village that barely clings to the blizzard-funneling notch between the Little Belt Mountains and the Snowies. Once a curse, the wind-tunnel topography is now a profitable blessing. You see, Judith Gap is now the home of one of the West's biggest wind farms.

The heart of the Judith Gap Wind Farm sprawls over forty square miles, about twelve miles due north of the front door of Wade's Drive Inn and Café at the junction of U.S. 12 and 191 in Harlowton, but you can see the mammoth turbines from Wade's front booth if you happen to stop for one of Wade's scratch cinnamon rolls on a June morning.

Even from a distance, we can see their three-bladed nacelles turning slowly like a field of spinning anorexic albino sunflowers.

Sitting atop sleek 260-foot towers, the slender blades reach nearly four hundred feet into the Big Sky—taller than any building in Montana and the five states that surround it.

"Can we stop?" Matt asks.

"Why not?" I say. "I always wondered what they sound like."

We split off the blacktop onto a dirt road that leads into the field of windmills. We come to an open gate and rumble across the cattle guard among the leviathans. Stopping at the base of one, we get out and snap a few pictures of ourselves beneath the giant blades, which emit an electric drone like an android's dream.

"Too cool," Matt says. "I feel so small."

Not a bad lesson, I think. I lay down on the road to get a shot of Matt with the enormous tower behind him, and he flashes the sign of the horns, a popular heavy-metal hand signal—uplifted index and pinkie fingers—as a symbol of his, I dunno, metalness? I just always thought it meant "two outs."

Just then, a wind rider's white company truck pulls up behind us. He looks official, with the wind farm's logo on the side.

"Private property here," he says. "You have to leave."

"Sorry," I say with an apologetic wave, still flat on my ass in the road. "Just taking some pictures."

He sticks around to make sure these two idiots—the old guy with dirt on his ass and the Satanic devil-kid—find their way out and move along to the next county, maybe even all the way to Great Falls.

Quixote, I think, wouldn't have given up without a fight.

At Sweet Grass, Montana, eight miles north of Sunburst at the bitter end of I-15 on the long, lonely northern border of Montana, we change our American dollars for Canadian cash—damn near one for one—at a little convenience store, then pull into the lines of cars waiting at the international border crossing.

Now, every journey is a story, and in every story there comes a moment when the hero crosses from his known, comfortable world into an alien, unsettling world where the rules and the limitations are different.

Some insufferable, monomythologizing, hermeneutic know-it-alls will pontificate about how this threshold is where our hero transcends the boundaries of his ego as he searches for identity and wholeness. The rules will change. This threshold is the gateway to a realm of darkness, they'll say, where our hero must confront his demons, seize his grail—whatever it might be—and be reborn.

. . . Dorothy goes all Technicolor . . .

. . . Leopold Bloom steps off his porch at No. 7 Eccles Street into Dublin on the ordinary morning of June 8, 1904 . . .

. . . Tyler Durden asks to be punched . . .

. . . Luke Skywalker's family is slaughtered on Tatooine . . .

. . . Thelma and Louise walk into this bar . . .

. . . Michael Corleone takes aim at Virgil Sollozzo and Captain McCluskey with a gun he found behind the toilet . . .

. . . Willie McCoy (down home they call him Slim) travels from south Alabama to 42nd Street to mess around with Big Jim Walker . . .

And they'll point out that the threshold is almost always protected by some kind of pathway guardian, usually someone of minor authority who blocks our hero from his adventure and warns him that the journey ahead might be harder than anyone expects. In order to pass, our hero must prove his mettle.

Whatever.

Sometimes a threshold is just a meaningless threshold, right?

These dog-eared archetypes don't exist in real life . . . right?

If any threshold marks the barrier between my old, comfortable world and a darker, more perilous one, it was the threshold of the Wyoming house where I raised my children, the doorstep I crossed on my way out of one life and into another.

Or maybe the jetway to the plane that took me to Panama, where ghosts, broken angels, and boa constrictors guarded the path.

Or maybe the crossroads between past and present, somewhere on the dirt road between the superslab and U.S. 24, where the shadow of a dreamer watches the road and yells down through his spectral megaphone, "Hey, Lone Star, stop for a spell and try to see two lives from the Tower! Look 10,000 miles into the future! And watch out for that dog shit!"

This threshold nonsense is what we make believe it is— nothing more and nothing less. Dream stuff. Plus, it's tough to imagine Canada as an alien, dark, or unsettling world, except to a ham-versus-bacon purist.

But here we are. When we finally roll up to the gates of Canada, I hand our passports to the uniformed bald guy at the booth window. Dark glasses hide his eyes.

"Why are you here?" he asks.

"Being tourists," I say. "Camping, eating, sightseeing, self-discovery. That kind of stuff."

"Ever been to Canada before?"

"I have, once. My son, never."

He looks long at the long-haired, lip-'stached, skater kid wearing a skully and a black Pantera T-shirt in my passenger seat, then back at me. I can't tell if he's suspicious or sorry.

"Where are you coming from?"

"Me, Texas. Him, Wyoming."

"Where you headed?"

"Yukon Territory."

"How long?"

"Three weeks."

"Do you have any liquor in your car?"

"Not yet."

The border guard doesn't smile. Smart-ass Americans. But we are passing Canada's best post-9/11 test . . . until the next question.

"Do you have any firearms in your vehicle?" the humorless guard asks.

I nod and smile. I expected this question. I knew we'd be camping, and I had planned to bring a handgun until a government clerk had told me that there was no way, no how I could bring a gun to Canada purely for personal protection. So the answer is easy . . . right?

"No," I said.

The uniform suddenly fixes his most suspicious gaze on me. "No?"

"No."

"Are you sure?"

Yeah, I was damn sure I didn't have a gun.

"No gun," I tell him.

"Well, when I asked you if you had a gun, you nodded yes, but you said no."

"I nodded because I was expecting your question," I try to explain, but all I do is dig a little deeper. "I was nodding because I knew it was coming. I mean, I was going to bring a gun, but I called somebody in Quebec or Toronto, and they said I couldn't. So I didn't. No gun."

He sizes me up, then hands me a yellow slip.

"You need to park your car and go inside to talk to our immigration people."

Krrrep.

Inside, the immigration clerk is a petite and pretty blonde whose nametag says S. Tundif. She asks more of the same questions, plus a few more that suggest she is a little more suspicious of us than I would hope any border agent would be.

"What's your relationship?"

"Father and son."

"What's your job?"

"Newspaperman."

"What does that mean?"

"I work for a newspaper in the States."

"Where?"

"Texas."

"When do they expect you back?" S. Tundif asks.

"About three weeks. I'm supposed to be back in the office on July, um, second, I think."

"You're not sure?"

"No, it's July second. Two days before the Fourth."

"Is that supposed to be funny?"

"No," I say. "It's just that the Fourth is . . . you know."

"What?"

This is Canada, you idiot.

"Um, it's a little local holiday. Nobody works."

Now she scrutinizes Matt, who must look to her like a terrorist refugee from a Palestinian skateboarding camp.

"Do you have a job that you must return to in the States?" she asks him.

"Uh, no. I'm in college. Nebraska. Go Huskers."

If I'd seen her next question coming, I swear I would have lied.

"Have you ever been refused entry to any country?"

I smile and suppress a little giggle. "Uh, yeah."

This gets her attention.

Note to self: Border agents don't want to hear you've been kicked out of other countries.

"What country?"

"Iran."

It was true, but nowhere near as swashbuckling as it sounds. After 9/11, on assignment in the Middle East, it could take days—or fat bribes—to get permission to travel to places like Egypt, Kuwait, or Iraq. I simply didn't have days—or cash—to waste while waiting for the sclerotic machinery of Arab governments and their avaricious functionaries to ooze enough ink and energy to stamp a passport. So it became my habit to just show up at international airports visa-less and plead my journalistic case to some harried immigration clerk, who was usually more interested in keeping the long, restive lines moving than sending an American journalist packing.

It worked every time—except in Tehran. Seems the mullahs had their standards after all.

"On what grounds did they refuse entry?" S. Tundif asks.

"I was a newspaperman . . . a journalist. I guess Iran didn't want American journalists in their country at that time, and they would not let me in. I didn't take it personally."

"For what reason?"

"I don't know, but . . . I guess nobody likes the media."

C'mon, a little self-deprecating humor; now that's funny. Real terrorists don't have a sense of humor.

The somber S. Tundif doesn't laugh. She doesn't even smile. She says nothing for several pregnant seconds, then disappears into a profoundly organized little back office, where I reckon she is telephoning one of her Iranian counterparts for his side of the story.

"I should have lied," I whisper to Matt. Not exactly the fatherly lesson I hoped he'd take away from this trip.

"No shit," he says.

S. Tundif finally emerges from her very tidy Canadian office. She still isn't smiling. She carries our whole adventure in her admittedly pretty little fingers, which hand me a new yellow slip and point us down the line to something called the Traffic Desk, where I am certain our car will be searched and we'll be sent straight home when they find some contraband bologna or suspicious sunflower seeds. The Sourtoe will remain an elusive prize, and the heroes of our story will have no story at all. Just a couple of misunderstood, white-bread, suburban badasses in a Subaru who are too wicked for Canada.

At the Traffic Desk, a trooper in a flak jacket glances at our passports, then hands them to another trooper in a flak jacket.

"Where are you headed?" he asks, never looking up.

"Yukon Territory," I tell him. "Dawson City, and then the Dempster Highway to the Arctic."

"You've got a long road ahead. A couple thousand miles. And on the Dempster, go slow. Take extra gas. Got spare tires?"

"Bad road?"

"Not good. It's gravel, you know, sharp shale. Hard on tires, and not many places to get help. Got a cell phone?"

"Yeah."

"Well, it won't work up there."

The trooper stamps something and hands us back our passports.

"Drive safe," he says. "Welcome to Canada."

That's it?

No cavity searches? No computer search for my permanent record? No exile to the Canadian Guantanamo? Just a warning to be careful on a freaking dirt road?

C'mon, I grew up in Wyoming. I've been on real dirt roads that were real dirt. Roads with names like Oh My Gawd and Turn Back Now. Roads with ruts that'd swallow my Subaru without belching. Roads where one guy has to back down the mountain if two cars meet. Roads where granny gear feels too dangerous. Roads where you only wear a seat belt to prevent concussions. Roads lined with oil pans and mufflers, where profanity still hangs in the air. Roads that are almost certainly unpaved switchbacks to the back door of Hell.

So really, how bad could a public, two-lane Canadian high-way that's paved with gravel be?

When the time comes, my friend, I will tell you.

Calgary is closed.

All along, we'd planned to end our first day here in the shadow of the Canadian Rockies, get a good night's sleep, then rent a small camper van for the rest of our journey north. But as luck would have it, Calgary is hosting the mother of all oil and gas conventions. A booked-solid Comfort Inn offers to put us on a not-likely waiting list for a double bed at a mere $209, and not even the cheapest flophouse has a room for any price.

It is getting late, but here in the northern latitudes, the sun is still high. Our bodies are fooled. After two hours of being turned away from a dozen inns, we are prepared to sleep in the car until a pretty young desk clerk—smitten with Matt—offers to call some roadside motels farther up the road for us. Nothing in Balzac, Airdrie, or Crossfield. But just before we resign ourselves to sleeping in a truck-stop parking lot, she finds the one last room in Carstairs, forty miles away.

We arrive after ten p.m., dog-tired, at the Golden West Motor Inn, a dowdy old motor court off the small town's main drag, but it's a dinner-hour light. The owner, a nice-enough old guy in red suspenders who reeks of man-sweat, checks us into a smoking room on the second floor, but thoughtfully puts a cheap air freshener in it for us. Even so, it still reeks like the smoking section in a burned-out Stuckey's. The toilet doesn't work, and to flush it requires one to actually lift the tank lid and reach into the water to lift the stopper. The postwar air conditioner oozes a death rattle. The phone doesn't work either, and there's no Internet. Only seventy bucks plus tax, and there are beds—the only proper beds we expect to see until we're almost home again in a fortnight—and that's all we really want.

Matt goes for a jog and I set out on foot to find a place to eat, but the sidewalks rolled up hours ago. I finally find some processed-turkey lunchmeat and day-old bread—no mustard or mayo, though—at a convenience store, but when I get back to the room, I am sleepier than I am hungry. We have driven more than eight hundred miles today, more than seventeen hours, and the thrum of the road is still purring in my bones.

I fall back on the bed and stare at the popcorn ceiling. I remember the sky still being light, even though it was nearing eleven at night. I remember smelling the foul plastic-wrapped turkey as Matt made himself a dry sandwich. And I remember picking up my cell phone to call Mary because I just wanted to hear her voice and to tell her we were okay, but it was too late in Texas to wake her.

I am suspended somewhere between Texas and a toe, between sleep and waking, between night and day. If home is not just where you live, but where you belong, it feels like far.

Last Exit to Valhalla

If death meant just leaving the stage long enough to change costume and come back as a new character, would you slow down? Or speed up?
— Chuck Palahniuk

By the way, the Golden West's alarm clock didn't work either.

We had planned to rise at the crack of sparrow fart, backtrack forty miles to Calgary to pick up our rented camper van and find breakfast, but it's after eight a.m. when I squint at the banjaxed clock on the nightstand. Matt's bed is a cumulus cloud of sheets and feet, and his laptop is on the floor.

I swing my legs to the side of the bed and realize I never took off my shoes. In fact, I never undressed at all, never took out my hearing aids, never even pulled down the skanky bedspread, which probably hadn't been washed or changed since the wreck of the *Edmund Fitzgerald*.

"Matt," I say. "Rise and shine."

The pile of bedclothes doesn't move. It doesn't even moan. It might be dead for all I know.

"Matt," I say a little louder. "We gotta hit the road, toad."

Oh man, an old home movie from another life. That's how I'd always rousted him when he was little so he wouldn't be late

91

for the school bus or a Saturday-morning soccer game. And it must have echoed somewhere in his slumbering middle brain, because the lump stirs.

———◆———

While Matt dresses, I carry our bags down to the car. A buzz-cut fortysomething guy in a striped polo shirt and a fishing vest sits in a plastic chair outside Room Ten at the bottom of the motel stairs, soaking up a Styrofoam cup of motel coffee, some cigarette smoke, and the morning sun.

"Good morning," I say.

"Guid morn," he replies. "Bonnie day."

"Beautiful. Edinburgh?"

"Ack, no. Glasgow. Ye?"

"Texas. USA."

"Oh, a cowboy . . . an' a lang way frae haem. Whaur ur ye gonnae?"

"Sorry, I—"

"Yer travelin'?" He steers an imaginary car.

"Oh, yeah. The Yukon." I chuck my thumb back over my shoulder, loosely northward-ish. "My son and I are taking a big trip together."

"Ah, 'at sounds guid. Ye hae a lang, lang road aheid."

"Yeah, a long road. I'm Ron." I hold out my hand.

"Aye, ah'm glad tae meit ye. Ah'm Davy."

Davy stands up to shake my hand. He's not a big guy, but his smallish hand clenches mine like a pair of little pliers.

He tells me he's a long-haul truck driver, trying to earn enough money to bring his wife and kids from Glasgow. He came to Canada last winter to find a better life for himself and for them, but so far he hasn't found it. Living in motels and truck stops, gutting out deadheads and turnarounds, sweating the ice and the emptiness. He knows roads, too, and none of them seem to lead homeward.

"Have you heard of the Dempster Highway?" I ask. "That's where we're headed. The Arctic."

His eyebrows rise.

"Aye," he says, "She's a hoor. Ah wooldnae drive thaur. Bad road, she is. She will kick yer crease."

It's just a road, dammit! Pussy Scottish truck driver!

"Then it will be a great adventure," I say. "Gettin' my crease kicked, and all."

"Yer gonnae in 'at?" Davy points at my Subaru.

"No. We're renting a little van. For camping."

"Guid. Make sure ye hae spaur tires. God disnae watch oer 'at road. Th' road is gravel, y'know? It doesnae go anywhaur, jist a deid end. Ack, ah wooldna. Wa in th' warld woods ye go thaur?"

"Say again?"

Separated by a common language. Eager for me to understand, Davy slows down and speaks a little louder.

"Wa . . . in th' warld . . . woods ye . . . go thaur?"

"Oh, we plan to go to a pub up there in Dawson where we will drink a mummified human toe," I explain, as if this would clarify our intentions in the slightest. "And then we'll go to the Arctic for a few days."

"A . . . wha'?"

I touch the tip of my Bass walking boot, then tip back an imaginary glass.

"A human toe. In the drink."

"A toe? A real toe? A deid toe? In the name of the wee man . . ."

I smile and nod. Davy scrunches his face. *What—you'll eat haggis but you won't sip a cocktail that contains an old toe? Braveheart, my ass.*

"Ack, yer a braver loon than me! Ur mebbe yer jist a bampot?"

"What's that?"

He twirls his finger at his close-cropped temple and whistles like a drunk parakeet. "An eejit."

"Ah, well, yes," I happily admit, "I am a wee bit crazy. Maybe I will be well again after I drink the Toe."

"Weel, if yer gonnae be a bampot, at leest hae fun," the Scot says as he claps my shoulder. "Yer a lang time deid."

———————

Back in Calgary, Sydney finds the camper-rental place without a hitch. (A little RV humor there.)

Months ago, we'd planned to drive the Subaru only as far as Calgary, where we'd trade it for a small camper van. Liberated from a dependence on expensive motels and restaurants, we could stop anywhere we pleased in the great Canadian Outback, cook our own food whenever and wherever we wanted it, and roll down the road, free of franchises and fecklessness. We'd have our little home to go to, a place to lay our heads down and figure the losses and gains that I knew were in there somewhere too, like Paradise and Moriarty, except that we are not them and chatter chatter blah-blah, and me swearing for all the time and money I'd wasted, and telling myself, I wanted to go north and west and here I'd been all day and into the night going up and down, east and south, like something that can't get started . . .

A tidy, well-groomed college kid named Daniel—I assume he's Mormon since he's got a preppy haircut, pressed trousers, and, oh, he's already told me that he attends Brigham Young University in the States—starts our paperwork. His perky attitude and his yellow golf shirt with the RV company logo inspire confidence and trust.

"You've got our deluxe Class B camper van reserved for, let's see, thirteen days," Daniel says. "Where are you headed?"

"We're going to the Yukon," I tell him.

Daniel pages through our reservation, then licks his manicured index finger and pages some more. He's looking for something and not finding it.

"Um, did you tell us that when you reserved the vehicle?"

"Where we were going? I don't know. Maybe not. Why?"

"Well, there's an extra charge if you go to the northern territories. I'm sorry, somebody should have—"

"Why extra?"

"The roads up there aren't as good as provincial roads," Daniel informs me. "Lots of potholes, rocks, logging trucks, ice, and rougher conditions. It's much harder on the vehicles, so we don't even let our brand-new vehicles go up there. For the rest, we charge extra."

"Define 'extra.' "

"Three hundred Canadian."

"What do I get for three hundred bucks?"

Daniel looks at me like I'm a stupid American or something. "Nothing. It just covers wear and tear on the vehicle for us."

"And if I get a flat tire . . ."

"Oh, you have to pay for that. It's not covered by insurance. Broken windshields either."

I'm a little startled. I mean, I was expecting to pay $122 a day plus gas, which had recently hit its highest prices since the discovery of the wheel. I kept telling myself it was all worth it for a once-in-a-lifetime road trip with my son.

A zaftig German tourist lady behind me in line—let's call her Helga—doesn't appear too happy that this particular train isn't running on time. Helga, who wears her Aryan white hair swept straight back like a Luftwaffe dive-bomber, also wears her impatience on the buttoned long sleeve of her starched linen blouse.

Maybe she's got a Metamucil monkey on her back, because she rakes me with a Teutonic death-glance and grouses something in German to her pasty, pension-age husband (who happens to be wearing a matching starched linen blouse) before she grabs a Banff camping guide and disappears into the women's restroom.

I grit my teeth and smile thinly at the bright-eyed, fresh-faced Daniel.

"Nobody told me, but okay," I tell Daniel. "In for a penny, in for a pound at this point."

"We also require insurance," he continues.

"That's okay. I have my own auto insurance."

"Will it pay in Canada?"

I look at Matt, who's been standing quietly at the counter with me.

"Don't look at me, dude," he says as he walks off toward a pyramid of septic-friendly toilet paper.

"I have no clue. How much would it be, the insurance?"

"Twenty bucks a day, Canadian, pretty much covers every-thing, with a five-hundred-dollar deductible," Daniel says. "And if you break down, it pays you up to fifteen hundred a day for interrupting your vacation."

"How thoughtful," I say as I finger the razor's edge of my Discover card . . . a potential murder-suicide weapon. "So that's another . . ."

"Two-sixty," Daniel says. "Canadian."

"Put it on my tab."

Helga and her impossibly high ass come out of the loo and she glances at her watch, which causes me to glance at mine. It's almost noon and we have five hundred miles still ahead of us today.

"We're almost finished here," Daniel says. "How many kilo-meters would you like to buy?"

"What do you mean?"

"We can sell you mileage in packets of five hundred kilometers for only twenty-nine cents Canadian per 'k.' Otherwise, it's thirty-three cents."

"Wait a sec . . . your daily charge doesn't include mileage?"

"No, sir. That's extra."

Krrrep.

"How many miles are we talking from here to Dawson, in the Yukon?"

The affably efficient Daniel punches numbers into a little calculator behind his desk. "That's about, oh, eighteen hundred."

See if you can follow my mental math: Thirty-three cents is one-third of a dollar, so I can go three miles on a dollar . . . eighteen hundred divided by three is six hundred . . .

"So less than six hundred bucks with the bulk discount, then, right?" I say, slightly proud of my extemporaneous math skills.

"No, sir."

"Whaddya mean?"

"You asked me about miles, not kilometers. It would be"—he *ticka-tickas* his perky little calculator again—"oh, make it twenty-nine hundred k."

Krrrep.

"Twenty-nine *hundred* kilometers?"

"Yes, sir. Or about"—*ticka-ticka-ticka*—"nine hundred fifty-seven dollars. Canadian. Or if you buy six packets"—*ticka-ticka-ticka*—"then it only costs"—*ticka-ticka-ticka*—"eight seventy. Canadian."

"So that's almost fifty cents a mile. Hell, I *live* in Texas, Dan. I don't *own* it."

Daniel smiles. "Sorry, sir, but that's pretty funny, the thing about Texas."

"Yeah, right. Okay, put me down for six packets."

"And back?"

"Back?"

"You have to come back."

Krrrep.

"We can't just leave the camper in the Yukon and hitchhike back?"

Daniel looks a little scared.

"I'm kidding, Dan," I assure him. "So it's not eight-seventy, but . . . double that?"

Daniel *ticka-tickas* some more. "Twelve mileage packs. Seventeen hundred and forty dollars," he says. "Canadian."

I've lost track of the charges. They're somewhere more than *krrrep,* just slightly below *You have exceeded your credit limit.*

"Is that everything I wasn't told about?" I ask Daniel.

"Did I mention the prep fee?"

"No."

Daniel turns sheepish. "Then no, sir, that wasn't everything."

"There isn't an extra charge to rent the key, is there?"

"Good one, sir," the perky Daniel smiles. "The key is completely free . . . but will you be needing camping equipment? Sleeping bags, comforters, towels, plates, bowls, cutlery, pans, coffeepot, broom, cups—you know, everything you need for eating and sleeping?"

I look around. Helga, the fubsy *hausfrau* behind me, makes no attempt to hide her irritation in whispers as she grumbles *auf Deutsche* to her fidgety husband. She doesn't realize that even a *dummkopf Amerikaner* knows what *dummkopf Amerikaner* means.

And now I've lost sight of Matt, who might be camouflaging himself among the Slunky sewage hoses.

Hell, I surrender. It's not like we can turn around and go home. *Sorry, kid, your dad's too cheap to take you on an unforgettable, life-affirming journey to the top of the world. How about we just head home and go bowling?*

"Why not? My wallet's still out. How much?"

"Only seventy bucks Canadian."

"A day?"

"No, sir, just once."

Finally, a bargain.

"Per person" he adds.

Krrrep.

The total estimated charges plus national sales taxes and a nearly one-hundred-dollar "preparation" fee come to a mere forty-five hundred bucks. Canadian. Which, at the moment, is almost exactly the same as American. And we haven't even pumped a single drop of gasoline nor driven one centimeter yet.

I hand him my Discover card.

"I'm sorry, sir, we don't take that card," Daniel says. I hear Helga behind me, huffing, "*Ach, mein Gott in Himmel!*" as I dig in my wallet for my backup Visa.

Daniel swipes my credit card—ironic phrase, isn't it?—for the full amount and gets me to sign several pages promising not to go to Mexico, not to let my nineteen-year-old son drive the van, and not to sue the company, even if the van turns out to be possessed by cliff-diving demons. Then he takes us outside for a crash course in operating a camper van.

Our Roadtrek 190 is just a tricked-out Chevy van, but this four-ton rolling dorm room is loaded, at least for a couple of single guys with quirky priorities: a home-theater system with built-in DVD, CD, dual rear speakers, flat-screen TV, and a remote control; a thirty-one-gallon gas tank; a three-cubic-foot refrigerator; a twenty-three-gallon water heater; three swiveling captain's chairs up front; a six-liter sequential fuel-injection V8 engine; two twelve-volt lead-acid auxiliary batteries for laptops, chargers, lights, and all-night fans; a computerized panel to monitor water, sewage, propane, and battery levels; an overhead air-conditioning system; a microwave oven, a two-burner gas stove, and a handy quick-connect nipple for a gas barbecue outside; a built-in coffeemaker; a private bathroom that converts to a shower, with a modest supply of that quick-dissolve toilet paper; a horseshoe-shaped sofa that morphs into an alleged king-size bed; and sixty-two cubic freaking feet of storage cubbies under the floor. She also hauls twenty-five gallons of freshwater, forty-five pounds of propane, and—if necessary—ten gallons of human waste.

Matt loads all of our gear from the Subaru into the van while Daniel issues me his final instruction: "If you get a flat tire, what-ever you do, don't try to change it yourself," Daniel says with all the gravity he can muster—which is to say that he sounds a little like an eighth-grade hall monitor. "Call our 800-number and we'll have a service truck sent to fix it wherever you are. These vans are extremely heavy, so for your own safety and to avoid damage to the vehicle, do not try to fix your own flats."

Much later, maybe too late, it will occur to me that he is so adamant about us not changing tires that he purposely didn't show us where the jack was hidden. Just a theory.

———————

And so our journey begins . . . again. The farther we go from here, the more civilization recedes and the wilder it gets. We've got a fresh mount and a new road ahead, and I am feeling like it all starts here. Now.

But it really started long before this, maybe even before I left Texas. I don't know when or where exactly. Maybe in the moment when some shopkeeper coughed up a flu virus that was breathed in by my great-grandmother. Maybe the day they sent Thom away. Maybe on the morning when my mother decided it was time for me to know I was a bastard. Maybe when I discov-ered Kerouac in college and read *On the Road* until dawn. Maybe the night Matt was born, or I was born, or *Mi Padre* was born. Maybe the morning I left my wife and children for the last time. Maybe when I died but my ghost kept moving. Maybe at some bleak crossroads where I turned west instead of east and unwit-tingly drove away from the Festival of All Answers.

Or maybe on the August night when I realized my son and I shared the same dream about the Toe.

So, you see, I don't know where this story starts or exactly where it goes along the way, but I know where it ends.

———•———

We return to Alberta's Highway 2, the province's main artery, but we don't get far. We haven't eaten a proper meal since the day before, since Montana, which already seems on the other side of the world.

In the small town of Innisfail, an hour up the road from Calgary, we stop at the first place that looks like a local sit-down lunch place because we came too far to eat at Burger King or Pizza Hut. I let Matt out to get a table at the Red Ox Steak House while I find a place to park the van. I chicken out and slide up to the long curb on an empty side street where I can avoid, for now, putting our boxy ride in reverse, or parallel parking.

When I get inside, a lithe, teenage waitress is already chat-ting up Matt at a corner booth. She's pretty enough and whole-some, albeit fashionably pale, with a Katie Holmes bob. If she isn't wearing somebody else's nametag, her name is Corrinna. After I sit down, Corrinna takes our drink order and leaves.

"Boy, you walk into a room and the girls start circling like horny fireflies," I tell Matt.

"Yeah, then you get here and they fly away."

"She's cute."

"Yeah."

"I think she likes you. Was she flirting?"

"I dunno. Maybe. I never know. I suck about that."

"Me, too."

"How the hell do you know? Girls haven't flirted with you in twenty years!"

I briefly consider feigning indignation, but it's a funny line . . . and he's right.

Corrinna returns with our drinks, and she hardly takes her eyes off Matt as she sets our glasses on the table.

"Where you coming from?" she asks him.

Matt answers like a cigar-store Indian.

"Me, Wyoming. Him, Texas."

"Are you cowboys?" she giggles.

We both laugh.

"Nope," Matt says. "Are you?"

"No, but I like 'em," she says. "Are you staying around here?"

Okay, even a flirtation-retard like me saw that one coming!

"Nah," Matt says. "Just stopping for lunch on the way to the Yukon."

"Too bad," Corrinna says as she flips out her scratch pad and scribbles out our order, a crab Caesar for Matt and a chicken cashew salad for me, then leaves.

"Geez, if you want to stay here . . ."

Matt slumps back in his chair. "My timing sucks. They never come around when I need them, and I never need them when they come around."

He's not talking about needs like air, water, and sleep. He's not even talking about sex. He is ruing the misalignment of small stars, wrong places and right times, songs out of tune, losing the road. I want to tell Matt that I know how it feels, but maybe it's best to let him think he's the first guy to ever get his stars crossed. And I want to lead him through the looking glass, where left and right is swapped but not up and down, where being needed is more necessary than needing, where needing to be needed— well, that's just weird. Anyway, there's plenty of road ahead to sort it out.

"Do you have a girlfriend right now?" I ask.

"Nah. I've asked a couple girls out, but they turned me down."

"God, I see these girls looking at you. You gotta have plenty of chances for dates. What's up?"

Matt shrugs. "They just aren't . . . I dunno . . . I can't find any that see things like me, like . . ."

Kelly.

Kelly was Matt's first love. Their high school romance fell apart, as they often do, just before he went off to college in Nebraska. Her idea, not his. This kid who'd watched his father and mother detonate, around whom shrapnel still fell occasionally, and who was still trying to put the fragmented pieces of himself back together, was blown up again. The one thing he thinks he knows, the one thing he can prove beyond any shadow of a shadow of a doubt is this: *Love never stays.*

But Corrinna comes back. She puts our lunches in front of us and flirtatiously tells Matt to call her if he needs anything else. He barely notices.

"Hey, Beavis," I say, "she told you to call her."

"Dude, if you think she's so hot, why don't *you* call her?"

"I would, but I don't think that's legal in Canada."

Equal parts hungry and eager to get back on the road, we barely talk as we inhale our lunches. Corrinna returns to check on us, but we're already done.

"Anything else I can get you?"

"Just the ticket," I tell her.

"What's that?"

"You know"—I do an air-scribble—"the ticket. So I can pay you.

"Oh, the check. That's what we call it in Canada. The *check*."

Matt smirks as the good-humored Corrinna rips our *check* from her pad, slips it facedown on the table, and wishes us a safe trip. He's mildly amused that his old man can't speak Canadian.

"Dude, you'll never get girls if you don't know how to talk to them."

———•———

After lunch, we're back on Highway 2. Alberta's main artery will pump us north, into the shiny steel heart of Edmonton, before it veers westerly through the east-sloping Athabasca River country, where the landscape slides away from the mountains into the muskeg.

Muskeg—from a Chippewa Indian word for "grassy bog"—is a fragile layer of swampy sphagnum moss and decomposing muck that's so wet, acidic, and infertile that only especially masochistic plants thrive in it. It embraces death, literally sucks it up. Dead trees and ground cover sink into the sopping, oxygen-starved, quickly frozen mire before bacteria and molds can digest them, and season after season, the dead debris piles up in thick layers of peat.

In this spongy subarctic swamp, decay is slow and man's influence even slower. Many roads and rails over the muskeg muck are laid on "corduroy," a foundation of felled trees laid side by side for miles and covered with dirt or clay. Legend has it that the muskeg swallowed a nineteenth-century railroad locomotive in northern Ontario, and construction equipment unwittingly parked on frozen muskeg in winter gets sucked down by every spring thaw.

One might think the road-builders diverted west here to avoid the muskeg, but it's really because there's little reason to go much farther north, which is a whole lot of beautiful nothing all the way to the Arctic Ocean.

So we set a course for Highway 43, a shortcut that will take us west across the upper reaches of the Athabasca River, through the broad plains of Alberta, tiptoeing past villages with British-sounding names like Glenevis, Mayerthorpe, and Whitecourt, and eventually dive into the splendid green wheat fields of the Peace River Valley and the boreal forests beyond. Except for the place names and the troubling fixation with the metric system, Alberta's not terribly unlike Texas in its landscape, economy, and people (many of whom are proud to call themselves—like Texans—"rednecks").

Sydney sounds disappointed we aren't muskeg-bound. "Recalculating," she fumes.

In Mayerthorpe, we stock up on food at the local co-op—staples such as hot dogs, sandwich meat and bread, a round tin of Danish butter cookies, string cheese, cans of chili, beef jerky, granola bars, crackers, condiments, and the like—and buy a case of Chilkoot beer and a pint of Yukon Jack at a strip-mall package store where Matt's delighted to learn the drinking age in Canada is eighteen. (Not that the legal drinking age in the States has thwarted him, but at least here and now, his father can only make lame moral, not legal, arguments against it.)

A few miles on, we stop for our first fill-up at a junction Esso station where a back road will take you to the unincorporated collection of 280 souls known as Blue Ridge. While Matt goes inside for a fresh energy drink, the frowzy teenage attendant washes my windows and pumps a little more than seventy-five liters of unleaded gas at a buck-eleven—or about twenty U.S. gallons at $4.15 a pop. The pump's cash meter finally stops rolling at eighty-three bucks and change.

I glance at the trip counter on the dash. *My God, we haven't even traveled three hundred miles in this freaking van!* I hand the greasy kid my Visa card and try not to think about how fast the meter will be spinning on the next four thousand miles.

Okay, breathe . . . Once in a lifetime . . . father and son . . . top of the world . . . you coulda gone bowling . . .

It's after ten p.m. when we back the van into an empty space in a secluded corner of the Williamson provincial campground beside Sturgeon Lake, but the sky is still smoky twilight blue. We're bushed, and the day has been 470 miles long, but we're barely a quarter of the way to the Toe.

Up here, a higher latitude than legendary cold spots like Vladivostok and the Aran Islands, evening temperatures typically drop into the mid-forties. Although tonight the still air hovers between sweatshirt and jacket, some tough-assed Canadian mosquitoes patrol the woods. I swat them back as I walk back to the campground's entrance to slide twenty bucks into the honor box. When I return, Matt is already building a smoky campfire with the free logs left for us by provincial woodcutters, who must certainly have the best job in all of Canada.

Awash in woodsmoke and mosquito spray, we blacken some hot dogs on the rusty fire grate and flush them down with a few Chilkoots—the first beer I have ever shared with my son. Alas, it is not the seminal moment to him that it is to me. He comments on the beer's body and aftertaste, and compares and contrasts it to a popular American lager. He appears to have done this before.

After supper, such as it is, we drag the heavy picnic table to the fireside, close enough to feel the prickle of heat on our faces as we poke at it, launching a shimmering mist of sparks into a sky that is still half day and half night. We sit there, mostly silent, the frontal lobes of our brains warmed edgeless by the fire in front of us.

When I go inside to get more beer from the van's mini-fridge, I find the contents of Matt's duffel bag spilled on the floor beside our sofa-bed. He's brought three books with him:

Chuck Palahniuk's *Rant*, a dog-eared copy of the unspoiled first rendering of John Fowles's *The Magus* (made less supple when he rewrote it years later in a prolonged fit of artistic pique), and Brian Greene's *The Elegant Universe: Superstrings, Hidden Dimensions and the Quest for the Ultimate Theory.*

I know my son's fascination with *Fight Club* author Palahniuk, the taboo-less, shape-shifting, malevolent Kerouac of his generation. And, in turn, he knows my own fascination with *The Magus*, a mythopoetic story about sense and sensuality that made me want to be a writer. But I don't know the Greene book, so I pick it up and read the jacket:

> *In a rare blend of scientific insight and writing as elegant as the theories it explains, Brian Greene, one of the world's leading string theorists, peels away the layers of mystery surrounding string theory to reveal a universe that consists of eleven dimensions where the fabric of space tears and repairs itself, and all matter—from the smallest quarks to the most gargantuan supernovas—is generated by the vibrations of microscopically tiny loops of energy.*

Rips in the fabric of space? Quarks? Vibrating strings of . . . what, exactly? I couldn't have been more surprised if I had found a baggie of pot in my nineteen-year-old son's luggage, although I must admit it's far less disturbing to find a book about theoretical physics and quantum mechanics than a stash—and far more difficult to talk about.

I shouldn't be surprised, though. Matt fell in love with books the moment he could look at a word and know how it tasted, smelled, and felt. From the age of six, he read almost every night before bed, and always stowed a book on the toilet tank. As a grade-schooler, he inhaled *Star Wars* novelizations, all the Goosebumps books, ancient mythology, and at thirteen, read—and mostly understood—his father's first novel, which was certainly not written for eighth-graders.

My son's literary tastes at the moment—dystopia, eroticism, and infinity—intrigue me. Maybe boiled down like that it sounds too much like late-night dorm-room prattle, but when the typical college freshman's leisure reading ranges from vampires to graphic novels . . . or nothing at all . . . it's comforting (and pleasantly astonishing) to know my son is delving deeper.

"I see you brought a Palahniuk book," I say as I hand Matt another beer. "Any good?"

"Freakin' cool," he says.

"What's it about?"

Matt shakes his head and pops the can open. "You wouldn't understand."

I am momentarily offended. Have I suddenly gone daft in my son's eyes? Does he see me as too old and senile to grasp "new" literature?

"Try me," I dare him.

He takes a deep breath, pokes the fire, and starts his book report: "It's like an oral history in the future with all these people getting interviewed about this kid named Rant Casey, which is just his nickname. His real name is Buster and he is born with this, like, Superman sense of smell, and he gets his jollies by sticking his arm down the holes of snakes and spiders and rabid animals so they'll bite him because getting bitten gives him a hard-on, but it also gives him some weird strain of mutant rabies that he passes on to all his friends, who sell him their teeth for these antique gold coins. And the people in his little town pay him to leave, so he goes to a big city where you are either a Day-timer or a Night-timer, because the day people are more of the, like, rich and upright people, and the night people are, like, poor and antisocial and persecuted and shit. The big thing to do for the Night-timers is to 'party-crash,' which is, like, these ginormous traffic accidents for fun where they chase each other through the streets and ram their cars in an all-night demolition derby so they know they're alive, which is what they do instead of this thing called 'peak-boosting,' where you just sit in this room by yourself with a cable in your brain that plays other people's experiences, sorta like TV except it's, like, this mainline into your brain, and everybody is not living a real life but are all virtual.

"So Rant is, like, this messiah who hates everything that's fakey and he falls in love with this Echo chick and they spread rabies all over and people turn into, like, zombies and shit, and the city makes a law that anybody with rabies can be shot on sight, so Rant straps this Christmas tree on top of his car and sets it on fire and drives off a bridge, but when they find the car, there's no body in it, but everybody believes that if you're in the right state of mind and you crash, you can be, like, totally jolted out of time, and if you kill all your ancestors you can have immortality—oh yeah, did I say he's already dead when the book starts?—well, anyway, so Rant could, like, kill his father and, like, re-create himself so he can live forever and be like a god. It's all like a story about vampires on LSD. But right now I'm at this part where Rant's mom is going to be raped by this other guy. That's all the farther I got."

Our campfire is burning fervently now, and swarms of glowing ash-sparks swirl and sparkle and rise on its column of heat toward the steely, half-lighted sky. I pick one out and watch it until it flames out and disappears against the dark background of the forest, an invisible ash. Gone. Unremembered, except right here.

"Let's play twenty questions," I say.

"You're not listening."

"Yes, I am. C'mon, let's play."

"I told you you wouldn't understand."

Matt throws a stick into the fire and says nothing.

"No, really," I say. "Let's play the game."

"No, fuck that. I feel like a douchebag."

"C'mon, chill. Just ask me a question."

Matt sulks for a moment, staring at the fire.

"Is it an animal?"

"No."

"Vegetable?"

"No."

"Mineral?"

"No."

"Come on! It has to be one of those! You suck. I'm not play-ing. You pretended you wanted to hear about the book, and now you're just fucking with me. I knew you wouldn't understand."

"Fire."

"What?"

"Fire. It isn't an animal, vegetable, or mineral."

"Fuck fire."

"Oooh, there's a painful image."

"You do this shit. You play around. You wanted to know about the book and I told you and now you're just making fun."

"No, I'm not. I'm trying to make a point."

"Bullshit," Matt grouses. "Not everybody writes books the same way you do. I like Palahniuk's books because they're never ordinary, and the endings are never what you expect. It's, like, sometimes the ending is a climax and everything makes sense right there at the end, but it's not a happy ending in the sense that the characters are all living happily—well, maybe—ever after, living the American Dream. I can't even imagine where this book is going or how it's going to end because he doesn't follow the rules. He makes his own rules. So it's not your kind of story, but I think he's friggin' cool."

Matt's angry, so we just sit for a minute, saying nothing. Best to let him think he's won. Lately, he's been sensitive about not being taken seriously because he wants desperately to be serious. I understand. Completely.

"Still, do you ever wonder what's in fire?" I ask. "I mean, what fire is made of?"

Matt pulls his skully down over his ears and mutters something under his breath that sounds like *Shit*.

"Think about it. We know what makes air, right? Molecules of different stuff. And we know what's in wood. More molecules of more stuff. So why don't we know what fire is made of?"

"No more beer for you, dude."

"Would you say fire is more like light . . . or like love . . . or life? Is it just particles of stuff floating through the air, or is it this kind of chemical reaction that creates something we don't understand? For that matter, what is time made of?"

Matt looks at me. I see the dancing orange fire reflected in his eyes.

"Are you having a stroke or something? Jeezus."

"It's just that we're surrounded by things we don't understand. I can't make fire without a match—or an electrical accident. I can't make air and I can't make time. I don't know where love comes from or where it goes. And I just got lucky both times I made life. There's just a lot of stuff that makes life worth living that we just don't understand, you know?"

"Do you have a point here or are you just jacking with me?"

"Palahniuk."

"What the f—?"

"That story about the kid with the rabies and the teeth and the car crashes and time-travel and reality . . ."

"Are you sure you're not having a stroke?"

"No, I'm fine. Just listen: Palahniuk is asking a question about something. I don't know about what. Maybe faith or love or what life should be. The bit where they can't find Rant's body? That's like Jesus and resurrection, you know? It's the old story about the hero's rebirth. No, I love your story, I really do. I can't write like that, and I don't understand where it comes from, but I love the story. And I especially love that you love it. But most of all, you don't have to explain it, and you don't have to worry that I won't understand. It's like . . . fire."

Matt leans forward to pick up the wayward remnant of a twig from the dirt between his feet. He tosses it in the fire.

"You suck," is all he says.

"What do you mean?" I'm a tad offended.

"Couldn't you have just said, 'Oh, that's a cool story'?"

Sometime after one a.m., with the sky still uncannily gray, we finish our beers, piss on the fire, and crawl into our allegedly queen-size bed.

Matt drifts off while I read his book about string theory, time warps, and other junk that I don't understand, and because I am pleasantly drunk, I won't understand in the morning, either.

But I am not looking for the keys to the universe. No; I am looking for my son, who is sleeping beside me in our cozy bunk on the same cheap foam mattress, not a stranger, but still enough of a man-cipher that I would drive to the top of the world to make sure he knew how much I loved him, and to make sure he still loved me, too.

I don't know how old this Brian Greene is, but judging by his picture on the back jacket, he's half my age and could be played by David Schwimmer in the movie. That—and a predictably gushy blurb on the cover from some guy at the *New York Times* who pretends to know exactly what it's all about when I don't—makes me feel a little impotent.

The basic conflict in this story is set up on the first page. Apparently, there's been a dustup between Einstein's relativity theory and quantum mechanics because, theoretically, both can't be right. Pretty quickly, the author dives into special relativity—how time and space are not experienced identically by everyone—and the faster and farther we go, the more we see things differently. And string theory—if we could prove it—could be the cavalry riding to the rescue of the distressed physicists, explaining everything about everything so we can relax and focus on the unsolved mysteries of Paris Hilton's celebrity, and why you can't take a close-up photograph of the horizon, which might also be explained by string theory as far as anyone knows.

I flip forward a few pages, maybe a lot of pages, to a chapter where Greene is discussing the possibility—no, the likelihood—that there are more dimensions than just width, depth, and height. Like, say, time.

Imagine you've got a four-dimensional, cosmic GPS. No, even bigger and badder than the two-dimensional Sydney. This magic machine would be able to pinpoint any place *and* time in the vast universe, then take you there. That's some deep flummadiddle.

At one point, Greene poses a tantalizing possibility: If we could travel at the speed of light, is it possible that we'd be able to reach out of our magical pickup truck and grab a big glob of stationary light?

This makes me wonder, in a vaguely beer-soaked way: If we could travel at the speed of time, would we be able to hold a completely motionless moment? Could we avoid moving another nanosecond into the future? And what if we could actually travel faster than time? Could we avoid all the fuckups that are coming up fast behind us?

Oh, it gets better. Throughout the book, Greene translates inaccessible physics into colorful metaphors that lesser beings can grasp. Space-time warps are like a bowling ball on a trampoline. He explains how the circumference of a spinning carnival ride can actually be greater than when it is not spinning, and somehow that's a big scientific thing. And he illustrates the inconsistency of time and motion this way: If you run away at twelve feet per second from a hand grenade traveling at twenty feet per second, the grenade is actually traveling toward you at eight feet per second even though it is traveling at twenty feet per second to a bystander (who must be retarded because he isn't running, too).

Briefly, he mentions Werner Heisenberg's Uncertainty Principle, which theorizes that the act of observing alters the reality being observed. In other words, just watching something changes it.

Then it gets weird. To illustrate the possibility of even more dimensions, Greene imagines a world inside a garden hose, where the inhabitants are merely wormlike beings with vacant eyes at both ends. Problem is, they think they only have one dimension: length. They can only go forward or backward, because in Garden-Hose Land, there is no up or down or sideways. They cannot imagine a world in which they could journey *around* each other, much less travel in time to a moment when they were someplace or someone else.

Oh, I get it! We're like the hose-worms! We're always looking the wrong direction, and we don't know what we don't know! Maybe we don't even know enough to run from a hand grenade! And this spinning carnival ride we call Earth might actually be bigger than it would be if it came to a complete stop! And thanks to Heisenberg, the simple act of regretting, dreaming about, or maybe just remembering every bad choice in life makes it different than it really was. Hallelujah!

I gotta pee.

I'm thinking this could be an embarrassing function in one dimension, where the eye of the guy behind you is always on your ass. As I squirm out of our archduke-size bed, trying not to wake Matt, I realize how lucky I am to have three marvelous dimensions to navigate. And when I'm finally peeing on the glowing embers of our smoldering campfire, I celebrate my freedom by spritzing up, down, left, right, and as far as my fifty-year-old bladder and three Chilkoot beers can muster. Three-dimensional urination is a gift from God.

Standing there in the middle of the slightly chilly night, going on three a.m., I realize the sky is actually getting lighter, although I don't plan to drag my butt out of bed for about five more hours. There are stars up there, but the sky isn't dark enough to see them. And if there's a moon out, it is obscured by the trees.

In a place where the sun barely sets on a summer night, dawn lacks confidence. It sneaks up early and lingers long. The dusky sky lightens in the wee hours, and the sun rises in its cockama-mie clockwise ellipse above the horizon, like a giant tetherball . . . *Oh god, now I'm starting to do it!*

I crawl back into bed beside Matt and turn off the overhead light. There in the half-dark, I think about time . . . tomorrow . . . and space . . . the miles we've come, the miles we'll go . . . as I reach over and rest my hand on my sleeping son's shoulder.

His skin is warm. I am reassured there's still a fire somewhere inside him.

———•———

I wake a little after eight a.m., but it seems later, a trick of this strange northern light.

The camper smells like woodsmoke, bug dope, electric heat, and sour socks. My neck itches from four unshaven days. A blood vessel behind my left eye, deep in my skull, is pulsating. It's not a stroke. It's Chilkoot.

In one of those brilliantly incoherent dialogues we have with our silent selves, I weigh the cost of sleeping off my hangover and decide to get up. I worm out of the little bed where Matt has sprawled, dead to the world, and slide into my dirty jeans and hiking boots. On the way out, I wash down two ibuprofen with a swallow of flat cola.

The morning is dewy and feels more like late fall than early summer. My breath comes out in vague, alcoholic vapors, like the ghosts of passing drunkards. The forest air is cleansed, except for the aroma of campfires I cannot see. Thin curls of smoke still rise from our fire pit, so I empty our leftover beer cans into the ashes. It feels like . . . revenge.

The road calls. Not far from here, just across the border in British Columbia, is Dawson Creek (a different place entirely from Dawson City in the Yukon), Mile Zero on the Alaska Highway, better known stateside as the Alcan. If we get rolling soon, we might make another five hundred miles—only half-way—before nightfall. Or what passes for nightfall in these parts.

We have the rest of our lives to sleep.

———•———

We build roads for many reasons: to make money, to reach farther, to claim what we reach, to find ourselves, or maybe just to return home.

But the Alaska Highway was built out of fear.

Years before Pearl Harbor, General Billy Mitchell warned that Alaska could be a key strategic prize in any future wars because it could control shipping and air routes in the northern Pacific. And after Pearl Harbor, American military planners suddenly got the message, fearing the likeliest Japanese invasion of North America would island-hop up the Aleutians into Alaska.

So two months after the Japanese attacks in Hawaii, the U.S. Army quickly approved the building of the unsurveyed 1,680-mile Alaska-Canadian Highway—or the Alcan—to bolster the so-called "Alaska Skyway," a string of Allied airfields from Edmonton, Alberta, to the Alaskan coast.

And not a moment too soon: Barely two months after construction began, the Japanese invaded Alaska's Aleutian Islands, partly because they feared any American attacks on Japan would likely be launched from the thousand-mile-long archipelago strung out only two thousand miles from downtown Tokyo.

Soon, 11,000 soldiers—a third of them Southern blacks, many of whom had never seen snow—and 7,500 civilians were literally plowing across the Rockies through truck-deep muskeg, heaving permafrost, endless ancient forests, precipitous river gorges, and man-eating weather. An advertisement for workers in the *New York Times* gave fair warning: "Men hired for this job will be required to work and live under the most extreme conditions imaginable. Temperatures will range from 90 degrees above zero to 70 degrees below zero. Men will have to fight swamps, rivers, ice, and cold. Mosquitoes, flies, and gnats will not only be annoying but will cause bodily harm. If you are not prepared to work under these and similar conditions, do not apply."

At the height of construction, the U.S. Army was using seven thousand bulldozers, trucks, and other vehicles to carve inch by inch through the wilderness, building 133 bridges along the way.

The cold was an almost-constant nemesis, not just for the men but also for their machines. Metal tools would snap at 40 below. Broken parts soon outnumbered spare parts, so broken-down hulks were left where they died and cannibalized to keep other vehicles running. If a bulldozer stopped its engine for more than a couple hours, it wouldn't start again, so men would sometimes build bonfires under them to warm them. And if they were forced to shut down any vehicle overnight, soldiers would often drain all the fluids into cans that they could rewarm on a hot stove the next morning.

At 70 below, a soldier risked frostbite if he took off his glove for even a minute, yet the Army, which had no experience with large-scale subarctic engineering, sent its troops into the Great

White North with clothing rated only down to 40 degrees *above* zero. The men bathed in hot springs and fifty-gallon oil drums. Digging a latrine in impenetrable permafrost was usually not feasible, so more often than not they just shit in the woods. They fought off blackflies and black bears. They slept on the ground in their bottomless tents. In summer, they slogged through swamps while thawing ice humped up the road behind them. They read the war news, which, in 1942, was not good.

One common injury reported was burned hands. Soldiers working long, grueling shifts would fall asleep while warming their hands at a campfire—and fall into the flames.

When they finished the Alaska-Canadian Highway eight months later, although it was one of the twentieth century's greatest engineering feats, it was no superhighway. In fact, it wasn't paved at all. The Alcan was just a serpentine, single-lane wilderness trail, gruesomely muddy and passable only by four-wheel-drive trucks, bulldozers, and half-tracks. Its treacherous switchbacks, pontoon or log bridges, suicide hills, steep grades, and lack of guardrails made the Bataan Death March seem like a cakewalk.

When nobody was looking, the Japanese abandoned the Aleutians and never came back. Suddenly, the road wasn't quite as urgent, and resources were redirected to more vital needs.

After the war, the cob-rough Alcan was turned over to the Canadian government, which straightened it out a little and tried to make it passable. Gas pumps were still few and far between as late as the 1970s, and, just in time for the highway's fiftieth anniversary in 1992, the last stretches of macadam were laid down.

Today, although the Alcan hasn't completely shaken its notorious reputation as the back road to Hell itself, it's so tame that grandmothers with their cheery little dried-apple faces peer down from the passenger seats of their forty-foot RVs as they zoom past. Campgrounds all the way to Fairbanks are filled with Good Sam Club life members who actually remember World

War II and are seeking one last great adventure or two before their time runs out.

But irony doesn't get old. Matt and I rolled into Dawson Creek around lunchtime and stopped at a local diner to eat something more than jerky and sunflower seeds. There was a long white tour bus in a side lot, and its roller sign said FAIRBANKS.

The place was small but clean, maybe a dozen crowded tables, all filled with hungry diners just starting to scan their menus. A frenzied waitress who looked to be past her Midol years saw us at the front counter, and her tired eyes telegraphed it would be a long wait.

Probably would, but the tourists had waited even longer to get here. They were all Japanese.

———•———

A warm rain spits as we hit the Alcan. These first few hundred miles of the highway plunge due north through a landscape that looks more like eastern Montana than the gateway to the Klondike. Up to Fort St. John, running parallel to the Rockies, low rolling hills unfurl in every direction, perfect for cattle ranching and a good life apart from whatever these hardy people came here to find or escape.

As the rain-washed countryside rolls past, Matt's head is bobbing to some scraping heavy metal that's buzzing in his earbuds while he reads the Palahniuk book. Here's a chance to have some of that father-son dialogue stuff . . . plus, I'm getting bored. I reach over and touch his arm.

"Yeah?" he asks, pulling out his earbuds.

"What are you listening to?"

"Megadeth."

"Metal, right?"

"Yeah, hot."

"How can you read at the same time you're listening to heavy metal?"

"How can you drive when you're listening to friggin' Elton John?"

"Driving and reading are different."

"Yeah, if you get distracted in a car, you die, dude. Get distracted with a book, the worst thing that can happen is you lose your page. Different all right."

"Yeah, but heavy metal is just a whole lot of distracting noise . . ."

This sends Matt into orbit. More of that "being taken seriously" stuff.

"Dude, metal is closer to classical music than most of the crap you listen to!"

This isn't going as well as I'd planned. I don't want to sound like, well, a middle-aged dad who is uncomfortable with his son's taste in music—which I am, just like my stepdad never understood The Rolling Stones—so I decide to at least appear open-minded.

"Okay, then let's listen together," I say. "Pick a good one, one you really like, and put it on the stereo."

Matt pages through his fat CD case and slides a new Megadeth CD called "United Abominations" into the dashboard player, then zips through the tracks to number eight, a song called "Tout le Monde." We listen for a while, and I must admit, it's rockin' good music, although the lyrics are somewhat obscured by all the screaming.

"What's it about?" I ask.

"It's a guy's suicide note to all his friends. He's telling them to smile when they think of him."

"No shit?"

"Yeah, and the chick who sings on it is hot, too."

"Pick another one."

Matt fast-forwards to a song called "Sleepwalker."

Mi Padre and Ron at a seaside jardin in Playa Venao.

Looking like his northern cousin, an *inukshuk,* this mop-and-stick man on a Panamanian beach points northward. PHOTO BY RON FRANSCELL

The World Wonderview Tower in Genoa, Colorado. PHOTO BY RON FRANSCELL

Along the quixotic highway, a windmill. PHOTO BY RON FRANSCELL

The Sign Post Forest in Watson Lake, Yukon Territory, was started by a homesick soldier in World War II and now features more than 65,000 signs. PHOTO BY RON FRANSCELL

A supper of caribou stew and musk-ox stroganoff in Whitehorse.
PHOTO BY RON FRANSCELL

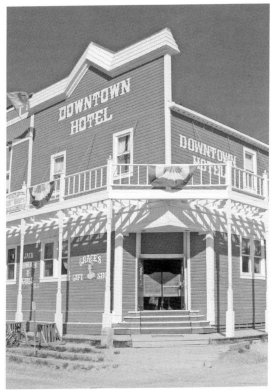

Dawson's Sourdough Saloon, home of the Sourtoe Cocktail. PHOTO BY RON FRANSCELL

Pieces of the past remain in Dawson City, Yukon Territory. PHOTO BY RON FRANSCELL

Captain Al Sider, the oath giver and Sourtoe keeper. PHOTO BY RON FRANSCELL

Ron with the infamous Sourtoe, just before he sipped the cocktail.
PHOTO BY MATT FRANSCELL

The macabre Sourtoe, complete with its jagged toenail.
PHOTO BY RON FRANSCELL

At the Arctic Circle. PHOTO BY MATT FRANSCELL

The Yukon's Dempster Highway is both tantalizingly beautiful and dangerous.
PHOTO BY RON FRANSCELL

A roadside *inukshuk* points the way. PHOTO BY RON FRANSCELL

The Dempster's devilish shale eats tires and windshields. PHOTO BY RON FRANSCELL

A peculiar road sign on the Dempster Highway. PHOTO BY RON FRANSCELL

Otherworldly landscape along the Dempster Highway. PHOTO BY RON FRANSCELL

Son and father—and white rock—at the spot where they buried the time capsule.
PHOTO BY RON FRANSCELL

"Okay, what's this one about?"

"This guy is in prison and he's dreaming about killing a girl in a bunch of gross ways, like choking her and throwing her in a ditch or throwing her off a bridge. Probably his girlfriend."

"Jeezus."

And so it goes, song after brain-melting song, a musical journey through strange death, perverse fantasy, ultraviolence, weird sex, and cranky political rants. Fact is, the whole album is a middle-aged father's worst nightmare. Its tracks include distorted ditties about the fall of America, angry stalkers, war crimes in Iraq, video games and modern weaponry, a prayer to the Four Horsemen of the Apocalypse, a celebration of senseless killing, the slow death of a crystal meth addict, and the obtuse lyric, *One day I'll dance on your grave even if you're buried at sea.*

"These guys seem a little angry," I say.

"You're just too old, old man."

"Yeah, but a lot of this doesn't even sound like music," I say. "Hell, I don't know a G string from a kite string, but I could stand up there and hack away on a guitar and be a heavy-metal hero, too. So if a musical idiot like me can do it, is it really music?"

"But, dude, you can't do it."

"Sure I can! If somebody would just show me where to put my fingers, I could just stand there and flail away . . . *jhu-jhu-jhu-JHU-JHU-BWOW-jhu-jhu-jhu!*"

"Oh yeah, that'd be awesome," Matt says, spluttering sarcasm down his shirt. "A bald, fat, old-fart headbanger who has to be shown where to put his fingers."

"Hey, it works for Ozzy Osbourne."

"He's not bald."

"Yeah, well, I don't eat bats, so it's a wash."

"Chill, dude," Matt says. "I like metal. You don't. You like James Taylor. I don't. You don't have to listen if you don't want to. Nobody's making you sing along."

"But I still don't get it," I say. "Why do you like it? Tell me that."

Matt breathes deeply. "I dunno. It rocks. I listen to the music more than the lyrics. The attitude and the riffs and the solos and the singing, and how they all come together to make a sound I actually can get into rather than just tune out. The same stuff everybody likes about their favorite music, isn't it?

"Plus, there's a whole bunch of different kinds of heavy metal. Death metal, thrash metal, speed metal, black metal, doom metal, folk metal, progressive metal . . . nu, funk, gothic, industrial, symphonic, alternative, power. Even Christian metal. So you can't even lump it all together."

I tell myself it's only rock and roll and he likes it. He even knows *why* he likes it. And come to think of it, that's why I like my fusty old rock 'n' roll, too. Still, there's a load of difference between Creedence Clearwater Revival and the headbanging Cannibal Corpse, between Springsteen's "Hungry Heart" and Glass Casket's "I Hate Almost Every Person I Come into Contact With."

I can't let it go.

"But the blood and the sex and the demons and the screaming and the same goddamned grating guitar sounds over and over and over . . . jeezus. It's just . . . well, it's crap."

Matt turns away and watches drizzled British Columbia blow by. Maybe he's contemplating this same conversation twenty years from now with his own son, who loves a kind of music he can't understand, but more likely he's telling himself he'll never be as uncool as his old man.

"Metal isn't crap," he says to the rain-spotted window. "Rap is crap."

———

The road to Valhalla is a dead end.

It's paved, unfurling north through drumlins and fields, past road signs that take on spiritual significance because you know you're on the road to Valhalla. One that says courtesy matters isn't about Canadian road rage (now there's an elusive concept), but must certainly point the way to salvation. And two crows on a fence post are just crows, unless you are hurtling toward the Vikings' heaven. Then they're Odin's ravens, living symbols of thought and memory who are dispatched every dawn to gather knowledge and return at dusk to whisper their news into the great Norse god's ears.

This town's name is all the advertisement it needs. Welcome to Valhalla. *Ride our boat . . . Don't mind the flames! Roasted boar every Tuesday in the Hall of the Slain! Live music by the Valkyries!*

This half-drizzled morning, focused on a farther destination, we blow past the exit to Valhalla. The sign itself doesn't register in my brain for a couple seconds, then I hit the brakes.

"What's wrong?" Matt asks, plucking his earbuds out and looking up from the *Scrubs* DVD playing on his laptop.

"There's a town back there called Valhalla," I say.

"No shit? Cool. Can we go?"

Matt's a hard-core mythie, and I, too, am drawn by the notion of visiting Valhalla, so I whip a U.

"Recalculating," Sydney huffs as we bounce off the four-lane blacktop onto the farm-to-market road, like tourists in Elysium. Sydney is a machine guided by man-made stars and couldn't know the raw magnetism of a sign pointing the way to a place called Valhalla.

"I hope it isn't far," Matt says as we roll down the narrow road. "I gotta piss."

"I don't know if there's a bathroom in Valhalla," I joke, but what bona fide eternal utopia wouldn't have toilets?

Mythology is the closest Matt comes to personal faith. Along the way, he asks me to pull off to the side of the Valhalla road not so he can pee, but so he can snap a picture of the two crows, but they decamp from their fence posts as he rolls down his window. Before he can get out of the van, they've literally disappeared into the blue British Columbian sky. On any other road, they'd have merely landed out of sight, or flown over the next hill, but here they are presumed to have vaporized into thin, Norse air.

The vanishing ravens of Valhalla spark a conversation about death and faith, but not before Matt pees in the barrow pit.

Matt's no more certain about death than about faith, and I'm no more certain than he. But being nineteen, he affects both the surliness and the naiveté of youth: When you die, everything goes black (probably). He doesn't care if he is remembered (except by his family and friends). And being remembered is different from being a legend (only people who knew you in life could truly remember you, and a legend outlives memory).

What makes us laugh and what makes us wonder are far more powerful forces in human passions, he once wrote in a college paper. He theorized that the surprise of absurdity and the certainty of mystery make life worth living, not the promise of forever in the clouds with God, St. Peter, and . . .

Jesus, don't get him started on religion. Matt calls himself a "weak atheist"—one who doesn't believe but fears he might be completely wrong . . . not at all like the narrow-minded zealots who believe passionately and couldn't possibly be wrong. Only unbelievers are wrong.

Maybe I'm an unbeliever, too. Or maybe I just think life is a road, and the road will just end someplace up ahead, someplace off the map . . . so I'll just drive 'til I lose the road. Or maybe I just imagine that Heaven and Hell are not places, but a single moment in time, the last twinkling of our earthly souls when we cannot change a thing, and we realize that we made good use of our existence (Heaven) or wasted it completely (Hell).

Eternity in a nanosecond.

All this talk about death and faith naturally segues to time-travel. It intrigues Matt, who now thinks he wants to be a history teacher. This might be the closest he'll ever come to leaping backward across the fourth dimension.

It also happens to be a plot device in the Chuck Palahniuk book he's reading. Plus, it's safer than talking about croaking or praying. Time-travel isn't easier to grasp than God or dying, but it's not as ominous.

Yet time-travel is, after all, a form of religion and death, isn't it? A corpus transcending the usual bonds of boring, linear time to enter a dimension where time itself is no more (nor less) restrictive than one or ten commandments . . . Well, hell, that describes a disembodied toe in a cocktail, too, doesn't it? Maybe for all good dead toes, Heaven is a saltbox under the bar in a Yukon saloon.

At any rate, we'd already spent sixty hours on the road, and we reeked of man-sweat, woodsmoke, and oversubscribed underwear. Time-travel was an especially appealing and hygienic concept.

"Where would you go . . . ," I start to ask, but edit myself. "No, *when* would you go if you could travel in time?"

Matt scratches the stringy mop under his skater's toboggan skully. "Not being religious, I guess I'd go back and see if Jesus really got resurrected."

Not the answer I'd expected.

"So you'd just watch him? Keep an eye on his corpse?"

"Oh, I dunno. Seems safe enough. The places where the really cool things happened would be too dangerous."

So I make a rule: You're merely a cosmic observer, invulnerable to bullets and bombs and arrows. You can't be wounded. You can only watch.

This emboldens Matt as a time-traveler. He quickly abandons his vigil beside dead Jesus in his tomb. "Okay, then, I'd go to World War Two, maybe. The Civil War. Thermopylae. Maybe Tenochtitlan as the Spaniards arrived . . ."

"Why wars?"

"Why would I want to go someplace to watch an old lady sitting on her porch?" he bristles. "Anybody who wants to go back in time would want to see men in motion—you know, to see action. Otherwise, just stay home in your time and don't waste the physics."

He slugs back a Red Bull in one swig. I wonder: If you time-travel hopped up on caffeine, does the clock spin faster?

"How 'bout you?" he asks. "Where would you go? No wait, lemme guess: You'd probably want to go sit and watch Hemingway write a book or something, right?"

My son associates me with Hemingway partly because I am a writer, and partly because he knows I admire Papa's work. He also knows I keep a signed copy of *For Whom the Bell Tolls* on a special shelf. And I have often said I'd like to share a beer or two or three with Hemingway, so his presumption wasn't unimaginable or even undreamed-of . . . just not my first choice today.

"No, I don't think so. Hemingway probably wrote books a lot like I and every other writer writes books. Hemingway's life offered much more interesting moments to watch, moments that shaped him, like almost dying when he drove an ambulance in Italy, or almost dying in an African plane crash, or really dying in Idaho. God, think of those stories he never wrote, all splashed on the ceiling."

"So you agree with me. A time-traveler should want to see men in action."

"Not always war, though. In peril, in life-or-death struggles, in desperate moments, yeah. But also in madness, in passion, in triumph, and in surrender. I think I'd like to see Cleopatra unrolled from Caesar's rug, or the killing of Bonnie and Clyde, or Rebel soldiers preparing to die in Pickett's Charge, or Martin

Luther nailing up his ninety-five theses, or the first time Gandhi ever got really mad. That kind of stuff."

Matt pops another Red Bull and sips.

"Well, I would like to go back to the moment you and Mom were having sex to conceive me," he cackles, "and I'd slap you on the ass and say, 'Hey, dude, I'm your son from the future!' "

"That'd be dangerous," I say, laughing with him. "I'd be so freakin' startled, I'd stop! You might interrupt your own conception."

Ah, the Grandfather Paradox.

That's the big wrench in this whole time-travel thing. Let's say you can travel in time and you go back to find your grandfather as a boy. If you killed him—let's presume it was an accident or self-defense—then you'd never be born. And if you're never born, then you are never able to time-travel into your grandfather's boyhood. But if you can't kill your grandfather, you will be born. And so on, until your head hurts.

So the past is a minefield. The future is a surprise.

And the present almost never seems good enough.

Matt spits some sunflower hulls in his empty Red Bull can, still smiling because he'd made me smile. Just like old times.

Up ahead is the city-limits sign for Valhalla. We stop to take some photos of ourselves, proof that we made it at least to the border of the place. Beneath the sign, I find a super-sized steel chain link, just one. *A link to Valhalla.* I slip it in my pocket and we get back on the road, which goes nowhere except Valhalla.

The promise (or the illusion) of a heroic, mythic place is all in our heads. It's a motley hamlet with gravel shoulders and clapboard facades, stuck irretrievably in another time, as we'd soon find.

There's a white church, a tiny white mercantile, the old white icehouse, some white houses, and fifty-seven Lutheran souls, presumably also white. And there's a white sign on the edge of town proclaiming Valhalla the home of Christine Nordhagen, a simple farm girl who grew up to be a heroic six-time world-champion wrestler who retired after the 2004 Olympics in Athens, another real place built upon a foundation of myth.

But I wouldn't have missed this detour for anything.

Time-travel, mythology, and dying were still on my mind as we tooled back toward the main highway, but Sydney was single-minded.

"Keep to the highlighted route," she commanded, and we both respond in unison, "Shut up."

"There's another place—or time—you can go," I say, picking up our conversation. "Forward. The future—to see how it all turns out. To see if this global warming thing is true. Or how we get Osama bin Laden."

Matt chuckles and spits some more hulls into an empty can, but says nothing.

"Isn't it funny we both answered the question with great events, not intimate, personal things?" I ask him. "Neither one of us wanted to see our great-great-grandchildren playing, or watch how we die. Why do you think that is?"

"Well, I talked about slapping your ass."

"True."

"I'd just want to go back and freak people out. I want to hear their assholes snap shut. That'd be fun."

"You can only watch events—you can't participate! That's against time-traveler rules."

"I'm talking about time-travel! I'm not gonna sit in a lawn chair in the middle of the Battle of the friggin' Bulge! That was your rule. I'm gonna get my own friggin' rules."

Matt's not keeping to the highlighted route.

"Okay, fair enough," I say. "Here's a different kind of time-travel: Imagine you're eighty years old and looking back on your life. What would a good life look like? What would have happened to make it good?"

My son is quiet for a long time—so long, I fear he's not going to answer at all. So long, I fear he's trying to imagine a life unlike his has been so far, or being a father unlike I have been. When he answers, it's a voice I've never heard before.

"I want to fall in love," he says. "Not necessarily get married, just fall in love. And I hope I have kids."

"That's it? That will make a good life?"

"No, that's not all of it," he says. "What will make it a good life are all the things I can't foresee. I won't know—and I don't want to know—until the end, you know? That's the awesome part."

My son surprises me sometimes. One moment, he's headbanging to the dark, distorted, subliterary lyrics of death-metal music, and the next he's the apparent love child of Werner Heisenberg and Hunter S. Thompson, celebrating the surprise of absurdity and the uncertainty of mystery as driving forces in human passions. To him, not knowing where the road goes is better than having it all mapped out.

And maybe he's right. Maybe what we fear most in life is that our destination won't be exactly as we'd hoped. Without preconceptions, it's hard to be disappointed. Without dreams, it's hard to have nightmares. A leaf with purpose is a leaf without a stream or a breeze.

A half-hour later, maybe less, we pull back onto the four-lane blacktop from Valhalla. The death-talk and the God-talk had petered out, and we spend most of our return trip trying unsuccessfully to reckon the formula for converting Fahrenheit to Celsius, a fool's errand.

But time-travel haunts me.

"We will do some time-traveling on this trip, I promise."

Matt shrugs and slips a new *Scrubs* DVD into his laptop.

"Yeah, yeah, yeah," he says. "Just keep your eyes on the road."

———•———

When we hit Fort Nelson, a one-time fur-trading outpost that's now the center of British Columbia's timber industry, we're famished. After we fill up with gas, we duck into a local pizzeria.

Matt orders a Guinness with spicy pasta and I have a Molson with a ciabatta chicken sandwich. While our waitress—a plain girl with an admittedly shapely butt—goes to the back to whisper about the cute guy who just sat down at table eleven, we scatter some pamphlets and maps across the table.

We've been averaging twelve hours a day on the road and we're a day ahead of schedule, so we decide to catch our breath in Whitehorse, which is still six hundred miles up the road. I point out there are museums, movie houses, tours, a hot springs, golf, Laundromats, and other ways we can spend our time, but Matt zeroes in on Mad Trapper Lanes, the only bowling alley in the Yukon Territory's capital city.

"Let's go here," he says.

"Yeah, right. We came four thousand miles to the Yukon to go bowling?"

Matt smiles.

"Who else are you ever going to run into who can say they did that? Only you. And me."

He is his father's son.

———•———

We hit the road again after dinner to find a campsite in the mountains. Soon, we enter a new world, some of the most vast and astoundingly beautiful wilds I have ever seen. We stop to take some pictures in the slanting light of the long sunset, but the mosquitoes are so thick that getting out of the van is risking a bleed-out.

The sun is still rolling around the sky, even though it's after nine p.m., but rain clouds loom on the western horizon and the whole landscape is cast in dull gray. Up ahead are Stone Mountain and Muncho Lake, a higher landscape where freakish storms rise quickly. So with the heavens already warning us to keep our distance, we scout a camp spot on the Tetsa River, only seventy miles west of Fort Nelson. We've been twelve hours on the road and traveled over five hundred miles today, counting the side trip to Valhalla.

Our camp beside a stagnant backwater is soggy and cold from a day of rain. We slather ourselves in bug spray and try to build a fire with damp twigs and skanky wood we scavenge from the surrounding woods. We never get a roaring fire going, but at least our smoky, smoldering pile of wet timber keeps the blood-thirsty mosquitoes at bay.

Mayflies hover on the water. They rise and fall in unison, males waiting impatiently for romance. They have just this night, this one night, to breed. By morning, they'll die. I stand on the bank watching them, pondering the compression of all time as they know it, of an entire life packed into a single day. Time travel, to the mayflies, would be yesterday and tomorrow. Life is now. No waiting.

Back at camp, Matt is struggling to keep our fuming campfire on life support. He wipes the gledgy top of the picnic table with the sleeve of his Husker-red Nebraska hoodie so we can play a few hands of Texas Hold 'Em for matchsticks.

While we sleep-walk through a few hands, I sip a Yukon Jack and Coke. At the same time, Matt throws back three cans of Bow Valley Lager, a bland Calgary brew just one step above near-beer.

"Do you drink beer back in the States?" I ask him during a break to count our matchsticks.

"I'm in college, Dad. What do you think?"

"Well, it's not legal back home, that's all. It's not good for you, and you can get in all kinds of trouble. That wouldn't exactly look good."

"What, you mean on my 'permanent record'?"

"You know what I mean. You don't drink and drive, do you?"

"No. Here, deal."

I dole out the cards for another hand of Hold 'Em, but I'm not finished with the beer yet.

"Hey, I'm not gonna preach. I drink. I drank in college, too. Fergawdsakes, we're on a freakin' round-the-world expedition so we can drink a cocktail containing a human toe! But I'm old enough now to know exactly what can happen—know what I mean?"

"Yeah, so you admit you drink."

"Yeah, and I'm fifty years old. I can barely face a hangover without a do-not-resuscitate order. I'm not telling you to never drink. I'm just telling you not to let the bottle suck you in. It's never good."

Matt just nods as he studies his cards.

"When did you start?" I ask him.

"After Kelly and I broke up," he says. "It hurt me. Bad. I drank for comfort. Or I thought it was comfort. I didn't know. I couldn't sleep. Probably wasn't a night for a long time that I wasn't fucked up."

"Matt, there's no comfort in a can of beer or a glass of wine. People get in trouble when they think they'll find something valuable at the bottom of the bottle, and they keep expecting to find it so they just keep looking, like kids hunting a pony in a pile of horseshit. It ain't there."

"Oh, c'mon, isn't that what this whole damn trip is about? Finding something in a glass of booze? You tell me, Dad—what is it you expect to find in the bottom of that glass? You think this is all about a freakin' toe? Shit."

Matt flops his hand on the rough green table—he's got three aces—and gets up to kick the fire. I gather up the scattered cards and say nothing.

"Look, I'm not an alcoholic, if that's what you're worried about," he says as he turns a sooty log. "I don't even drink every day. I'm just a typical college kid. I go to parties. I have a beer when I sit around the room on Sunday, watching football and playing XBox. I know when to stop. It's not controlling me. I can control it."

"Good," I say, raising my can of Chilkoot to him. I know him and trust him. " 'Nuff said."

"Now, the heroin, that's a different story . . ."

I nearly choke mid-swig. For the first time in my life, I have beer in my nose.

"Psych!" Matt belly-laughs. "Dude, you should have seen your face! It's good to finally get you back for all those stupid, lame jokes you pulled on me when I was a kid."

—•—

The next day, we plunge deeper into the Canadian Rockies, where an emerald mantle of old-growth cedars drapes an infinite landscape of majestic peaks, jade-colored lakes, and alpine meadows, all carved by tectonic folding and glacial abrasion over millennia. The immensity of the space, the forces, and the time is beyond my pitiful grasp. It is bigger than my imagination.

But for all its vastness, this surreal terrain's real beauty is in the smallest details, things I can touch. Early in the morning, we happen upon a bighorn ram licking remnant road-salt from the highway. Wild lupines mass in clouds of blue and pink on the roadside, their leaves following the sun as it circles the wide sky above. Ghostly hoodoos—totem-like spires of stubborn rock rising from broken land—haunt unexpected places. And man, pathetically unable to inflict a lasting wound on this immortal landscape, spray-paints graffiti on rocks that will not just outlast the markings themselves, but the next thousand or so generations of the painter's descendants.

Animals surround us. Enormous cartoon road signs appear regularly to warn MOOSE ON HIGHWAY, and buffalo, caribou, stone sheep, even bears appear from forest shadows, grazing on sweet shoulder grass or crossing the road for whatever reasons wild animals cross roads.

Even the little steering-wheel blister that's developing on my right palm from more than sixty hours of driving so far is a tiny testament to the enormity of this place.

I stop frequently to take photos, and Matt is growing more annoyed. After the first few times, he doesn't even get out of the camper anymore, and just sits in the passenger seat listening to his music or watching *Scrubs* reruns. But every bend in the road reveals something new and even more magnificent than the last bend.

We stop for an early lunch at Toad River, a one-time road camp that is now one of the few service stops for travelers on this stretch of the Alcan. Some sixty people live here, most of them highway maintenance workers. The rest tend to be travelers like us at the funky Toad River Lodge, where there's a grassy airstrip (which made us happy to be driving), post office (where I bought stamps for postcards), a souvenir stand (where I got a Canadian pin for my hat), a dump station, some cabins and kitchenettes with satellite TV, a six-calendar diner with soft-serve ice cream, and, surprisingly, an Internet hot spot.

The Toad River Lodge is just one of a few dozen roadside service stops that popped up on empty stretches of the winding gravel road known as the Alaska Highway after World War II. In those days, the military still controlled the road, but it wasn't an enormous inconvenience: Even if civilian traffic weren't severely restricted by the Canadian government, there were simply no services for casual travelers in their laughably inadequate family cars.

In 1949—the year the Alaska Highway finally opened to foolhardy civilians—fewer than fifty roadside businesses operated outside the cities of Dawson Creek, Whitehorse, and Fairbanks. Most of these were mom-and-pop lodges strung out at interminable intervals along its nearly sixteen hundred butt-clenching miles. More prevalent were horror stories about travelers who were lost and never found, flash floods that swept mountains (and cars) into mile-deep canyons, and breakdowns at 30-below. And just when a shiver was set to roll down a spine, some party-pooper would ask, "Where exactly does this hellish road take you?"

While most lodges-cum-oases advertised "good food" and "indoor plumbing," they were often rather primitive structures hurriedly converted from derelict army barracks or log cabins where meals were served in canvas tents. Because milled lumber was in short supply after the war, some lodge-builders scavenged materials from abandoned road camps.

But in the early days of the Alaska Highway, bone-rattled adventurers didn't expect four-star elegance. They wanted food, some gas, a man who could fix a tire, a place to warm up, maybe something resembling a clean bed, and the reassurance that humans could survive in this godforsaken wilderness. The meals were simple; a roast beef dinner might cost a buck. In bad blizzards, two strangers might share a double bed, or sleep beneath a dining-room table. And like today, gas was expensive—fifty-five cents a gallon in 1948—because of government taxes and the expense of transporting it into this netherworld.

As the highway evolved, so did the lodges. The least fit died. Heated by wood-burning stoves, many lodges burned to the ground on frigid nights. Others were shuttered as the road was straightened and improved, allowing motorists to go faster and farther between stops. In recent years, government regulation has done more damage than fire, forcing many of these historic ramshackles to close because they can't afford the cost of a twenty-first-century septic system, gasoline storage tanks that don't leak, or urbane health codes.

But Toad River survives.

Most small towns boast they're a good place to raise kids, but I'm not so sure about Toad River. Only about twenty-five students attend the little school here, from kindergartners to high school seniors, all taught by just two teachers. Some live as far as fifty miles away. Because there's no school bus, they come to school by any conveyance available, including horseback, ATVs, snowmobiles, and bush planes. Although registered sex offenders and roving bands of felonious youths are nonexistent, subzero temperatures, rutting elk, and grizzly bears can make walking to school slightly more dangerous than a midnight stroll whistling "Yankee Doodle" in downtown Baghdad.

Nobody really knows why it's called Toad River, but our waitress, a pretty thirtysomething in worn jeans and a plaid cotton shirt—she's distant and beyond knowing, really, like rain on another roof—prefers this theory about a colorful misspelling: When the Alaska highway was being built and a bridge hadn't yet been constructed on the nearby river, the only way across was to be *towed* on a ferry.

I suspect that the actual Toad River, like many rivers across the western half of North America, actually got its name from somebody, an early explorer or local, who merely associated it with some odd observation or memory for future reference. In this case, it was probably just a river where somebody saw a toad they didn't expect to see. But I like the waitress's story better, even if it's a made-for-tourists fantasy.

One genuine thing about the Toad River Lodge is its collection of seven thousand hats. Legend holds that the lodge's two proprietors were drinking one night; when one left to piss, the other tacked his hat to the ceiling. Now everybody does it.

"Don't take much to get something started around here," our waitress tells us. "So you won't wanna take yer eyes off yer hats."

We order our burgers while we check our e-mail for the first time in more than a week. My laptop—or, more accurately, the dulcet, digitized declaration of voice-over actor Elwood Edwards—announces to the entire Toad River diner: "You've got mail."

"Oh good! I love mail!" the waitress hollers from the kitchen.

My mailbox contains 286 e-mails, 271 of which are spam. Among the rest is a matter-of-fact note from my editor that the upcoming paperback version of my latest book will have a different title than the hardcover ("Something more arresting," he says, which in publishing terms usually means using the words *blood, death,* or *fatal*).

But there are also a half-dozen e-mails from Mary about nothing more significant than the sweet, ordinary life I'd be leading if I weren't waiting for a short-order burger in the Canadian-wilderness equivalent of a truck stop. In an odd way, I miss its daily inevitability, the reliability of sunset and the lines outside of which one cannot color. It is one thing to gather stories, another to gather friends. As much as I love the road, it is meaningless without home, without sanctuary, at the end of it.

While Matt chats with an elderly American couple eating chili at the next table, I find the only pay phone in Toad River. I call home collect, but Mary doesn't answer and the operator won't let me leave a message. I would have told her we were safe, and the road was longer than I expected, but we were closer. And that I was thinking of her.

So we wolf down our delightfully greasy burgers and fat fries, pay the ticket (er, check), and load up. We're hundreds of miles from our next camp, and the road is slow.

Outside, a behemoth RV with naked-girl mud flaps and Texas plates blocks one whole side of the Toad River gas pumps in front of the lodge. A man wearing a white cowboy hat and his wife sit in lawn chairs beside it, drinking American sodas. Funny place to stop for a cold drink, I think, so I wander over and introduce myself as a fellow Texan—although, in truth, I merely live in Texas. Neither I nor any self-respecting native would consider me a true Texan.

Turns out, it's a retired Odessa oil-field roughneck and his wife heading to Alaska, but Toad River is plumb out of gas. He's waiting for the next gas delivery at four p.m. and, by God, he's gonna be first in line.

"How long you been waiting?" I ask.

"So long I'm fixin' ta put out roots and I got moss on my north side," the old guy says.

"That long, eh?"

"Ten more minutes and they'll be swearin' me in as a damn Canadian citizen," he continues, on a Texas-sized roll. "It didn't take the Messicans this long to whoop them boys' asses at the Alamo. We was on our honeymoon when we got here, and now we're fixin' to celebrate our fiftieth weddin' anniversary . . ."

Lordy, if it weren't for shameless hyperbole, a Texan would just be . . . well, a loud Oklahoman. And the fact that I'm not exaggerating proves my unsuitability for membership in the exclusive club called Texas.

———•———

Beyond Toad River, the Alaska Highway tickles along the ribs of the Rockies, along the shores of the majestic Muncho Lake, imbued with an otherworldly blue-green color by the sky and the copper oxide in the water. Its invitation can be deceiving: Winds blasting between the barren Sentinel Range and the forested Terminal Mountains whip up deadly whitecaps in less time than it takes to run for shore.

And magnificent storms rise suddenly here, especially in summer. Flash floods course unchecked through the steep, treeless Sentinels, sweeping sand, gravel, and boulders down unrooted limestone slopes into cracks that become ruts that become canyons, then burst out in a torrent upon ancient flats in splendid deltas known as "alluvial fans." These alluvial fans are common in desert areas for the same reasons they are found in this relatively arid subarctic region, where the annual precipitation is less than Arizona: intermittent and intense cloudbursts over patches of sterile landscape.

The difference here, though, is magnitude. These bucketing floods can disgorge boulders bigger than houses. They spew out in great fans that cover more earth than most international airports. They can be seen from space.

Matt and I stop along the Liard River in northern British Columbia to marvel at one such alluvial fan that lies across the water from the road. Even at this distance, it is epic.

We clamber down a talus shoulder to the river. The sky has lowered and we are engulfed by the grayness of the claustrophobic sky, the mountains, and the water. Here we stand at the foot of this immense stone ramp into the clouds, throwing little pebbles into the shallow, swift Liard.

"How many individual stones are there, do you think?" I ask my son.

"Just there?" Matt asks, gazing at the fan. "I don't know. Counting every grain of sand? More than a billion billion billion. More than I can count. More than stars. I feel so small here."

"Me, too."

Across the road, a cataract overflows over a wall of tumbledown rock, so we decide to climb as high as we can. Matt scrambles up the steep lower slope, where the scree tumbles in little

landslides in his wake, while I ascend more slowly and deliber-
ately behind him, dodging sharp rocks from above. The higher
we go, the more the falls beckon us to go higher, until finally we
are at least three hundred feet above the road with a spectacular
view of the entire alpine valley.

I can't go farther, and needn't. I sit breathless on a flat ledge
beside the waterfall, kneading my knotted leg muscles while I
watch a small group of stone sheep watching me from higher
up. The only sound I hear is the cold, cascading water, but I can
taste rain coming.

Matt goes higher, and I catch only fleeting glimpses of his
black Pantera T-shirt or his black cap in the rocks above. I lose
sight of him altogether as the clouds descend and a fine mist
floats in the thin air.

I wait. Until he's gone high enough. Until he finds whatever
he seeks. Until he can go no farther. Until there's nothing else to
see. Until he no longer feels small. Until he comes back to me.
I tell myself that a father probably should always let his son go
farther, and to do that, he must be prepared to wait.

I listen for his voice up there, or the sound of falling rocks,
but I hear only the water rushing past. There's no telling how
high he went, or when he will be back.

So I wait, although I'm no good at it. Now is better than
then. Sooner is better than later. I am the mayfly.

I once knew a patient man who stood on the same street
corner every day for seventeen years (and another one across the
street for twelve more), looking for one face in the great river of
humanity that flowed past him. He had loved her and lost her.

He saw her face in his mind, framed against hazy memories
of San Francisco's Haight Street in the sixties. That picture flick-
ered through his brain every time he saw a middle-aged woman
who might have once been the frail, pale, blonde foundling he
had lost.

"This guy Carl once told me, when he was tired of hearing me whine about her, that if I stood in one place long enough, everybody in my life would pass by," he explained to me.

So he found a place to stand from which the world would not move him.

My friend, whom I knew only by his street name—Babe Rainbow, after the Melanie song—wasn't the kind of guy people would normally cozy up to. He looks like an outlaw Hells Angels biker with spidery tattoos wrapped around both forearms. He wears dirty jeans, T-shirts, and a leather vest, and his long straight hair is parted by a razor-sharp face, overgrown with wild sideburns and a prodigious handlebar mustache. His dark glasses perch on the tip of his hawkish nose as he studies the faces of passersby, making them a little nervous. Nobody exchanges unnecessary pleasantries.

Brainwashed by beach-party movies, he had run away from his home in New York at sixteen and landed in Haight-Ashbury, where he got a job managing a rickety apartment house. His tenants regularly left without notice, got busted, or overdosed, unwittingly leaving all their worldly goods to . . . Babe Rainbow. He had a good thing going.

That's where he met her, a girl he knew only by her street name: Spooky Boots. Their meeting was a bizarre fantasy that might or might not have been influenced by an acid trip, but Spooky moved in with Babe soon after. Babe's life and love changed; Spooky changed it.

When the love began to drain from the Haight, the young couple decided to move to New York. Spooky urged Babe to travel on ahead and find them a pad, but he hesitated to leave her. She insisted. Their parting had a sentimental twist, though: He gave her his purple sunglasses to wear until they could be together again, sort of like a groovy St. Christopher's medal.

"I might as well have cut off my arm or cut out my heart and handed it to her and told her 'Here, keep this 'til I get back.'"

He begged her from New York to hurry and join him, but Spooky put him off gently. She had taken over his job managing the apartments, and wanted to save as much money as possible for their life together.

Then one night, SFPD rounded up all the tenants of that old flophouse. Spooky, too. Nobody knew what happened to her after she was loaded into the paddy wagon.

"I just wanted to die," he told me. "I just sat around the house eating Twinkies. I don't mind dying, but I don't want to go crazy."

That's when this dwarfish street bum planted himself on a downtown corner in a bustling Southwestern city . . . and waited. Most nights, he slept in his truck ("The first thing I ever owned with a decent paint job"), and when the sun came up, he'd be back on the sidewalk.

Seventeen years.

Then it happened.

No, Spooky Boots didn't pass by. Babe just decided to move to a different corner, a move I couldn't fathom. I mean, what if she walked past the *old* corner the very next day? This guy Carl said, "If you stand in one place *long enough*." How long is *long enough*? Could it be one more day?

"Yeah, sometimes I think about that," he said. "I mean, like, what if she's standing on a corner someplace in South Dakota, waiting for *me* to walk by?"

The existential irony of it all didn't matter. Babe moved. He crossed the street to the opposite corner where he stood for another twelve years before he gave up on love, on patience, on Spooky. Maybe this guy Carl was wrong. Or maybe Babe just got over her.

"It kinda sounds like I'm obsessed, and maybe I am," he admitted to me once, many years after we'd first met. "But what else is there to do?"

What else, indeed.

Still, I once asked him if he'd ever imagined that magical moment, if and when he saw Spooky again.

"Yeah, man, I've dreamed about it," he said, his rheumy eyes going a thousand yards off. "I see her and she sees me, and we slo-mo into each other's arms for about an hour, and then we go off into the sunset . . .

"But I have another dream, too. We see each other and she comes up to me and says, 'I've been looking for you for a long, long time.' Then she reaches into her purse, pulls out a gun, and *blam, blam, blam.*"

Yes, it's a weird story, but Babe always wore a button on his stained black leather vest that said BEING WEIRD IS NOT ENOUGH.

Sadly, Spooky Boots never came, or never knew, or never even remembered. Patience might be a virtue, but for my old friend Babe, it simply wasn't good mojo. When I last saw him a few years ago, he wasn't healthy and had stopped waiting, except maybe for death. I asked him if he regretted standing in the same spot for almost thirty years for nothing.

"It wasn't for nothing," he told me over a coffee and pastry not twenty paces from the faux-adobe corner where he'd spent most of his life. "I got a lot of good sun."

In time, my son returns to my safe little ledge at the shallow end of the mountain. It's getting cold—time to move.

"What could you see up there?" I ask him as we start back down.

"More," he says. "Just more."

On September 24, 1942, road-building soldiers from the U.S. Army's 35th Regiment, coming from the south, and soldiers from the 340th Regiment, coming from the north, met near the Yukon–British Columbia border. In less than seven months, they had laid almost a thousand miles of road over some of the wildest territory in North America, and their Promontory Summit was a stream originally named Beaver Creek—although today it's called Contact Creek, for obvious reasons.

After the war, the ever-fastidious Canadian government straightened the Alaska Highway and paved it, literally shortening the old military road. But history is hard to come by up here, so some of the original highway's miles are still marked, often alongside contemporary mile-markers—confusing for travelers who measure their adventures by mileposts.

There isn't much to see at Contact Creek—oh, a couple miles up the road, there's a funky postwar lodge that offers pricey T-shirts and snacks, gas, a tow truck, and a mechanic—but there's a historical marker that celebrates the joining of the Alaska Highway at this spot, Mile 588 in 1942 . . . but Mile 565.5 today.

A more-important clue to the Canadian mind-set, though, is that this is the first of seven times the northbound traveler will crisscross the Yukon border before he sees the official WELCOME TO THE YUKON sign about forty miles farther down the highway. But we don't care about unofficial crossings. We don't want to come through the back door.

So we travel on to the exact spot where they've put up a big sign so thousands, maybe millions, of adventurers just like us can get out and take pictures of their beaming selves for their scrapbooks, blogs, game-room walls, and maybe books about sons and life and dead toes.

Rare Earth North

*And then it comes to be that the soothing light at the end of the
tunnel is just a freight train coming your way . . .*

—METALLICA LYRIC

L et's get this straight right off the bat: The Yukon is not in
Alaska.

For the past year, I've endured (and gently corrected)
the misimpression—even from college-educated newsroom
colleagues who should know better—that the Yukon is just a
shrewdly marketed region of Alaska, like California's Wine
Country, except with a growing season measured on a stopwatch.

True, the enormous Yukon was Ground Zero for the Klondike Gold Rush after salmon fishermen found gold in Rabbit
Creek near the ramshackle northern village of Dawson in the
summer of 1896. In their stampede to the gold, some 100,000
gold-fevered prospectors from all over the world disembarked
at Alaskan ports like Skagway or Dyea at a time when most
nineteenth-century Americans believed Alaska was nothing
more than a grotesquely frigid wilderness full of ice and Eski-
mos. But Alaska was just the gateway, not the destination. The
gold was still hundreds of miles away, in a remote corner of
Canada.

And that's where a century of confusion begins: The words *Alaska, Yukon,* and *Klondike* got all tangled up, as if they were the same exact place on the miniature mental maps of North America. And nothing has happened since then to dispel the muddle.

In fact, the Yukon is a Canadian territory, foreign soil for Americans. It is separated from Alaska by an international border, so for Yukoners—as they call themselves—Alaska is a foreign country, too.

Without getting into the rather complex differences between Canadian provinces and territories, the Yukon functions more or less like an American state, except that stepchild territories have less sovereignty than provinces, and are more directly managed by the federal government (which, in Canada's case, also has certain obligations to Her Majesty the Queen, Elizabeth II of England).

But politics are far less important than scale in visualizing the Yukon. It's a fool's errand to try to condense this colossal space into a digestible paragraph, but chew on this: From top to bottom, the triangular territory is 700 miles long—about the distance from Chicago to Mobile, Alabama. At its fattest point, the Yukon is almost 600 miles wide—try to imagine the length of a rope (and the social differences) between Los Angeles and Salt Lake City. And the uppermost spine of the Rockies forms the raggedy-ass 800-mile hypotenuse of its eastern border.

The 1,980-mile Yukon River, from which the territory takes its name, is longer than the Rio Grande, Ganges, Danube, Rhine, and Tigris rivers, and carries more water than the Nile.

In square miles, the Yukon Territory is much larger than the State of California, but has fewer citizens (31,587) than Apache Junction, Arizona. Or North Tonawanda, New York. Or Butte, Montana. Or Tuckahoe, Virginia. Or Pflugerville, Texas. That means every man, woman, and child in the Yukon has about six square miles all to himself—a "personal" space five times bigger than New York City's Central Park. Imagine, if you can, only four people occupying the entire island of Manhattan, and you'll have some idea of the average Yukoner's legroom.

Of course, they don't live lonely and scattered, but huddle together in a handful of settlements where they share the sundry hardships and body heat. Three out of every four Yukoners live in Whitehorse, the territorial capital and the largest town in the Yukon. By comparison, the territory's fifth-largest municipality has a grand total of about four hundred citizens, which is roughly the number of people *on the field* at a typical Texas high school football game every Friday night.

In all of the vast Yukon, there are 91 frost-free days, 4 newspapers, 6 radio stations, 2 television stations, 1 college, 400 licensed fur trappers, the world's smallest desert, 14 native tribes, 18 total legislators, less annual precipitation than Arizona, 448 motorcycles, 7,168 trailers, 190,000 caribou, and not a single authentic igloo.

And now, two American *cheechakos* who want to sip a cocktail containing a mummified human toe.

———•———

The Yukon border town known as Watson Lake didn't really exist before 1942, when the U.S. Army invaded Canada to build the Alaska Highway. Back then, the road crews established one of their supply bases on the southern edge of the still-untamed Yukon Territory, 635 miles from Mile Zero in Dawson Creek, farther north than Leningrad and Stockholm, much closer to the Arctic Ocean than to the American border—already much farther than most people would someday go to drink a cocktail containing a human toe, which is still two days' drive north from here.

To us, it was just another way station, an afternoon gas stop. But when I go inside to pay for gas, the kindly c-store clerk says my credit-card company has refused to pay. From a pay phone next to the bathrooms, I call back to the States, where I try to talk calmly to a young woman who insists my credit card is perfectly usable. So I hang up and ask the gas clerk to try again.

The card is refused. Again.

I call again back to the States and another earnest young woman tells me her computer also shows no problems, but that it's possible the company has put some kind of security hold on the card since they were seeing significant charges being racked up more than two thousand miles from my billing address in Texas.

"I'm on vacation in Canada and I need this card," I tell her. "I can tell you my mother's maiden name, the city where I was born, and the date I lost my virginity, so please—can we clear this up?"

"Did you alert the company before you started your trip?" she asks.

"Did I ... *what?* No, I didn't. Honest to Pete, I didn't know I was supposed to call and share my travel plans. Can I just send a nice postcard from the road?"

"Well, we encourage our cardholders to let us know in advance when they expect to have any charges that are out of the ordinary. I'll have to transfer you to our security office. Please hold."

The credit-card company's security phone is answered by another earnest young woman who confirms that my card was clamped when they started seeing thousands of dollars being spent on RVs, gas, and food in a foreign country. To get it unclamped, all I must do is answer two questions.

"What's your dog's name?"

"Cagney. Like Jimmy."

"So is it Jimmy?"

"No, Cagney. Like Jimmy Cagney, you know?"

"No, who is that?"

"He was . . . look, the dog's name is Cagney, and you've asked three questions. Are we good?"

"No, sir," she says, earnestly. "Two of those didn't count. I'm looking at your charges right now. Where did you spend the night last Tuesday?"

I'm stumped. I've lost track of the days. Nights, too. It's not hard when only a slight variation in shadows separates day from night. But I'm not even sure what day of the week this is, much less what time zone we're careening through. I check all my pockets and come up with . . . today's lunch receipt from Toad River. Which is stamped. With a date.

"Let's see . . . this is what . . . Friday?"

"Yes, sir."

"So Tuesday would be . . . ?"

"Three days ago, sir."

"Can you give me a hint?"

"No, sir. That would defeat the purpose."

"Right, well . . . We've been camping, so the last motel charge you'll see on my bill is from a motel in a little town north of Calgary . . . named . . . Carson, or Car-something."

"Carstairs?"

"Yeah, that's it! Carstairs. And the motel was the Golden Something. Sunset? Corral?"

"Golden West?"

"That's it! The Golden West in Carstairs. The Scottish guy and the stinky sandwiches with the toilet ball that didn't work . . ."

"Close enough, sir," she says. "We'll unlock your account and you may continue to use your card. It could take up to thirty minutes for this to go through. Is there anything else I can do for you today?"

"Watch a Jimmy Cagney movie," I tell her before I hang up. "He was good."

I notify the gas clerk it's going to take up to a half-hour before the credit-card snafu is un-snafu'd, and I offer to leave my driver's license with her while Matt and I scout for signs of life in Watson Lake. But the pleasantly Canadian clerk brushes me off and points the way to the biggest tourist attraction within, oh, ten kilometers (if you don't count the Northern Lights show at the planetarium): the allegedly world-famous Sign Post Forest.

This is the godforsaken spot where, in 1942, a homesick American soldier named Carl Lindley dreamed of home. So he posted a crude sign on a post, pointing the way to Danville, Illinois, 2,835 miles southeast of where he was freezing his ass off. Soon, other soldiers did it, too . . . CORINTH, MISSISSIPPI, 3,020 MILES . . . DEEP CREEK, VIRGINIA, 3,412 MILES . . . NORFOLK, NEBRASKA, 2,176 MILES . . . More and more posts were added to accommodate more and more signs, until a small grove of these odd trees had flourished.

Problem is, when the road was finished and the homesick Americans finally went home, pesky passersby kept putting up signs. In time, the forest expanded to include thousands of other distant places, like Lyons (Colorado) and Tigard (Oregon) and Baer (North Dakota). Oh my.

Today, more than 65,000 skewed signs from all over the world festoon the two-acre downtown park, and they are diligently maintained by the town fathers, who know a tourist trap when they see it.

So it's hard to miss the biggest attraction in this little town of fifteen hundred souls. There's the truck scales, the campground, the bus depot, the variety store, the liquor shop, the town hall, a little lake, the Pizza Palace, a couple motor courts like the Cozy

Nest Hideaway and the Gateway, and . . . oh, the Sign Post Forest, where all the tourist cars are bunched up.

We park the van at the first open spot down a side street and walk a block or so to the Sign Post Forest. Dozens of other travelers are already wandering in the mind-boggling maze of stolen street and city-limits signs, markers snatched from farm-to-markets, provincial and township roads on five continents, license plates going back forty years, hand-carved and wood-burned cabin plaques, missing mile-markers, no-parking placards, pilfered phone-booth and toilet devices, official-looking signs in various languages, some possibly original Route 66 signage, all manner of municipal seals, Red Cross emblems, warnings from black-diamond ski slopes—even a boulder pointing the way to some small town in Vermont.

Several prestigious universities are clearly missing some dorm and stadium signs, and a confounded grandmother from Enum-claw, Washington, can't help but wonder aloud: "Griff, how do you reckon they got this Autobahn sign all the way from Germany? It must be ten-foot wide!"

Matt and I stroll among them, calling out when we see a sign from someplace we recognize. Like Shoshone, Wyoming, a town of, oh, a hundred people, where in my past life we'd always stopped with the kids for the best hand-mixed malts in the universe. Or Petaluma, California, where we lived when Matt was born. Or Idaho Springs, Colorado, the sanctuary where I'd run aground and then eventually abandoned to move to Texas. There are a hundred way markers in our memories from another world, as if we needed to come this far to remember where we've been.

But thousands more signs remind me there are places yet to be seen. This place is a travel agent's dream, better than any four-color brochure. Oh, how I want to journey to Ulysses, Kansas. Eat an apple in Garden of Eden, Nova Scotia. Wear my sunglasses in Cool, California. Get a flat tire in Nojack, Alberta. Lose my temper and stomp off in Fugit, Kentucky. Do something stupid in Embarrass, Minnesota. Just to say I did.

We had nothing to post. No sign of our passing, literally. If I'd known, I might have filched the street sign at the end of my block, or sacrificed one of the dozen or so old license plates that are just taking up shelf space in my garage because, as pathetic evidence of my ceaseless comings and goings, I can't throw them out.

After an hour or so of wandering the Sign Post Forest, we return to the convenience store to properly pay my gas bill and resume our journey, guilt-free.

Maybe every road leads here, or maybe this road goes everywhere. Carl Lindley, of course, only dreamed that it led home to Danville, Illinois, but it was still a dream. This peculiar roadside attraction is nothing if not a place to contemplate where we belong and how far we've come.

And how far we still must go.

———•——

Deep in the mountains west of Watson Lake, we stop for dinner at a roadside diner and tavern. It's almost nine p.m., and back in our low-latitude world, the sun would be setting, but the sky here is afternoon bright.

The Upper Liard Resort is another of those long-suffering postwar lodges, most of which are apparently clinging to the precipitous edge of the road by whatever tenuous ties bind families together. The proprietors, like their lodges themselves, are pragmatic, tough, and comforting to see after vast stretches of nothingness. They are often running family businesses, with Dad fixing blown tires or guiding hunters, children pumping gas or serving lunch, and Mom cooking and making beds (although she's likely capable of fixing blown tires, too).

Not much separates these people and places from one another, except the road itself.

We're led to a small table in the empty dining room by a dark-haired and startlingly pretty girl about Matt's age. She hands us our menus and smiles flirtatiously at Matt, who is suddenly bashful.

"What's your name?" I ask her.

"Jessica."

"Jessica, I'm Ron, and this is my son Matt."

"Americans?"

"Does it show?"

She winks and smiles. "A little."

"Well, then, no American beer for us! You must have a couple of cold Chilkoots back there someplace, eh?"

"I'm sure we can find one or two," she says, and cheerfully disappears into the adjacent tavern, where a jukebox plays "Sweet Home Alabama" and three plaid-clad guys who look like out-of-work ice-road truckers nurse Molsons in the neon shadows. I watch them watch her as she leans across the bar in her tight jeans. To them, she must be the most beautiful woman this side of Moose Jaw, a prize harder to win than the Stanley Cup, and warmer. To her, they are just customers and . . . well, a Canadian team hasn't brought home the Stanley Cup in fifteen years.

"She's cute," I say to Matt, who pretends he hardly notices.

"Calm down, Dad. You don't stand a chance. Maybe that butterface at the pizza parlor, but not her."

"Butterface?"

"You know the one," he says. "Everything was hot but her face."

After a few minutes, Jessica plunks our beers on the table and I catch a whiff of perfume I didn't smell before. We make small talk and find out her mother and father, both Czech immigrants, have owned this place for twenty years. In summer, she is the restaurant manager, head chef, and, on some nights, the hostess, waitress, and dishwasher, too. When the tourist season ends and the long night called winter begins, she goes back to college in Calgary where, like Matt, she has already flitted through several majors, the current one being veterinary science.

"Those guys in the bar—do they bother you? I mean, well, this is a lonely place and . . . you know."

Jessica laughs.

"Most of them have known me since I was a baby. They're more like uncles than anything. They watch out for me. Right now, they're probably worrying that you guys are bothering me."

I glance into the bar and, sure enough, they're watching. So I smile and wave. With typical Canadian courtesy, they smile and wave back.

"Okay, well, we better order before they get too nervous," I say. "Do you have a menu?"

"Not really. It's kinda whatever I got, and tonight I've got chicken souvlaki, which is chicken on skewers and rice and salad. I have chicken wraps with salad and fries. A chicken basket, which is fried chicken and fries. And that's about it."

Luckily, we like chicken and we're hungry. Jessica disappears back into her kitchen to fetch souvlaki (Matt) and a chicken wrap (me).

"So, you oughta ask her to the movies," I joke with my son.

"Sure," he says. "The only theater is, what, four hundred miles away?"

"It's tragic, isn't it? The farther you go from home, the less you risk."

"That's not it."

" 'A pain stabbed my heart, as it did every time I saw a girl I loved who was going the opposite direction in this too-big world,' " I say without decoration.

"Did you just make that up?"

"Nah. Jack Kerouac."

"Who's he?"

"Are you kidding? He wrote . . . oh, never mind."

"Well, that's not it either."

"C'mon, she goes to school in Calgary, and you go to school in Lincoln. What if you called her up and reminded her of tonight and asked her to meet you halfway, like, say, in Billings, for a concert or something? You could go to see, I dunno, Pantera or something."

The mere mention of the apparently unresurrected godband Pantera raises Matt's hackles.

"Jeez, dude, there are just so many things wrong about that. First of all, there is no more Pantera. There will never ever be another Pantera concert. Ever. Dimebag Darrell was Pantera, and he's gone. You went to his grave! You saw him dead. How could there be another Pantera?"

"Rock and roll loves dead guys! There's still a Lynyrd Skynyrd and a Grateful Dead, too, fergawdsakes. And Buddy Holly's been moldy for damn near fifty years, but we still have the Crickets! And Keith Richards died but there's still a Rolling Stones."

"Keith Richards isn't dead!"

"No, not technically; I'm speaking metaphorically."

"For Christ's sake, Dad, Pantera broke up. They're gone. They don't exist *at all*."

"Oh. Okay, fine. My bad. I just know you like music, and maybe she likes music, too. Maybe you could go to one of your headbanger things, like a Megadeth reunion tour."

"Aack, god! Megadeth is still together—they never broke up! Oh, you are fucking frustrating me! It drives me crazy! See, this is exactly why I need a girl who likes the music I like, but I'll never find one."

"Is that it? Your perfect girl has to be exactly like you? You're kidding, right? Because you like what you like and you're never

going to compromise. Oh, yeah, there's nothing more important than music. She has to be a headbanger. Is that what you're
saying?"

If Matt wasn't on the defensive already, he is now.

"No, I'm saying she has to have similar interests. I'm willing
to compromise, but I'm never gonna find a girl like that, because
girls these days aren't like that, and it pisses me off."

"Girls these days? What, did the species mutate drastically
since 1999?"

"Well, I met one girl who was, but she was a lesbian."

Whatever I'm about to say doesn't come out. My brain's hard
drive is still downloading an image of my son and his lesbian date
in a mosh pit, and my tongue can't upload until it's finished. My
mind flashes the blue screen of death. I reboot.

"Look, forget the music stuff for a minute. I'm not talking
about music. I'm talking about taking a risk, about seizing the
moment, making the most of the light. Just to make a connection. You could call her up and find out if there's something
there. Wouldn't you hate to die and find out she was The One
and you just didn't have the balls to pick up the phone?"

Matt smiles.

"Trust me, I'd do it," he says. "Romance is cool. But I'm just
not into her. She's kinda hot, but I guess I'm not seeing everything you're seeing, dude. Or maybe I'm looking for something
else. The prize has to be worth the risk. That's all."

Fair enough. Maybe he understands more than I give him
credit for; maybe I don't understand at all. Or maybe we're just a
couple of wounded hearts sitting in a lonely place, drinking beer,
talking trash and lamenting bad love, and hoping we haven't for-
tified our hearts deep inside walls that have no doors.

Jessica returns.

"Can I get you guys anything else?"

Matt shakes his head while I hand her my credit card.

"No, thank you," I say. "You've given us plenty."

———•———

That night, somewhere in the lower Yukon, we cross the Continental Divide, where rivers change direction. Ground fog seeps into the road hollows, and here on the roof of North America, late on a summer night when the sun is still up, we seem to be traveling on clouds.

Around midnight, when the chilly northern Canadian twilight is already turning to dawn and skipping the dead of night altogether, we pull into a campground beside Teslin Lake, an eighty-mile-long finger lake on the gnarled hand of borderland tarns and rivers clutching the crotch of the Klondike.

This night is the coldest so far, and it's starting to rain. So after we find a place to park for the night, Matt unlatches the little metal plate over the back bumper that protects the propane knob and opens up the gas for our space heater. We've been driving all day, but we're not sleepy. A trick of the light, maybe. Without undressing or waiting for the van to warm up, we crawl straight into our sleeping bags and Matt puts a DVD into the player.

And that's how I meet the serial-killing Firefly family, who'd been riding in back the whole time. You simply haven't lived until you've traveled a few thousand miles with a family of serial killers.

Maybe you know them: Otis B. Driftwood, an on-again, off-again albino serial killer who makes sculptures out of his victims, or skins them to wear as costumes; Baby Firefly, the bloodthirstiest hot chick since Patricia Krenwinkle; and Captain Spaulding, Baby's creepy clown father and the white brother of a black pimp. Yes, they're all named after Groucho Marx characters.

This ever-so-extraordinarily dysfunctional family is the creation of monster-metal auteur Rob Zombie—the former front man for a shock-rock band called White Zombie, and the son of ex-carnies—in his indie horror flick, *The Devil's Rejects,* a sequel to the missed-an-Oscar-by-a-hair *House of 1,000 Corpses.*

And, yes, they are the *heroes,* not the bad guys. They rack up more kills in this blood-spattered film than Ted Bundy, Dirty Harry, and George Custer put together. They butcher an entire country-and-western band, and a revenge-obsessed sheriff (they slaughtered his brother in the first film), and the blood spurts more than drunken teenagers upchucking on a Tilt-a-Whirl. Their methods, ranging from very sharp knives to speeding eighteen-wheelers, simply don't tolerate subtlety. They make Hannibal Lecter look like a Peace Corps volunteer.

Anyway, the road-tripping Firefly clan survives every attempt to capture, prosecute, and kill them . . . until the final scene, when they go out in a slo-mo blaze of glory, speeding their car toward a phalanx of state troopers and firing every weapon in their considerable arsenal. To the heroic, romantic strains of "Freebird," no less.

Freeze frame. Serial killers fade into heavenly bright light as cops' bullets tear them apart. Smiling. Angelic.

"So, what'd you think?" Matt asks me when it ends in the wee hours. "Cool, huh?"

"Are you freakin' kidding me?" I come up out of my sleeping bag growling. "This is just more of your heavy-metal, bomb-throwing, iconoclastic crap. Fergawdsakes, they made those sideshow freaks into heroes!"

"No, they didn't. It's just that not every story has a happy ending"—adding, for effect—"like *your* old movies."

"Hey, not every old movie had a happy ending. But almost every old movie had a message that was worth pondering. This one had no message. It had nothing but blood and guts."

"It had a message."

"What was it? Serial killers are fun people, too?"

"Jeez, they get killed at the end," he says, angling like a lawyer for anything that will stick. "Who would want to be like them?"

"That's not a message!"

"How about . . . Not every movie has to have a message?"

"That's not a message either."

"Who says? That's the message I got. Everything in this movie could happen. Probably has at some time. Just because this isn't a movie that looks like all the movies you ever saw doesn't mean it isn't a valid work of art."

"Art? Fuck me dead. Now you're just being a contrarian. Every story has something—you know, a journey, a resurrection, a resolution. When it's over, things will never be the same again. We see ourselves in the heroes. They are us and we are them. Criminy, a story has to mean something!"

"Why? Who says a story has to mean something? Is that like a law or something? I thought art is about making people feel something and sometimes breaking rules. Obviously you feel very strongly about this, so hasn't it accomplished its goal?"

Oh, he's good. But, goddammit, I refuse to be outmaneuvered. I have to stay in this game. Losing would be intolerable.

"Oh, c'mon! Serial killers who chop the faces off people and wear them aren't heroes! You can't have them being admired at the end of the movie. You can't make them look like marines charging into a machine-gun nest on Iwo Jima for God and country! They're freakin' serial killers! You can't have this slow-motion sequence that transforms them into mythic heroes! And 'Freebird' . . . jeezus criminy. This isn't revolutionary filmmaking . . . It's just sex-and-shoot-'em-up exploitation thumbing its nose at convention and anybody over eighteen! It's just like your goddamned heavy metal music, with all its fuck-everything bullshit! You can't tell kids that crime is cool."

Okay, now I am starting to sputter and spit, but I've got him here. I'm on the side of the angels. He lines up with the devils and/or Black Sabbath—either way, a bad choice. Anybody who thinks a dad shouldn't take some pleasure in checkmating his smart-ass college-kid son is plain flat wrong.

Matt just smiles. *Smiles*, goddammit.

"Oh, you mean like *Bonnie and Clyde?*"

Krrrep.

———— • ————

On the road early the next morning, Matt's cell phone rings. We have been without bars for days, and then suddenly a call inexplicably bounces off a strange satellite and slips through the ether.

It's his mother.

"Hey . . . just getting started . . . I don't know, somewhere in the mountains in the friggin' Yukon . . . Good . . . What? I can barely hear . . ."

For a long time, Matt listens but says nothing. He turns toward the window. Without saying another word, he closes his phone and puts it in the cup holder.

"Everything okay?" I ask.

"Lost the signal," he says, still facing away from me. "She was just calling to tell me they're gonna put T.J. to sleep."

T.J. is Matt's dog, a border collie so smart we named him "Thomas Jefferson," or T.J. for short. I brought him home as a puppy many years ago, an anniversary gift to my wife, and he quickly became a part of the family. T.J. and Matt grew up together. They both had far more energy than our modest backyard could comfortably hold, so they were kindred spirits from the beginning. After the split, Matt clung to his dog even more.

In the past several months, T.J. had developed a tumor in his jaw. When it first appeared, he hadn't been expected to live long, but he was irrepressible. He defied the odds. And he continued to brighten when Matt came home on college breaks.

"I'm really sorry, Matt. T.J. is a great dog. I've missed him myself for a long time."

Matt clenches his jaw and wipes his eyes.

"She said they'll try to wait until I get home before . . ."

"I thought he was doing better. Has he gotten worse?"

"Another tumor in his mouth. I guess it's . . . bleeding. He has to sleep in the garage because of the blood. The vet says it'll only get worse, and when it gets to his brain and lungs . . ."

Matt fights hard to keep from crying, or at least to keep me from seeing it.

"God, sorry. I know how you felt . . . feel . . . about him. I hate to think he's suffering, but I hope you see him again. Sorry. Just . . . sorry."

I reach over and squeeze my son's arm, just to make some kind of contact. For the rest of the morning, we mourn separately and silently.

In the abstraction of a heavy-metal song, a slasher flick, a graveyard, or even a Yukon road-trip book, death is made romantic. Memory tangles up with immortality, myth with poetry, illusion with theatricality, ghosts with whimsy, until we sometimes forget that a lot of unpoetic stuff like maggots, pain, grave wax, putrid stink, carnivorous bacteria, suffering, oozing death-juices, and toxic rot are part of it.

Man is the only animal that simultaneously doubts and fears death's finality, and then makes death and resurrection a part of every story he tells. Come to think of it, man is the only animal that tells stories.

I don't know if Matt understands death, although I know he understands loss. Some people are just too young to absorb death seriously, and that's not all bad. Time wounds all illusions. For our own sakes, we transform death from its sickening reality to something more abstract and metaphorical. But here it sits now, a profound chunk of concrete death in his lap.

In a way, the idea of drinking a cocktail containing a long-dead human toe no longer feels like the heroic quest it started out to be. But in another way, if you believe in metaphor, we will get our chance to push back, to appear for one shining moment as if we aren't scared shitless of dying.

————

We are bone-tired after driving almost three thousand miles in four days. The days have been too long and the twilight-nights too short. After cussing and discussing father-son stuff like the history of heavy metal, what you can tell from a kiss, the real-life manifestations of the mythical hero's journey, Panama the place and my own private Panama, the merits of farting as a male-bonding experience, profanity as an art form, why choosing a college major before graduating is probably a good idea, dissociative personalities, love in lonely places, the inevitability of his baldness, carburetors, whether poker is a sport, strip steak versus sirloin, the subtexts of Adam Sandler movies, butts versus boobs, the keener elements of dystopia, the intrinsic efficiencies of roadside peeing, Bam Margera and the *Jackass* jackasses, why gray water from the sink and black water from the stool can't go in the same tank, why Macs suck, whether crepes are just thin pancakes or a completely different dish altogether, the dangers of earbuds, why yawning is contagious, BluRay versus DVD, the Denver Broncos' collapse since Elway retired, the agony of depression, how cool it would be to have a pet monkey, whether women prefer a chest that's hairy or shaved, high school misdemeanors I've never heard about, the best comedy films ever made, why some scars are innies and some are outies, whether it'd be better to die in your sleep or doing something (or someone) you love, whether Achilles and Darth Vader were cut from the same mythical cloth, the purpose of golf, whose

job it is to squeegee the windshields when the driver is filling the gas tank, the wisdom of picking up discarded shoes
and dirty clothes when a camper van doesn't have much room
for maneuvering, and fergawdsakes, why it would be better to
look at the majestic landscape that we're passing through than
to watch smarmy *Scrubs* reruns on the laptop . . . Well, we are
past ready to put this circus down for a couple days of R&R
in Whitehorse.

At the edge of town, we pull into the Pioneer Campground,
an honest-to-god RV park that advertises hot showers, an Internet hot spot, a Laundromat, gas, food, a sewage dump, water
and electrical hookups. The Korean lady at the front desk gives
us a parking slot between a couple of half-block-long, three-
bedroom, aluminum highway mansions where we felt—and
probably looked—like a kayak moored among a fleet of aircraft
carriers.

The first order of business is to hook up the water and elec-
tricity while Matt levels the van so the refrigerator will keep our
beer and bologna cold. Simple enough.

The retired undertaker in the enormous motor coach next
door is washing his tow-behind Jeep with Texas plates. His name
is Howard, he lives in some little Panhandle town I've never
heard of, and he wears a greasy Bass Pro Shops cap, which marks
him as a real road man. If he is entertained by the two newbies
in the toy RV that is smaller than his toolshed back home, he
doesn't show it.

That is, not until it comes time to empty the shitter. I hook
the big slinky hose up to the sewage pipe and the poop tank,
then yank the handle that should release a week's worth of crap
safely into the underground septic system but . . . nothing. Not
a (literally) guttural torrent. Not a gurgle. Not a drip. Nothing.

I jiggle the handle. I lift the hose to a comfortable angle. I
gently rock the van. I question whether the laws of gravity might

be somehow warped at these latitudes. I question my mother's morality. Nothing works.

"Y'all wanna borrow some rubber gloves?" Howard asks.

"Thanks," I say, "but it doesn't look like it's gonna work."

The fellow saunters over and bends down to take a quick peek at my plumbing.

"Y'all are hooked up to yer gray instead of yer black," he says. "Jes' switch her over and I bet she runs like the mornin' after Jalapeno Night at Luby's. Hold on, son, and lemme git you some gloves."

While he goes off to find gloves, I decide to get a jump on the switchover. I unlatch the hose from one tank and lock it into the other. Simple enough. *Aw, hell, I'll just open it up and let 'er rip . . .*

Nothing.

Again, I jiggle the handle. Shake the hose. Rock the van. Nothing.

I decide the hose must be plugged, so I lift it out of the dump hole and smack it against the ground a couple times, then stretch it out flat on the ground, in case it just needs to get some siphoning action going. Nothing.

I am aiming to re-insert it into the disposal pipe when the slinky hose gets strangely heavy. Just before my brain solves the mystery and just after my helpful neighbor comes 'round the corner with fresh new latex gloves—PHLOOSH!—my jeans and hiking shoes are drenched in gledgy, week-old poop water, fermented man-piss, and gloppy flecks of used toilet paper.

While the damn hose gushes raw sewage, I manage to aim it more or less at the dump hole, but not before sliming the entire area (and myself) with an indelicate glaze of human waste the color of liquefied month-old latte with white chocolate bits.

And the smell. Such a rich bouquet could only be rivaled by the worst prison outhouses.

Howard stands there watching it all with a big Texas smile on his face.

"That there is what my wife'd call 'self-defecating humor,' " is all he says.

After hosing away all evidence of my sewage misadventure, I shower and shave for the first time in a week at a coin-operated lavatory, where I can hear somebody down the row of private stalls singing a song I can't recognize. The soothing hot water makes me wonder what else I take for granted back home.

Cleansed and renewed, I go back to the van, where Matt is napping with his buzzing earbuds in his ears. I fetch my laptop, my cell phone, and every unfolded piece of clothing in the van—which is pretty much every piece of clothing—and schlep it to the campground's launderette. A washload costs one Canadian dollar, a coin known as a "loonie" because its reverse side features a loon. One dryer cycle costs two loonies, or a "toonie," a two-dollar Canadian coin with Elizabeth II on the front and a polar bear on the back (some Canuckleheads call it "the Queen with a bear behind" or a "moonie").

Even here in the Yukon's biggest city, an ordinary American cell phone can't get out through the local network without extra fees arranged in advance, so I boot up my laptop on a bench beside my two swish-swashing washers, amid the floating lint, the artificial baby-fresh scent of fabric softener, and the invisible fog of wireless Internet.

It's been a couple days, so my in-box is awash with opportunities to commit at least three of the seven deadly sins, by fattening my penis (lust), losing weight without actually changing my eating habits or walking farther than the refrigerator (sloth or gluttony, take your pick), and getting obscenely wealthy by conspiring to transfer a deposed African bureaucrat's loot to the safety of my savings account (greed, or *oju kokoro* in Yoruba, one of 521 languages spoken by Nigerian Internet scammers).

After deleting a few megabytes of spam, I'm left with a few notes from my daughter, my literary agent, some friends, and a cluster of daily e-mails from Mary. I read each one. They are my only connection to the life I interrupted for this journey.

I save for last an e-mail Mary had sent just a few hours before. Her messages were our only communication in the past head-long week, and I felt her presence in every one. But this one . . .

She has been offered a new teaching job in San Antonio, five hours west from Beaumont, and she must give them an answer before I get back. It is a bigger school, lots more money, a better city, a chance to teach at a higher level . . . a different and better existence. In the past few years, she has made some good friends in Beaumont, but the oppressive humidity, the bugs, the hurricanes, the small-town politics, the unconcealed racism that is as corrosive and stinking as the chemical air, even the blaring night-trains have prevented her heart from settling in. Except for me, she would never have gone there at all.

I tell her to do what she thinks is best. I'm happy for her. I tell her it's a good opportunity.

We had long ago settled into a relationship that was neither fish nor fowl, neither committed forever nor easily abandoned. She had followed me to Texas from Colorado, desperately wanting an *always,* but settling for *a while.* Our friendship grew closer, but when it came to marriage, I kept an uneasy distance. I just wasn't ready to put my fears and dreams in another woman's hands again.

It wasn't an ultimatum, just good news. I always knew she was unhappy; I'd encouraged her job search, and I even relished the idea of going with her, but . . . *Oh, fergawdsakes, was there really a "but"?* She is in my pores, and this trip has already proven it to me. But I'd be leaving a good job for no job, and it unnerved me. It isn't loving her that I fear. It is the mistakes so-far-unmade or yet-to-be-remade. The return of the black dog. The exhaling.

I fear becoming *Mi Padre*. How odd, wouldn't you say, that ordinary risks everyone else takes—like saying "I love you" to the woman who has stuck by me for the past few, rough years, or committing myself to her for anything more than a Friday-night movie—scared the hell out of me?

Maybe I fear my son becoming *Mi Padre,* too. I regret my failure as a husband and a father, a failure that has made me emotionally risk-averse. And maybe I fear being forgotten—that the damned Toe would be more immortal than I. Might I cast no more shadow across this Earth than the stories I tell?

Mary wouldn't leave without me, so my choice was to anchor her in her misery, or to leap off the cliff and hope to grow wings before splashing flamboyantly at the bottom.

I hear cars on the highway, always moving. I miss her, and it's not just a fear of being alone. The farther I go, the more important is her lifeline. I don't want to go back to someone else, or a string of someone elses. I want her. She's good company.

Out here, I stopped letting my relationship with Matt happen to me, controlled by my dislocation in his time and space. And maybe I stopped letting my relationship with *Mi Padre* happen to me when my questions were finally answered. It's time to stop letting Mary happen to me, too.

For the first time in many days, maybe months, I don't want to be on the road. Distance is suddenly a barrier, no longer a sanctuary. I want to talk to her, but I can't. And even if I were holding her close and whispering in her ear, I'm not sure what I'd say.

———————

I bump into Howard outside the campground office, where he bought his wife a souvenir Yukon spoon for her collection, and where I must make change for more loonies and toonies. They plan an early getaway in the morning, hoping to hit the road before all the "other" lumbering motor coaches clogged the road to Alaska. Apparently, Howard belongs to the NASCAR chapter of the Good Sam Club.

"Where y'all fixin' to go from here?" he asks.

"North," I say. "Dawson City. Then to the Arctic on the Dempster Highway. For the solstice in a few days."

A smile crinkles across Howard's sun-cracked lips like a trickle of rainwater in the badlands.

"You sure?" he asks.

"Yeah. Why?"

"I'd sooner sled nekkid down a mountain of broken glass. Without a sled."

There's an image that will haunt me for the rest of my days.

"Bad road, eh?"

"Badass road. Badass maintenance. Badass attitude. It goes nowhere, so after y'all drag your bare balls across that bed of nails, y'all gotta turn around and drag 'em back."

This guy is good.

"So I should take it easy, huh?"

"Me? I wouldn't take it at all. It's all gravel for hundreds of miles, ya know? Might as well just shoot out your own tires and take a hammer to your own glass. Save on gas. I wouldn't take my own vehicle unless I owned one of them Sherman tanks."

"Well, good thing our little camper is rented."

"They're gonna hate y'all. Got extra tires?"

"There's a spare on the back."

"Ain't enough, son. Go find you a tire shop and get another one. Or two. And a jerry can for extra gas. And enough food to last y'all 'til next spring in case you get stuck, cuz nobody's comin' to git y'all. Ever skinned a caribou?"

"No."

Howard winces. As a mortician, he's probably seen the results of many foolhardy decisions.

"Well, ain't my place to tell y'all what to do," he says, as if he really doesn't believe it. "Y'all are free. I really hope y'all find whatever you're looking for up there . . . before it finds you."

I am beginning to think the Dempster is a bad idea. We haven't yet crossed paths with anyone who recommends it. Even the guidebooks sound subtle notes of caution.

"Thanks for the advice, man," I say. "Maybe it wasn't a good idea. I'll think about it."

"I reckon that's why they call it adventure. Wouldn't be much fun if y'all always knew how the story ends, would it?"

He sticks out his bear paw of a hand. I've always been a little squeamish about shaking morticians' hands, but I shake Howard's and tell him to be safe as he shuffles off with his wife's new spoon.

"Hey, Howard," I call to him. "You ever been on the Dempster?"

He stops and turns around, that trickling smile spilling across his craggy face.

"Not yet," he says. "I'm savin' it for last."

———•———

Matt awakes hungry from his afternoon nap, so we unplug the van from its water-and-electric life support and explore White-horse's modest downtown, looking for a local place to eat.

Whitehorse owes its existence to man's willingness to take risks—but only up to a point. During the 1898 Gold Rush, the nearby Yukon River was the main river route into the Klondike gold fields in Dawson and beyond. But just south of where the town sits today, dangerous whitewater rapids (whose crests reminded travelers of the flying manes of wild white horses) stopped would-be miners dead in their tracks and sunk more than three hundred boats in a single year.

Rather than brave the single most perilous obstacle on the trail, the stampeders paid three cents a pound to be carried around the rapids by wagons or horse-drawn trams. In time, a railroad was built from Skagway, and its northernmost terminus was a new boomtown that took its name from the raging rapids it bypassed, Whitehorse.

By early 1900, Whitehorse was roaring bigger and faster than its infamous rapids. Tents, log huts, and tumbledown shacks were thrown up on every flat patch of earth—including a cabin built by a starry-eyed Canadian prospector-poet named Sam McGee, who, it turns out, didn't come from Tennessee (Robert Service needed a name that rhymed for an unfinished poem), didn't die in the Yukon, and (thus) was never cremated on "the marge of Lake Lebarge." Damn poets.

In 1907, Service's first book, *Songs of a Sourdough,* with its macabre poem about the incineration of Sam McGee's frozen corpse, made Service a literary luminary—but it made the real Sam McGee the butt of countless cremation jokes. He came to hate the classic ode that made him famous.

In 1938, the authentic Sam McGee returned to White-horse and, again, he left empty-handed—except for a poke containing "Genuine Sam McGee Ashes" that he purchased at the tourist gift shop in his old cabin. When Sam died of a heart attack two years later, he was buried in an Alberta churchyard, and legend swears the bag of his fictional ashes was buried with him.

Anyway, to take the money of dreamy stampeders like Sam McGee, the main street soon featured a few mercantiles, several saloons, a bordello, two pharmacies, a telegraph office, a hardware store, six large hotels, a brickyard, three churches, an athletic club, an electric light plant, and a tent-frame bakery.

They're all gone now, except the bakery building, which is still on Whitehorse's main drag. By 1930, a couple barnstorming entrepreneurs bought it and painted KLONDIKE AIRWAYS on the side because they dreamed of someday buying an airplane to transport mail and freight into the Yukon's nether regions. But they never bought the plane, and went belly-up in a few years. In the mid-1930s, a carpenter named Jack French opened a woodworking shop there, specializing in fine coffins for a local mortuary.

Which brings me to my roundabout point: Today the old place is one of Whitehorse's favorite local diners, the Klondike Rib and Salmon BBQ, where they specialize in northern ocean fish, wild game, and other Yukon delicacies. The place is packed, but we get a table with a checkered tablecloth in a back room, where we order beer to go with our extraordinary supper of musk-ox stroganoff and caribou stew.

"You're quiet tonight," Matt says.

I shrug. "The food's too good. No need to waste time talking."

"You always talk, dude. You don't stop. What's up?"

It eventually pours out of me. I tell him about Mary's job offer, and how I've come to another crossroads. How I don't want to fuck up another relationship the way I might have banjaxed my chance to be a good father. How I might've lost the road. How I fear I'm still dead, which might be slightly better than being resurrected unwhole.

"Is that why you wanted me to bring a shovel?"

The question doesn't just come out of deep left field, but beyond the bleachers, beyond the batting cages, beyond the snack stand, from someplace in the next county—and it blows right past me.

"What the hell are you talking about? A shovel?"

"You know, the camp shovel. I was wondering why it was so important, and now I know."

"What do you know?"

"You want me to kill you and bury you, right? You can't go on. Can't run with the big dogs anymore. Dude, there's nothing left to live for. You got no love, no future, no dreams, and no balls. Am I right?"

The twerp is mocking me! This is where a no-spanking policy leads.

"No. Not even close."

"So what the fuck are you whining about, old man? Jeezus. If you think there's nothing left, let's just go out and find a little hill and get it over with. You can even pick the hill. We'll dig a hole—well, *you'll* dig a hole—and I'll dump your body in it. Too bad we couldn't bring that gun. I'll mark the spot with a rock in case anybody wonders whatever happened to you, but you probably won't get many visitors up here. No biggie, because it sounds like nobody cares anyway. I might even pray a little prayer because you've been an okay dad. Whaddya say, dude?"

"You're an ass."

"Yeah, I inherited it from my dad."

A woman at the next table glances at us so I smile wanly, as if to reassure her it's all in fun, like a father and son in a popular TV sitcom where the audience is supposed to laugh, not glower. Then I lower my voice, to more the level of a primetime drama.

"Don't joke about this stuff. It's not funny. I tell you I'm a little afraid and I don't know what comes next, and you just make jokes."

"It's all a joke, dude," Matt says. "You're all, like, poor me. You're the smartest guy I know, but you can't figure out that you've got a great life and great stories . . . and a great son and daughter. You are invisible to yourself. That's pretty damn funny."

I am caught with nowhere to maneuver, a skunk in the head-lights. Our waitress saves me by clearing our plates and gently seducing us into ordering a dessert of bumbleberry pie. Neither of us has ever heard of bumbleberries, much less tasted them, so we presume these native fruits must be as rare as African horned cucumbers or Hottentot figs. When it finally arrives, the still-warm pie is treacly and mysterious.

So after Matt gulps the last little bit of pie, I beg our waitress to tell us more about these exotic Yukon bumbleberries, which I imagine are only picked by Inuit virgins on the first full moon of spring, or are propagated by sweet-toothed caribou who scat-ter their precious seeds across the tundra in their steaming dung.

She just giggles her courteous little Canadian giggle.

"There's no such thing," she says. "The chef just uses what-ever berries are in season and mixes them all up. So I guess a bumbleberry is whatever you want it to be."

Sometimes we happily, willingly, allow ourselves to be fooled. Prairie wizards, perpetual motion, broken angels, the scent of distant women, reanimated fence posts, a morning in Valhalla, talking mummies, Sam McGee's ashes, time travel, empty graves, rumors of gold, tilting at windmills, ordinary bumbleberries, dead human toes floating in glasses of rye, the one-in-a-million chance of a tiny resurrection . . . we want to believe it all. Not because we're dense, but because it's our detour around the real obstacles, the roaring rapids of decomposing love, the parts that stop working, and the gut-clenching fear of being alone and unremembered when we die.

Oh, hell, who am I kidding, besides myself? This isn't about life and death. That's an abstraction bigger than me. No, it's about *my* life and *my* death. It's about driving until you lose the road. It's about living until I die. I've had it backwards for too long, being dead and hoping to live. Dead guys don't worry about tomorrow.

I am the bumbleberry.

The next morning is Father's Day. We loiter in the campground, where cottonwood wisps float in the sun-drenched air. By ten a.m., we are nearly alone as the veteran road dogs, including our neighbor Howard, have pulled out for parts unknown.

While Matt cleans up the cumin-scented splatter left by an exploded can of chili con carne inside the kitchen cabinet, I find a picnic table beneath the pines where I can make notes on my laptop. The shade is refreshing.

About noon, Matt wanders over and sits with me under the trees.

"You hungry?" he asks.

"Yeah. What sounds good?"

"Crepes. We passed a French place downtown last night. Looked good and classy on the outside."

"You buying?"

"No, it's Father's Day. Dads buy. It's a Canadian tradition."

"You don't have any money, do you?"

"Dude, I'm a college kid. That's why we celebrate fathers."

"God knows there aren't any other reasons."

Matt smiles and a comfortable silence settles between us like the soft seed-tufts in the air.

"Hey, sorry about last night," he says as we walk back to the van. "I didn't mean . . ."

I shake my head and wave him off. "You were right," I say. "I'm okay. Sometimes I forget how lucky I am, that's all. I just hope someday you have a good son who thinks you're an okay dad. It's nice to know. Really."

That afternoon, after our long crepe lunch in a quaint but almost empty bistro, we visit the Yukon Beringia Interpretive Center on the western edge of Whitehorse, a museum about the

Atlantis-like land bridge that spanned the Bering Straits during the Ice Age, enabling Asian migrants to populate North America, then disappeared.

Here, we learn to hurl spears with ancient atlatls at imaginary targets and are dismayed to discover that we'd definitely go hungry if our survival depended upon actually hitting a distant animal with deadly force. In fact, we might be the crappiest father-and-son atlatl hunting team since Peking Man and his kid were forced to invent egg noodles to avoid starvation.

Luckily for us, French crepes are stupid animals and easy to kill.

———•———

After a day of exploring and a dinner of roadhouse burgers, we return to the camp and turn in early. The huge bowl of sky above us remains in perpetual twilight, so we button up the cheap shades to seal out the light, which leaks in anyway. Matt puts in his earbuds and covers his head with a pillow.

Tomorrow, we light out for Dawson, where we'll sip the Sourtoe Cocktail to prove our manhood. And after that, we push north into the Arctic on a road that apparently no sane person willingly travels. Without doubt, this relates to our manhood, too.

I lie here around midnight, examining the minute wrinkles in my hands by the light of night. Fifty years old and I am just now beginning to understand the relationship of the Earth to the sun. Granted, it's a poet's view, not a scientist's, but you might not have read this far in a science text.

Only a poet could be intrigued to know that the ethereal boundary between day and night is called the "circle of illumination."

To the metaphor-addicted right brain, it sounds like someplace as magical as the Fortress of Solitude or the House of the

Rising Sun, as if it might not be just a place of light, but also of enlightenment. This is, of course, ludicrous, since some of my best work is done at night. Plus, left-brained scientists, who used their appendixes more often than their sense of humor, are quick to point out that the world isn't perfectly round, so it's not really a circle, which somehow skews the whole astro-geometric theory in their minds.

So anyway, half of the Earth is always in sunlight, half in darkness. At any given moment, one is either literally looking on the bright side or on the dark side of the Earth. Half the Earth is always visible from some distant perspective, half invisible. Every human on the planet technically spends part of every day in some light and some dark—except for two extraordinary days of the year at the figurative edges of the Earth, the Arctic and Antarctic. On those two days, the summer and winter solstices, the sun never rises or never sets.

The word *solstice* is apt. It comes from the Latin for "the sun stands still," because the ancients couldn't see much difference between the spots on the horizon where the sun set every night during the beginning of summer and winter.

On the date of the summer solstice, just four days from today, the North Pole tilts toward the sun, which means its rays strike far north of the equator, and the bulk of the sun's light and heat is concentrated in the Northern Hemisphere—and we have summer. Six months later, on the winter solstice, the North Pole tilts away from the sun—and it's winter.

But while the rest of the Earth continues to rotate in and out of the sun's light like the scrupulously faithful wheel of an old clock, the entire Arctic remains inside the circle of illumination for the entire day. The sun never sets.

Thus, it is possible, through no particular magic or will of our own, to stop a sunset. But you must go to the end of the Earth to do it.

And that's why we came to this place at this moment in time.

To consider that we are all just revolving in lonely space, half light and half dark at the same time, sharing orbits with the occasional satellite or shooting star.

To dance along the edge of daylight.

To slow down a sunset.

The Toe

When you're traveling, you are what you are, right there and then. People don't have your past to hold against you. No yesterdays on the road.

—William Least Heat-Moon in *Blue Highways*

The next morning, rolling north on the Klondike Highway toward Dawson City, an earnest announcer on the CBC-FM station out of Whitehorse poses a whimsical question for groundling superheroes like us: Would you rather be able to fly or be invisible?

Matt, ever the contrarian, answers first and fast, as if it were a game show.

"Neither," he says with his best scurfy smile. "I'd be immortal."

"That's not one of the choices."

"So what? You're making up your own rules again?"

"It's not my rule," I say. "The guy on the radio only gave you a choice of being able to fly or being invisible."

"That's a stupid choice. What good is a superpower if you can still be killed?"

"No, stupid is that guy whose only superpower is being able to turn blue," I say. "What the hell good is that?"

"That's stupid, too, unless . . . crap, I can't think of any good reason to turn blue."

"So if somebody offered you the power to fly, you'd refuse because it was stupid?"

"Not necessarily, but I'd probably ask what other powers were available. Maybe the sales guy has some extra instant healing or mind-reading or super strength. Those would be better. Doesn't hurt to ask."

"Okay, so some guy walks up and offers you a free superpower that no other human has . . . and you want to bargain?"

"Think about it, dude! You might be able to fly, but somebody could still shoot a heat-seeking missile up your butt unless you had stealth powers or something. And being invisible—well, that just sounds creepy."

"Really? I think I'd choose to be invisible," I say. "I could find Osama bin Laden or fight crime, and nobody could find me when I didn't want to be bothered . . . and I guess if I was invisible I could get on airplanes and fly free anyway."

"See, that's what I mean! Most people wouldn't use their invisibility for good stuff. They'd sneak into girls' locker rooms and theaters and go places where they shouldn't go and steal things. People suck."

"Oh, you'd never, ever misuse immortality, right?"

"Yeah, sure, Dad, all my friends love practical jokes about immortality," Matt says, rolling his brown eyes. "Dude, I just think being un-killable would be the coolest superpower to have. Sue me."

"Wouldn't it suck to watch every single person you ever loved die? And think about if you live, like, oh, a hundred thousand years. After four or five millennia, will you remember the sound of your mother's laugh? What your children's names were? The things that make you smile? Would you just slowly forget, piece by piece, everyone you ever loved?"

"You'd get used to it, I suppose. If you were immortal, you just couldn't look at life and death like a mortal. There'd be . . . adjustments."

"And a day wouldn't really be a day, would it? I mean, wouldn't time pass differently? Would any single day be more special than any other? If not, why look forward to tomorrow—or a million tomorrows?"

"I could live with it," Matt says, mindless of the irony in his words.

"Yeah, but living forever? Seems like you want to live forever just so you won't die prematurely. I don't want to die prematurely either, but I'm not sure immortality is the best solution. So is it death or just fear of death that's the problem? Would it be just as good if we could just be unafraid of dying? Maybe a better superpower would allow you to live until you *want* to die."

"You suck."

"That's it? That's your argument?"

"I'm not arguing. You always do this! You get so damn serious, it pisses me off. We're talking about make-believe superpowers here, not where you want your ashes scattered. Forget it. I'm out."

Matt turns away, silent. We are passing through a narrow canyon of boreal forest, so close to the roadside that the eye cannot focus on a single tree, only a blur of forest. I can see only the back of his head, a tangled ruck of buffalo belly-wool.

Until this moment, it doesn't occur to me that my son might fear all kinds of endings, up to and including death. But no superpower will protect you from your parents' divorce, a foundered first love, or losing faith, so maybe it's safer and easier to wish for everlasting life.

And maybe our fanciful choice between flying and invisibility is a little like choosing between absence and presence, between memory and the fear of being forgotten, between life and death. It's hard to hide as you streak across the sky, but if you're invisible, you also risk being unremembered.

My son is telling me something, but I'm not hearing. There's more to say, more to hear.

"Oh, jeez, lighten up," I say. "You can be immortal if you want."

"No, I don't want to be immortal anymore. You ruined it."

"I ruined immortality? C'mon, you can be immortal if I can travel in time. We'll be Doctor Perpetuous and Mr. He-Was-Here-a-Minute-Ago. Whaddya say?"

"Sounds gay."

"Are there any father-and-son superheroes?"

"What kind of a nerd would want to see his dad in tights and a cape?"

"There you go—a first! We could have our own comic book. *The Dynamic Dudes* . . . or *Duds.* You can even have a sidekick— Ozzy Girl, a hottie Goth chick whose superpower is knowing everything about heavy-metal music. Whaddya say?"

Matt shakes his head, then leans back in the passenger seat to stare absently at the real world streaking past. The radio guy has moved on to some other nonsense, and Matt says nothing for a long time. After a dozen miles of silence, he speaks again.

"I think if I lived forever I would always want to know whatever I had ever learned or knew," he says, not looking at me, but his eyes lost out there somewhere a thousand yards ahead.

"Well, we don't live forever, and we already forget a lot of the long-ago stuff," I tell him. "Forever is a long time. Remembering might be a whole different kind of superpower."

"Okay, so then maybe that's what I'd choose," he says, his air thoughtful. "Memory. Forever. I don't want to forget anything or anybody."

I want to warn him about the Kryptonite called pain and regret, which are also memories. I want to beg him to forget the times I disappointed him. I want him to detour around the bad memories that can nail your foot to the floor. I want to tell him that someday it will be more important to him to be remembered than to remember. I want to focus him on the road ahead, not the road behind. And I want to make secret handshake deals for him with the superpower salesman . . . well, because it doesn't hurt to ask.

But my son doesn't want to forget, and right now, right here, neither do I. Someday, when it hurts again, when I think dying is better than being forgotten, I will remember this moment.

I hate flying anyway.

———•———

We are following, very roughly, a historic path paved with gold dust and broken dreams.

From Alaska, each *cheechako*—newcomer—would carry his requisite one ton of supplies over the treacherous, muddy trail of White Pass (where the air was soon filled with the stink of rotting horses that had died of exhaustion or were shot where they fell by overloaded stampeders) or climbed Chilkoot Pass's "Golden Staircase" (fifteen hundred steps carved from solid ice over the summit, where the prospectors flew down the other side on frosty ice-slides) on their 600-mile, backbreaking, finger-freezing trek to the Canadian headwaters of the Yukon River.

Some never made it past the Chilkoot. Others got to Dawson to find all the best claims already staked, so they left. A few found gold, but most didn't.

Some among them struck gold without ever turning a single spadeful of Yukon soil or panning a drop of frigid creek water: They mined the frenzy of dreamers. In Dawson, they opened saloons, brothels, gambling halls, theaters, hotels, newspapers, mercantiles, and mortuaries, and they grew fat on other miners' gold.

Within a year, the former mud bog in the crooked elbow of the Yukon and Klondike rivers was a thriving city with phone service, electric lights, and steam heat. Two newspapers slugged it out. During the day, two banks took all the money left over from the nights' entertainments. The pastors of Dawson's five new churches must have felt a great deal of pressure. And temptation.

At the height of the rush, one fresh egg cost a dollar (more than twenty-five dollars today), and a five-minute bath, a dollar fifty. A bowl of hot mush in winter ran five dollars. A shipment of watermelons sold for almost thirty-five dollars *each*.

In June 1898, the arrival of a live milk cow in Dawson made headlines in the local papers. A miner paid thirty dollars in gold for the cow's first pail of milk, and subsequent milkings were expected to fetch up to one hundred dollars. The cow's owner even sold ice cream for ten dollars a glass—more than any pint of hand-mixed boutique ice cream costs today.

A single, spartan room rented for a hundred dollars a month, at a time when a four-bedroom apartment in New York City went for a hundred and twenty. Thanks to a law against carrying guns and a very visible contingent of Mounties, not a single person was murdered in 1898, even though nearly 150,000 gallons of alcohol were drunk and almost everyone carried gold in his pockets.

Oddly, companionship was comparatively cheaper than milk, eggs, whiskey, or mush, but the wages of sin were still pretty good. One dance cost about a dollar. The going rate for one of Dawson's two hundred-plus hookers might range from about three dollars for a back-alley quickie to sixty-four dollars (about four ounces of gold, usually weighed on the working girl's own crooked scales).

One of Dawson's most popular burlesque entertainers was a singer named Cad Wilson, who reportedly was neither pretty nor a very good singer, but drunken miners would reward her racy humor and naughty songs with a literal shower of gold nuggets. Once, a miner paid twenty dollars a bottle so he could watch Cad bathe in French wine—but he wasn't allowed to touch her.

Wyatt Earp and Calamity Jane came. William Randolph Hearst dispatched six reporters. Thomas Edison brought several film crews to record the mass dreaming. A Greek waiter named Alexander Pantages opened a brothel and burlesque theater in Dawson, his first foray into the North American theater business—which he would ultimately transform into big business back in the States. The infant Jimmy Doolittle traveled to the Klondike with his restless father. Augustus Mack sought his fortune here before deciding that designing a powerful truck was probably a better use of his time.

A few poets came, too. Robert Service and Jack London never found gold, but they found something else, something that made them immortal. London, in particular, almost died in the Yukon, and he couldn't have known that a little boy would read his Yukon books fifty years after he died, dream of being a writer, and someday get the crazy idea to go to Dawson, too. Not for gold, but for immortality.

Suffice it to say, anybody who survived the Chilkoot and a Yukon winter had some sterner stuff than greed or lust keeping them alive. Maybe it was a dream. Dreams are better than nightmares, but not always sane.

At one point, some thirty thousand people lived in Dawson, the biggest city north of San Francisco. Some began to call it the "Paris of the North," a mythic place over the rainbow where all dreams came true and riches beyond imagination literally lay on the ground.

And for some, the myth proved true. By 1903, less than five years after the rush began, more than $96 million worth of gold had been panned from northern Yukon creeks.

But dreams die. A series of devastating fires in Dawson City and the discovery of gold in Nome, Alaska, in 1899 scuffed the thrill. Ten years after gold was found, the Klondike rush was over. A few stayed, but most went home with empty pockets, or just empty.

The Klondike rush was, in many ways, more than the sum of its parts. In fact, stampeders are estimated to have spent at least as much money getting to the Klondike as they ever took out of it. Most took nothing from the Klondike. For every stampeder upon whom history and the Midnight Sun shined brightly, a thousand went home with nothing more than a few stories and, if they chose to put the brightest spin on their misfortune, knowing a dream was definitely lighter than a year's worth of supplies.

Today, only about thirteen hundred hardscrabble souls scrape out a hard-fought existence here, mostly in gold-dredging and tourism. Most of its streets are still gravel and dirt. Tourists come in the summer, but winters are dark, lonely, and subzero cold. Most of Dawson's buildings date back before Lindbergh. And in 2004, the whole town went bankrupt.

In winter, Dawson is a frozen ghost of itself. Most of the stores are shuttered. Through the season's interminably long nights, the only lights burning are in the homes and dashboards of the year-round miners and trappers. And the insane.

And where else would you find a pile of dirt that's a historical site? For a half-century after the Klondike gold rush, gold mining continued. Big mining companies brought in massive dredges to scoop the river bottoms, and water cannons powerful enough to reduce entire mountains to parking lots, literally leaving no stone unturned.

The monstrous, river-eating dredges dug and dumped 'round the clock, recovering as much as 800 ounces—50 pounds—of gold from 16,000 cubic yards of Klondike river muck and gravel every day.

Every scoop was separated from its gold nuggets by a system of sluices and screens. Then the lifeless, worthless waste, the "tailings," were carried by a long conveyor belt to be dumped in gigantic piles taller than any building in Dawson. By 1966, the corporations turned to new methods and walked away from the whole mess.

But these tapeworm-shaped piles of gravel still slither across the flats east of town, where they are occasionally picked over, again, by pick-and-shovel prospectors who hope to see what the machines missed. Far from being an eyesore, they are celebrated as evidence of the Yukon's literally golden age.

That was then, and this is now.

Now, Dawson City isn't even big enough to be an official Canadian city, although the word *city* is as much a part of its name as gold is part of its history. All told, it's just fifteen blocks wide and eight blocks deep, plenty of room for its thirteen hundred citizens.

Nonetheless, its century-long decline from boom to bust is spelled out in big letters on signs at the edge of town, where road-worn travelers are formally welcomed to THE TOWN OF THE CITY OF DAWSON.

We have arrived. Somewhere in this little town is a big toe with our name on it.

———•———

After we scout a parking spot in the local RV camp, we wander downtown for a look-see and a late lunch at Klondike Kate's, a California-style diner in a gold rush–era mercantile just two blocks off Front Street, Dawson's main drag.

It's part funk, part frontier, with century-old dark wood floors, swirly antique café chairs, probably original fixtures, oh, and a birch-bark canoe hanging from the ceiling. Not a stick of blond wood in the joint. On summer days, waitresses prop the front door open, so it's inviting outside and cool inside. From the sunny window table where we sit, I can see at least six calendars, but nothing notably extravagant happens here.

History records at least seventeen Klondike Kates, but this place is named for Kathleen Rockwell, an adventuresome Kansas-born redhead whose exotic dances amid endless billowing yards of red chiffon earned her another nickname, "The Flame of the Yukon." In Dawson, she became the lover and partner of penniless bartender (and future theater mogul) Alexander Pantages, who eventually stole her money and dumped her for a violinist. In her later years, she literally added to her legend by making up stories about her adventures and promoting herself as the Queen of the Klondike—and died poor at eighty-four.

While we wait for our sandwiches, Matt drinks his water, and I pull aside the lace curtain to see a poem painted on a clapboard wall of a stately but vacant building across the dreary gravel road known as Third Avenue. It's Robert Service's "The Spell of the Yukon," an appropriate verse in an unexpected place.

> *I wanted the gold, and I sought it;*
> *I scrabbled and mucked like a slave.*
> *Was it famine or scurvy—I fought it;*
> *I hurled my youth into a grave.*
> *I wanted the gold and I got it—*
> *Came out with a fortune last fall.*
> *Yet somehow life's not what I thought it,*
> *And somehow the gold isn't all.*

Matt bobs for an ice cube with his forefinger. In the two minutes it takes me to copy the poem into my notebook, our waitress delivers lunch.

For some strange reason, the verse speaks to me. We came here seeking something akin to transformation or renewal or epiphany, but none of them are just lying on the ground like gold nuggets—which, the chagrined stampeders discovered, don't just lie on the ground, either. Still, these fortunes all seem a little too big to have escaped our notice, if they existed at all. If there's more, something unexpected, time is running out. Back in the lower latitudes, night returns, and it's harder to see what might be found.

Matt drags me back to the moment.

"Maybe I'm just stupid, but what's the difference between a poem painted on a wall and graffiti?" he asks as he takes a bite from his grilled chicken sandwich.

My kid's a bomb-thrower, but he makes me think. I never know if he really believes some of his bombast or is just needling me to get a rise. I know the technique all too well. I'm a pro.

"Permission," is all I say.

Pffft is all he says.

———•———

It doesn't take long to walk the streets of Dawson City. There simply aren't that many. A walk from one side of town to the other takes less than ten minutes, even if you stop for ice cream.

After lunch, we wander aimlessly for a while, peeking in windows and soaking up the slanting sunlight. We foray quickly through a trapper's boutique, where we try on big fur hats and marvel at snowshoes and mukluks, and duck into a gift shop where they offer back massages twice a week. There are more gift shops in Dawson City than gas stations, more entrepreneurs offering gold-panning than groceries.

We pass an Internet café and I think of Mary as if she exists somewhere in the ether, but Matt has other plans. He's already scoped out a hotel that sells genuine Cuban cigars, forbidden in America but available in Canada. Sort of like cheap pharmaceuticals.

"You smoke cigars?" I ask, a little bewildered as he walks on.

"Only when I play poker."

"You play poker?"

He turns and smiles as he backpedals up the boardwalk.

"Only when I smoke cigars."

We agree to spend the next few hours on our own, apart. While Matt goes to buy his stash of contraband cigars we probably can't smuggle back into the States,[2] I check my e-mail in this fluorescent little salon that smells like coffee and banana muffins. Forty-two junk e-mails, and nothing from Mary. No word about the job offer, about her choices, about us. So I send a quick note, telling her we're in Dawson City, hours away from sipping a dead toe, and . . . that I am missing her.

And it's not just a lie from the road. I *am* missing her.

Alone now, I wander the dusty streets of Dawson, looking for nothing in particular, thinking about the life that waits back home as if it were an escaped reality, which it is. At least now I can admit to myself that I have always escaped certain painful truths by ducking into a pleasant state of unreality. Not crazy dissociating; more like poetic, selfish dreaming. This whole adventure started off being about a father and a son, about coming back to life, about changing the future because I can't change the past—fantasy shit—but somewhere in the past four thousand miles, the concrete reality of the life I was evading caught up. So I go farther, faster.

But now, for the first time in a long time, I feel I have left something or someone behind. I might have gone too far.

So I stroll down to the spot where the Yukon and Klondike rivers mingle and I keep walking downstream, out to Dawson's western limits, where the lonely highway dead-ends on the riverbank. From here, you must cross the Yukon River on a ferry to continue on to Alaska, through a big sky and a hundred thousand cast-off dreams.

2. Later, I discover that private citizens bringing Cuban cigars into the United States face up to $250,000 in fines and ten years in prison.

I walk farther and emerge on a high bank. Back the other direction, a few miles upstream from here, there's a spot where the wild terrain is just as big, but the remnant dreams are, well, smaller.

Exactly one square inch.

In the halcyon days after World War II, nestled in the comfortable bosom of 1950s America, children raced home from school to listen to the radio, mostly because televisions were scarce, and video games, text-messaging, portable DVD players, and Internet porn hadn't yet been invented—which is just one reason we call them "halcyon days."

And the most popular kids' radio programs of the day featured Flash Gordon, the Lone Ranger, the Green Hornet, Buck Rogers, Captain Midnight, and an intrepid Mountie known as Sergeant Preston of the Yukon (with his stalwart steed, Rex, and his "wonder dog," Yukon King).

Sergeant Preston was a stud—a superhero who possessed no superpowers whatsoever, except a faithful husky with an uncanny sniffer for bad guys. The sergeant was merely a corporal until he tracked down the man who'd murdered his father, a beloved Mountie. He became known for two things: He always got his man, and he's the first guy to say, "The view only changes for the lead dog." And he owed his airtime to Quaker Oats, the show's sponsor.

But by the mid-1950s, television and an explosion of sugary new kiddie cereals containing cheap toys in every box were taking a big bite out of radio and Quaker Oats. Ratings and market share were falling faster than a Yukon thermometer. The peril was beyond Sergeant Preston and Yukon King's mere mortal powers to fix.

Ah, but a different kind of superhero rose, a dream maker in the age of dreaming. In 1954, a Chicago ad man named Bruce Baker concocted one of the most successful promotions in

American advertising history, bigger than the Yukon itself: He put free Yukon land deeds in a million boxes of Quaker Puffed Rice and Puffed Wheat!

That's right. In less than a month, millions of American kids became proud owners of Yukon real estate, and started dreaming about going there someday to meet Sergeant Preston, nuzzle Yukon King behind the ears, and maybe find a gold nugget on their own land. Okay, maybe their lots weren't as big as the Yukon. Or as big as a small lot in downtown Dawson. Or even a parking space. Or half a parking space. Or even a boot print in the snow. Or a paw print. Or a postage stamp.

Fact is, every deed provided just one square inch of land.

Baker had paid a thousand dollars for 19.11 acres of land on the west bank of the Yukon River just upstream from Dawson City, and formed an Illinois holding company known as the Klondike Big Inch Land Company. He printed 21 million fancy deeds with ornate borders and official-looking seals and fine print. These deeds were numbered consecutively starting in the northwest corner of the acreage. Any kid who wanted to actually stand on his "lot" could start at the northwest corner, count X number of inches east, then X number of inches south, and he'd be home. Literally.

The land rush was on! Quaker Oats' offices were deluged. These pint-sized landowners had a lot of questions about location, value, and—the dream of dreams—whether there might be gold in them thar postage-stamp lots. One kid reportedly mailed in four toothpicks and some twine, asking that his inch be properly fenced.

A slick-talking prepubescent speculator might trade this new kid Koufax's rookie card for a Yukon deed, but the Yukon land was so valuable it usually took at least a Ted Williams and maybe a Duke Snider. One Michigan guy wanted to establish the world's smallest national park. Legend has it that one fellow scoured America to buy up 10,880 one-inch deeds, which he reckoned to be about 75 square feet worth of land.

Imagine the look on his face when he discovered that in 1965, Quaker Oats forgot to pay $37.20 in taxes and the Canadian government seized the land, which still sits undeveloped, a stony, riverine beach about a hundred feet wide, garlanded with some of the same jack pine, spruce, poplar, and birch that were there when Bruce Baker nearly froze off his feet in 1954. Once owned by millions, still unspoiled.

That hasn't stopped the dreamers. They still show up occasionally to see their land. And today, one of those "worthless" old deeds can sell for as much as forty dollars on eBay, a good deal more than one share of Quaker Oats stock is worth.

But in the end, it's not about the real estate.

It's about halcyon days.

———•———

On my way back to camp, I stop in at a little gold shop on Front Street, seeking a gift for my daughter Ashley, whose twenty-fourth birthday is coming up. Something gold.

The scraggly goldsmith, his hands grotty with god-knows-what heavy metals and his voice thick with an Eastern European accent, rises from his cluttered bench and walks over.

"Someting you vood like to see?" he asks.

"Maybe some earrings," I say. "Or a necklace. In Yukon gold. For my daughter."

He shows me several matching sets, some just gold and others with gems, and tells me about each one.

His name is Andrew Kuczynski. He was born and raised in Poland, where he grew up to be a high school history teacher. Although he wasn't Jewish, he says his mother fought for the Jews in the Warsaw Ghetto uprising. He grew frustrated with the half-history he was expected to teach, ignoring the Soviet aggression that harmed Poland almost as much as the Nazi occupation. He wanted to tell the truth, he says, to live freer than he was. So in 1987—before Solidarnosc and Lech Walesa won their revolution—he fled Poland to England as an apprentice jeweler, then to Canada, where he now owns three gold shops like this one.

"So where do you belong—Poland or Canada? Which one is your home?" I ask him.

Andrew shrugs his whole face as if it might go either way.

"Ees not easy to say. Poland ees homeland if I veel nevermind da heestory," he says, "but Canada ees my home for twenty year, and now fameely live good vit da gold. I em heppy. So . . . ees two homeland and ees none. Nic big."

Nothing big. That's easy for him to say, and not just because it's Polish. I buy a pair of Andrew's Yukon gold earrings for my daughter, and as I shake his hand, I think some roads lead so far that you don't know where you belong anymore. A cautionary tale for road men and selfish dreamers.

All is not gold.

We meet for a pre-Toe dinner at the Downtown Hotel.

It's hard to miss, there in the heart of town with its blood-red paint job, red-white-and-blue bunting dripping from ornate white balconies, and fluttering flags amid big P. T. Barnum lettering painted high up on the outer walls, a two-story backdrop straight out of a Tombstone parody. It even sits next door to an abandoned old-time mortuary, where several hideous tools of the cadaver trade are still displayed for tourists in the front window.

At one end is the Jack London Grill, a tribute to the young American who came to the Klondike at age twenty-one to seek his fortune, and nearly died of scurvy. He still hadn't published a single word in his life, but the adventure that would make him a literary giant was frozen in his bones in the winter of 1897.

So we order a pint of a local Yukon brew and toast Jack London, the beautiful scurvy bastard. I stand and recite his words (somewhat errantly) with a grand flourish:

I would rather be ashes than dust!
I would rather that my spark burn out in a brilliant blaze than
be stifled by dry-rot.
I would rather be a superb meteor than a sleepy and perma-
nent planet.
The function of man is to live, not to exist.
I shall not waste my days trying to prolong them.
I shall use my time.

"To Jack!" I say rather loudly. Matt raises his glass and, head low, peeks around to see who might be watching his idiot father.

We order another round of ale with our dinner of baby back ribs and char, and again, I raise my glass of beer.

"To Jack!"

"You already did him," Matt reminds me.

"Then . . . to Buck!"

Matt doesn't look up, just lifts his glass about two inches off the table and sets it back down while he forks his fish.

We talk about nothing and everything over dinner, and when it's over, we skip dessert in favor of a third round and another salute.

"To Jack!" I say, no less enthusiastically but without the recitations.

Matt tosses his napkin on the table and cocks his head sideways, like the RCA dog trying to read an emoticon.

"Jeez, dude, you already toasted Jack and some guy named Buck. They're gonna cut you off. And we haven't even got to the Toe yet."

"Buck is a dog. *Call of the Wild*. Sorta like *Old Yeller* meets *Rambo*. Or *Where the Red Fern Grows* if Jim Harrison wrote it. Goddamned good book. You should read it. I've got it at home. Someplace. Anyway . . . ," I pause mid-toast, "here's to . . . I dunno . . . the Snark!"

"Dude, you're drunk," Matt says, smiling. "I never heard of Old Yeller or the Snork or whatever. And who the frig is Jim Harrison?"

Pffft is all I say.

———·———

Fortunately for us drunkard Jack London admirers, it's a short walk to the other end of the hotel to the Sourdough Saloon, home of the Sourtoe Cocktail.

We step through the old-fashioned swinging saloon doors like a couple drunken rookie gunslingers in cargo shorts and funny hats. Our eyes require a few moments to adapt to the dark interior, one of those little realities Hollywood Westerns always overlook. I wonder how many sun-blind shootists were ground-sluiced in the doorway because their eyeballs' rods and cones were slower than their trigger fingers?

But once our eyes have adjusted, we see it's just a pleasant small-town tavern, albeit cobbled together from different alcoholic epochs: walls bedecked with flocked Victorian wallpaper and T-shirts for sale, red velvet upholstery and laminate tables, gilt-framed mirrors and neon beer signs, a mirrored back bar clustered with every imaginable variation of booze since the invention of sacramental wine, a few hunched-over Carhartt backs at the bar and Eddie Bauer tourists wearing Nikons playing

"Brown Sugar" on the jukebox . . . All that's missing are gaslight fumes and slutty city girls in Prada slurping Cosmopolitans.

We sidle up to the bar, where a couple fur-bearing, barrel-chested locals are bitching about "clown shoes," their label for the mushroom-pickers and hippies who migrate like trash birds to the Yukon to live off the grid for a season or two before going back Outside—which is what Yukoners call the world beyond the territorial borders.

"Fucking clown shoes comes out of the woods and whips out his dick and takes a piss in the river like I wasn't even there," one of them says, pinching an imaginary joint to his lips while his buddy laughs. "Fucking gearbox in his own little faggot world, if you know what I'm sayin'."

I step backward and sideways to block their view of Matt, whom I feared might cause a clown-shoes flashback, and I hail the bartender over their shoulders.

"We came for the Toe," I say when our eyes meet. Without a word, he points toward the back of the bar, to a solitary table in a dark corner where a forlorn and peculiar little bearded man was sitting in a sea captain's hat, hands in his lap like some nautical-themed guru in the Shangri-la Saloon at the top of the freaking world, waiting.

For us.

Many stories are told about the Toe, which only adds to its mythos. Fact is, nobody is absolutely sure how or why these crazy Canucks started putting dead human toes in cocktails, but the yarn almost everybody believes is this: During Prohibition, bootlegging brothers Otto and Louie Liken were hauling contraband rum from Dawson to Alaska with dogsleds when Louie stepped in a puddle hidden by ice and snow. Suspecting the Mounties were close behind, they didn't dawdle in a sub-zero blizzard. The rumrunners escaped the posse and returned safely to their isolated cabin, but the headlong chase had its price: Louie's big toe was frostbitten.

Knowing the dead toe would soon rot and deadly gangrene would set in, the brothers decided to amputate. With Louie anesthetized on 180-proof rum, Otto whacked off the toe with an ax. For possibly sentimental reasons lost to history, they embalmed the toe in a bottle of their illegal hooch and hid it in the cold, dark space below the cabin's floorboards.

There it remained for the next forty years, long after Otto was dead and nine-toed Louie was dying in a Dawson old folks' home. Likely never to return to his home, Louie sold the tumbledown cabin in 1973 to a colorful local riverboat captain, Dick Stevenson, who hoped to renovate it into a fishing lodge.

Louie told him about the hidden toe, too. Sure enough, while cleaning the place, Stevenson found the bottle and took it back to Dawson as a macabre conversation piece.

One night, somebody mentioned "The Ballad of the Ice-Worm Cocktail," a Robert Service poem about an uptight British major tricked into drinking a strange cocktail containing a rare "ice worm."

Their bellies were a bilious blue, their eyes a bulbous red;
Their backs were grey, and gross were they, and hideous of head.
And when with gusto and a fork the barman speared one out,
It must have gone four inches from its tail-tip to its snout.

Taunted by the rugged denizens of Dawson's fictional Malamute Saloon, the delicate major waffled at the sight of the cannibalistic, red-eyed worm curled in his glass, but finally swigged it—and ran outside to puke in the snow. The bar erupted in hilarious celebration because, it seems, the "ice worm" was just a piece of spaghetti with two ink dots for eyes.

Inspiration isn't always pretty, but there it was. The lightning in Stevenson's bottle was a black and wizened dead toe. He cajoled a Dawson bar into letting him plunk his black and wizened old digit into the glass of anybody who (for a small fee) wanted to earn his stripes as an authentic sourdough without actually staying all winter. But the bar owner warned Stevenson that if the grotesque drink chased away even a single customer, he'd be out on his ass.

The rules were simple: The Toe must be dropped in a beer glass full of champagne and, whether you drink it fast or drink it slow, your lips must touch the Toe. Anyone brave enough to do it would be granted membership in what promised to be a very small and exclusive club. After all, not too many folks passed through Dawson, and not many of those would pay to touch a dead toe to their lips, right?

In September 1973, eight people—all locals—came lip-to-nail with Louie Liken's pickled toe and became the founding members of the Sourtoe Cocktail Club. Their names were entered in Captain Dick's big leather logbook, and over the next few years, a handful of plucky tourists would belly up to a Sourtoe Cocktail, but not enough to make Captain Dick rich. Barely enough to keep the free drinks flowing.

Then disaster. In 1980, after only about 725 Sourtoes had been served, a local miner decided to go for the single-night record. As he chugged his thirteenth Sourtoe of the night, he keeled over backwards and accidentally swallowed Louie's toe.

Hearing of Captain Dick's potentially career-ending tragedy, an Alberta woman donated an amputated toe she'd kept refrigerated for thirteen years, but the bar soon lost it. Then a trapper from Faro mailed his frostbitten big toe, but it was stolen by some drunken soldiers from the Royal Canadian Horse Artillery.

Temporarily toeless, Captain Dick invented a substitute: the Better Bitter Bear Ball Highball, made with a black bear's testicle and swizzled with the unlucky bruin's penis bone. It was a modestly popular drink for a spell, although disgusting animal privates just can't compete with the pseudo-cannibalistic allure of pickled people feet.

But it wasn't long before Captain Dick enjoyed a toe surplus. An anonymous donor sent a replacement toe, and the Royal Canadian Horse Artillery grudgingly returned the previously stolen toe; however, the glut didn't last long. A baseball player from Inuvik—an Arctic shantytown on the edge of the Beaufort Sea, and the unlikeliest place on Earth to find a baseball team—ingested one of them, and a big-game hunting Texan stole the other.[3]

In the meantime, the Toe's fame was growing. Magazines, newspapers, and TV shows told the strange story all over the world. Jay Leno invited Captain Dick to appear on *The Tonight Show*, but U.S. Customs agents wouldn't allow dismembered human remains across the border. Morbid curiosity attracted more onlookers than actual drinkers, but membership was mounting, sometimes by a hundred a night.

In case you were wondering, yes, the Toe is real. Many people think it's not, merely a playful joke with an artfully whittled chunk of jerky or nonhuman meat—just like the "ice worm." Some cosmic performance art, they think, solely for their amusement. But suspicion is a two-edged sword: Many self-deluded Sourtoe sippers only did it because they were certain it was a faux toe. They were wrong, although more than a few probably never knew it.

So why is the notion of touching a mummified toe with your lips so off-putting when we stick far more virulent things in our mouths every day—and on some hot, randy nights?

3. Unmasked in a two-week investigation by the Royal Canadian Mounted Police, the toe-rustling Texan eventually returned it to avoid international body-smuggling charges.

Our atavistic fear and loathing of dead human parts, as well as our taboo against eating dead human flesh (or just sipping around it), inspires a pretty natural revulsion to using a desiccated toe in a drink where there should be a little paper umbrella.

The grotesquerie is all in your mind. Sure, the ritual cannibalism, the specter of blood-borne disease, the insalubrious appearance of the Toe, and the fact that it's been in other people's mouths arouses a certain physical and intellectual distaste. But these donated toes are usually shipped in some sterilizing preservative like medical alcohol, stowed in rock salt 99 percent of the time, and then immersed in straight liquor. Can you say the same about the last ballpark hot dog you ate?

Plenty of people have weighed the risks and tippled the Toe anyway.

There was the octogenarian grandmother who downed the Sourtoe, then cuffed her adult son for chickening out. Captain Dick even relaxed his champagne rule so an underage Boy Scout troop could drink the Toe in soda pop. The youngest clubber was fourteen-month-old Stewart Tyson Morgan, whose father held a glass of ginger ale to his lips outside the bar; the oldest was a ninety-four-year-old woman. One guy slurped it in a bowl of soup ("Hey, waiter, there's a . . ."). An Amazon parrot named Waldo even touched the Toe while dipping his beak in a White Russian.

Oh, and consider the fellow who popped out his glass eye and dropped it in Captain Dick's Yukon Jack. The one-eyed gent drank the Toe as Stevenson drank the first-ever Sour-Eye Cocktail.

Of course, there's also the guy who tried to swallow the Toe on purpose, but ended up vomiting on the table. Luckily, Captain Dick rescued the Toe unharmed from the puke to be used again . . . and again . . . and again.

Over the years, members of the Sourtoe Cocktail Club have paid their dues in an unusual way. Some have legally willed their cadaver toes to the cause. Others' occasional lawn-mowing accidents, inadvertent frostbite, monster corns, or diabetes-gone-bad have provided a never-ending source of amputated toes for the drinking pleasure of future pledges.

By the time Captain Dick retired to Whitehorse in 1993, more than ten thousand Sourtoe Cocktails had been served. Soon, the owners of Dawson's Downtown Hotel leased Captain Dick's five marinated toes—a whole foot's worth—for about five thousand dollars a year (Canadian), making him the only man in the world whose retirement is funded exclusively by mummified toes.

But the Sourtoe lives on, in a manner of speaking. Actually, there are several toes—at least one of each from big to little—that rotate into the nightly game like ghoulish relief pitchers. They're all bullpenned in jars of rock salt within a gnarled wooden box about a foot long and seven inches wide. It's kept safely in the hotel vault with the other, um, valuables.

These days, Yukon Jack is the traditional mixer, but you may drink the Toe in your straight liquor of choice, although three decades of experience have proven that beer, milk, and sweet, creamy liqueurs are unhealthy for the Toe. For the teetotaler, the underage, and the still-drunk-from-last-night, a glass of soda pop or water is allowed.

Every summer, the Downtown Hotel hires a "Toe captain" to administer the solemn oath in sonorous tones, monitor the actual lip-to-toe collision, issue membership certificates (and wallet cards that guarantee a lifetime of free Sourtoe Cocktails), and dutifully update the logbook. The primary qualifications for the job appear to be a strong stomach, a head that fits the old sea captain's hat, and the rare ability to fake dignity.

And tonight, that's "Captain" Al Sider, a funny little man whose whaler's beard is rimed with gray. A shock of nor'easter hair blows over the blue-piped collar of his off-brand golf shirt, which drapes from the sloping shoulders of a lifelong deckhand. He wears big bifocals and a slender sailor's kerchief knotted around his skinny neck, and I wonder if he knows it's black as a tribute to all dead sailors (and, presumably, their toes).

Probably not. Al is a recovering alcoholic, clean for the past twenty years, who grew up in a small town in southern Ontario, near Niagara Falls. In fact, Al's never really been to sea. He's descended from Pennsylvania Dutch who emigrated to Canada a long time ago. All his life, he's knocked around Canadian construction sites and odd jobs, mostly, making just enough to scrape by. In his forty-eight years, he's evolved into something more than a drifter, something less than a homebody. His gray eyes and the distant lilt in his voice say he hasn't yet hit the end of his road.

A few years ago, he was hired over the phone as the Downtown Hotel's new janitor, and before long, he was filling in as the Toe captain when the regular guy was missing in action, sick, or hungover. Now he's the captain of captains, the Toe's go-to guy, although he still mops the floors.

Ah, but the star of this little burlesque is the Toe itself.

This mummified big toe rests regally on its throne of rock salt in the middle of the table, easily three inches long from bone-stump to the tip of its ghastly, jagged toenail, and as fat as a fusty kielbasa. Death has shriveled the flesh and turned it leathery brown, until it looks more like a deformed smoked prune. The nail, which appears to have continued growing for at least a month after its amputation, bulges from its dead, black cuticle and curls unnaturally to one side.

(At this point in the narrative, Herman Melville or James Michener might have launched into an exhaustive and meticulously researched medico-historical treatise on toes, but I will not. It must suffice, dear reader, to know that humans have historically paid little respect to toes, which never developed the usefulness of fingers. Nonetheless, toes play an important role in balance, traction, and forward movement. Practitioners of an ancient Eastern healing art called Jin Shin Jyutsu believe that squeezing the big toe helps you breathe better, as well as lubes your stomach, spleen, liver, and gall bladder. Although toes aren't exactly vital organs, legendary whiskey maker Jack Daniel reportedly died of blood poisoning that started with an infection of his big toe. Fortunately, toe scientists have found that amputating your big toe really has no serious impact on your life, except that the calluses on the second and third toes of your unlucky foot get thicker, and you'll wear down your shoes faster on that side. Oh, and the medical name for a big toe is *hallux,* and in 90 percent of humans, the hallux is longer than the second, or "pointer" toe. But if your pointer toe is longer than your big toe, take heart, you mutant: Most classical Greek and Roman sculptures—as well as the Statue of Liberty—bear a similar genetic deformity.)

"That's just butt-freakin'-ugly," Matt says, leaning in for a closer look.

"Yeah, but if it was cute, I don't think this would be such a big deal," I say, close to laughing but settling on a smile.

If Matt is thinking about aborting this mission, he doesn't show it as he eagerly grabs a chair at the next table. And while I readily admit I hadn't considered the toe's repulsive appearance—*What, I was expecting a delicate digit illuminated by a shaft of heavenly light?*—I'm ready to do this thing, too. The feeling is sudden and good. Our hearts are finally beating in the same rhythm.

"How does this work?" I ask Captain Al, who seems affable enough.

"You buy whatever spirits you're drinking at the bar, then come back and pay me five bucks so we can have our little ritual and you can join the club," he says. "But no beer or milky drinks. Bad for the Toe."

"Whose toe is it?" Matt asks.

"No idea. I could make up a story if you want, but the fact is, these things just show up in the mail. This one came about a year ago. It's a good one. Looks like he was a big fella, eh?"

"And it's real, right?"

"Totally," swears Captain Al. "Just lift up that toenail and you'll see."

I'm not yet ready to be that intimate with a lifeless toe. I take his word for it.

"Do you treat it or anything?"

"We serve it the way we get it."

"So you don't know how, er, why it, um . . . died?" I ask.

"Nope. But don't worry; nobody has died. Yet."

"Hey, there's a great advertising slogan," I say.

A few minutes after nine p.m., the Toe-seekers begin to dribble into the saloon in twos and threes or more, but never ones. There must be witnesses in case nobody believes them, bulwarks in case they chicken out, someone to take the picture. Men and women, young and old, dainty and rugged, husbands yearning to relive younger days, and wives who'll refuse to kiss them for a week. Within fifteen minutes, the bar is humming with the half-soused, nervous excitement of a bachelor party before the strippers arrive.

Soon, the pilgrims form a raggedy line and, one by one, Captain Al launches into his oath-swearing with a delightful Shakespearean flourish. One by one, he plunks the Toe into their drinks. And one by one, they examine the turd-looking thing floating there, look around fretfully for a familiar face, then tip back their glasses until the Toe loses its gummy grip on the bottom and tumbles down to bump against their lips.

The crowd quickly joins in chanting: *Drink it fast or drink it slow, but your lips must touch the Toe!*

A cocktail waitress who's flirting with Matt buys us a couple more beers as we watch this perverse party. We conspire to go last, if only to make the night last longer. It'll be a while. We've got plenty of beer and we can wait.

After the Iowa church lady who will never tell a soul back home what she's done tonight. After the Montreal hairdresser who bailed out at the last minute and gave Matt her glass of tequila. After the tour guide who lost a mysterious bet and would soon dive, fully clothed, into the frigid Yukon River. After the movie stuntwoman who was, oddly, a little squeamish. After the three Oklahoma fishermen who'd accidentally wandered into the bar after a day in the backcountry, never imagining they'd have a dead toe in their mouths tonight. After a dozen people who journeyed to the Yukon for a few moments of a life that isn't really theirs.

And after Emery Huber, a kindly German shopkeeper who told me he has been diagnosed as being in the earliest stages of Alzheimer's disease, and is determined to live the last cogent moments of his life to the fullest. Just when I was worrying there was a danger in taking this Toe thing too seriously, Emery gives me a reason to think about how this insignificant little risk might be more important than I know. I buy him a drink and promise to remember him. When he takes the Toe, we toast again and I wish him good spaces as he wanders off into the twilight of this night and his days.

Somewhere around midnight, when the sun was still shining outside, after a half-dozen rounds of Canadian beer and random shots of whiskey, our time has come.

I go first.

Captain Al drops the Sourtoe into my double shot of Yukon Jack, neat. While he delivers his stentorian oratory, I swirl it around in the honey-amber liquid and smell it. Nothing but whiskey; no death, no rot. The Toe just stares brownly and blankly back at me. I'm just making it dizzy.

Before I drink, I glance at Matt, whose eyes are bright and alive. I imagine him, much younger, imagining this moment. If he ever has a son, I hope he sees that look someday. Maybe here, or maybe some other road. By then, he'll be fading as his own son blossoms, and he'll know why we came, and he'll pray that his flaws haven't broken the chain, and wish for just a few more days of immortality to see how it all turns out.

As some amorphous rock anthem blares from the jukebox and the vibrating hum of the bar swirls around me, I throw back the Jack and the Toe rolls into my open mouth.

With the Toe wrapped in my lips like a fat stogie, my tongue can't help but diddle the blood-blackened bone-end. No smell. No taste. Just a rubbery hunk of dead meat long ago leeched of its marrow and soul.

Finally, I pluck it daintily from my mouth and drop it back in the empty glass. The whiskey is still smoldering a hole in my gut but I have conquered the Sourtoe.

Captain Al sticks out his hand. "Welcome to the club!"

"Well, I'm glad to be here, dammit!" I say, shaking it.

Matt bellies up and after a quick swig, clamps the Toe between his teeth and growls like a madman before doing his victory jig. We slap high fives and hug tight. We're drunk on our asses, but we're now Members No. 24,694 and No. 24,695 in one of the strangest clubs in the world. The Vatican's College of Cardinals has had more members! That's gotta be worth something.

"Remember, your membership card entitles you to free Sourtoe Cocktails for the rest of your life," Captain Al reminds us as we stagger toward the door, my arm around my son's shoulder. "It's a lifetime membership!"

Matt turns back to him and smiles.

"I'll be back," he says. "I promise."

Sometimes—more than sometimes—he surprises me.

The brassy blue sky is too bright for the moon and stars, even though it is past midnight when we spill out onto the dirt streets of Dawson City. The surrounding hills reflect orange light from a barely concealed sun skipping the light fandango somewhere between east and west, across the river, where the dark, slow water sparkles with copper and azure.

The midnight sun is out just for us. Something quite extraordinary has happened, but we are both intoxicated, without the wisdom or clarity to know what it all meant. Artless? Yes. Decadent? Yes. Symbolic of nothing? Maybe. Maybe not. Someday, I will run with the bulls and maybe it will be the same. Or eat a gorgonzola sandwich at Davy Byrne's Pub in Dublin, like Leopold Bloom. I've already been to Dime Box, Texas, but maybe I will ride a streetcar—no, a goddamned bus—named Desire just to say I did, even though I don't know what the hell it means or how it changes anything. It's a drunken poet's promise.

"Oh shit, I should have drunk the Toe with grappa!" I say, drunkenly exasperated. "Or, oh, oh . . . absinthe!"

"Grappa sucks," Matt sneers. "That shit's worse than turpentine."

"Yeah, look who's talking—a guy who just put a dead toe in his mouth. But it was amazing, wasn't it? Grappa would have made sure it was dead, and absinthe would have been good, even though it's green and maybe it's illegal up here. I dunno. Amazing, wasn't it? Too freakin' cool."

"Yeah, dude, we did it. We did it."

"Fucking amazing."

"It was."

We can't sleep. Too high and too sillydrunk. We stumble aimlessly through empty streets and end up at the little casino, Diamond Tooth Gertie's, where I kiss a sixty-something mother and her homely daughter beside a plywood cutout where you stick your head and somebody takes a picture, then go inside amid the ringing and the music and the laughter and the blinking lights and the uncluttered lust and order a rum and Coke for the road. No lime.

Leaving the casino, we drift through the day-night, weaving down dusty roads, light-headed and loose-jointed. When we stop to piss in the weeds of a vacant lot on the edge of town, I spy a conspicuously white stone the size and shape of an unbaked loaf of boule bread or a sleeping snow-white cat. It stands out among the universally gray and angular shale, as if a stranger had transported it a great distance and just dropped it there when it no longer made sense to carry it any farther.

I turn it over and heft it.

"Dad, what are you doing?"

"Just looking at this rock."

"You're drunk," he says. "I can't believe this. It's a stupid rock. Let's go."

"It doesn't belong here."

"Dude, it's a rock. It's happy being with other rocks. You can't keep it. Jeezus, it belongs to Canada."

"But it's different."

"You're different, too. And the other rocks don't care. Dad, no . . ."

I shamble off down the road with my new rock. Matt follows, but a few steps behind, making his final arguments on the move.

"What are you gonna do with a goddamned rock? Are you joking? It's not even that good of a rock. If you want a souvenir, there are better rocks. I hope nobody sees. Dude, you look like some crazy guy right now. Jeezus, if I was doing this, you'd bust a vein . . ."

I stop in the middle of the road and look at him.

"Chill. The rock just stood out," I say, trying to sound humorless but failing. "I'm not stealing it, but I don't know why I am borrowing it either. Let this be a little crazy thing between us. You'll laugh about it someday. But if a cop stops us, just say we brought it with us."

"From Texas?"

"Shhhh."

Night means day. Son means father. Dead means alive. Sure, it is alcological, but I have grasped some of my best paradoxes, I think, under the influence. I might give you a thousand examples of it, but I recall practically nothing except that Zen lunatic Kerouac suddenly makes sense when he writes about the mad ones, the ones who are mad to live, mad to talk, mad to be saved, desirous of everything at the same time, the ones who never yawn or say a commonplace thing, but burn, burn, burn like fabulous yellow Roman candles exploding like spiders across the stars and in the middle you see the people exploding like spiders across the stars and in the middle you see the blue center light pop and everybody goes "Awww!"

And why Kerouac shows up at this moment of madness, I haven't a clue, except maybe this will be recalled forever as the night Matt and I went mad together.

He follows me all the way back to the camper, where I put the rock on the floor at the foot of the bed and fall facedown like a cartoon dead man on top of the blankets and pillows and Matt crawls in beside me. I close my eyes and I dream of sleep, but I suddenly realize we'd walked past a pay phone during our meanderings.

I pull myself together and go back out into the day-lighted night to find the phone, which luckily isn't far.

I have a couple Canadian coins, but not enough for an international call, so I dial the operator and fumble with a number in my rummy head. It rings four or five times before someone answers.

"Will you accept a collect call from Ron?" the operator asks.

In a sleepy voice, Mary says she will.

"Honey, is everything okay? It's . . . what . . . gosh . . . almost four-thirty in the morning here."

"We did the Toe. It was amazing."

"Oh, good." She sounds relieved, at least to a drunkard.

"Fucking amazing. The whole thing . . . together. The sun is out right now. We did it . . . just amazing."

"You're drunk. Was it worth it?"

"Not bad drunk. Good drunk. Every inch."

"Of the Toe?"

"Of the road. The Toe . . . fucking amazing."

"You need to go to bed, sweetie. You need some sleep."

"Yeah, yeah. Hey, you should know . . . I miss you, and I'm not just saying that because I'm drunk. I'll be back and, you know, we'll figure everything out. I promise."

"I know."

"And," I say, as I steady myself against the phone's protective hood, "I love you."

"Now I know you're drunk" is all she says.

In the Circle of Illumination

And the end of all our exploring
Will be to arrive where we started
And know the place for the first time.

—T. S. ELIOT

The next morning—or what passes for morning—I awake early. Or at least one of my eyes awakes and peeps at my watch.

It's been just three hours since my body drooled like lumpy broth across the thin Scotchgarded mattress. I blivet my pillow to find a cool spot for my feverish head, careful not to disturb the rusty spike spearing through my eyeball into my spongy brain. There's a high-pitched scream in my head-meat. At this moment, I'm thinking death has an appealing upside.

Morning is an abstract concept up here, particularly on the morning of the eve of the longest day of the year, when there is, technically speaking, no night. After a night that was day all night. Or a day that was day all day.

And especially when a dead-toe hangover is involved. But for once, I know why my mouth tastes like I've been sucking on an elderly stranger's raunchy corn pad. After a pus-weeping toe infection. Still soggy.

Something black wriggles in my gut, too. Maybe toe parasites, maybe drunkard's bile, or maybe just a shadow of unsynchronous anxiety about the road ahead. Today, we light out for the Arctic on the bluest of blue highways, a monster road that nobody willingly travels, to learn the magic in a day without darkness. The Toe? Well, it was just a test of our spirit, a gut-check of our worthiness to enter whatever dark forest lies ahead in this landscape of light. At this moment, I feel adrift.

Worse, I gotta pee, and I'm seriously weighing the pros and cons of bed-wetting. Cons win, but only by a hair.

Matt's still asleep. Or dead. Not sure. Either way, I don't want to disturb him as I ooze out of our peasant-size bed onto a dog-pile of dirty shoes, smoky underwear, disconnected power cords, empty luggage, beer cans, stray pillows, various electronics, and a big white rock—*Wait a second . . . Why is there a big white rock on the floor of the van?*—that's barricading the door to our toilet. Rather than bend over and risk a busted vein in my hot, throbbing head, I instantly choose to use the campground porta-potty. Luckily, I never took off my shoes last night, so if I'm still wearing my pants, I'm already dressed for the trip.

Stepping out of the van, the sunlight needles like a black widow spider into my sole surviving eyeball. My sweat starts to sweat. The gravel under my feet grinds up through my soles into my soul, which is now only loosely tethered to my bones; a stiff morning breeze would disconnect me completely from my pith.

I've lurched halfway to the plastic loo when I realize it's not a loo at all, but a phone booth. The loo, it seems, is at the other end of this friggin' aluminum ghetto.

Krrrep.

After what seems like forty days in a subarctic desert (where the coinciding forty nights are just like forty more days), I find the unshaded latrine empty. My shaky hand on the door, I thank God for leading me out of the RV wilderness and delivering me from evil toes as I trespass against those who are probably already driving through the Valley of the Shadow of . . . *Dear God in Heaven and all that is holy, did someone die in here?*

The relentless sun has awakened the fetid cesspool below, and the heated stink-demons are trapped in the confined space of the porta-potty, waiting for some unsuspecting outlander to open this scatological Pandora's Box and release god-knows-what (plus several fleshy flies) into the atmosphere.

But I still gotta pee. I suck in a half-minute's supply of fresh air and duck into the stifling, toxic sweatbox. Unfortunately, my zipper is balky and my bladder is bigger than my lungs, so I am suddenly forced to breathe hot poop-air. That's all it takes: I double over with a sploogy retch, my flushed face just a couple inches from the unwashed communal toilet seat . . . *Oh my god, is that . . . ?* I puke again.

Back at the van, the guy in the next camp space is preparing to pull out but having trouble with his GPS unit. Although my head throbs and my mouth tastes of swarf, I fetch Sydney and, being adult road males, we both pretend to know something about this geosynchronous latitudinal space-geometry shit.

We take a simultaneous GPS reading of his fifth-wheeler's front step so we can compare Sydney's accuracy against his nameless, pouty receiver. The coordinates differ slightly, and like two cavemen arguing about whether our new stone wheel is supposed to go backward or forward, we don't know which of us is right.

Just then, a few feet away, I hear Matt rustling inside our van. His stirring sounds more like a giant fart rumbling through a hungry man's bowels as he rolls from the bed, stumbles over the detritus, rams open the bathroom door, and hurls a righteous barf. With an encore.

For a stillborn moment, I don't know why we're here, why we're going someplace farther, why we're not going home. Two pilgrim strangers seeking . . . *what, exactly*? Some little Yukon knickknack to fill an empty shelf in their incomplete hearts? Another adventure story to tell? Escape?

The van's side door slides open and Matt sits on its muddy threshold, barefoot and ashen, as if he might walk to his own funeral. His rumpled black T-shirt and Charles Manson hair make him look even deader. He rubs the slits of his eyes and splurts a toxic glob of spit toward the back tire.

"You alive?" I ask.

"Barely."

"Hungry?"

"Not anymore."

"Thirsty?"

He flips me off.

My neighbor uses this heartwarming moment between father and son to say good-bye. We wish each other luck as he and the missus head off on the Top of the Road Highway, the back road to Alaska. When they're gone, I lean against the dusty van beside Matt.

"Really, are you feeling okay? I have some Tums in the first-aid kit, if you . . ."

He waves me off.

"I'm fine."

The Arctic sun loiters in the midriff of the sky, like it might come to a dead stop. The slanting light is somehow uneven.

"Look," I say, "we did the Toe. That's what we came for. It's gonna take us a long week to get home. We could get back and . . . I dunno . . . be back."

Matt looks up, a little angry. "You're wussing out? You want to bail out now? This far?"

"No, I just—"

"What a pussy. We're not done. I want to see the longest day. We came for that, too."

"Hey, relax. I'm no pussy. I'm just saying it's an option."

Matt doesn't look at me straight on, just at his bare feet. He speaks coolly, deflated. "Dude, you want to bail."

"No, I don't."

"It's what you do. You walk away. You're good at it. It's your superpower."

"Hey, c'mon. You're going way too far."

I turn my back on him and walk a few aimless steps toward . . . I don't know.

"Or not far enough. Dude, you talk all big about your dad's flaws. You, like, write 'em down. Well, you aren't the only friggin' son in the world. Write that down."

"I never said I was perfect, but this isn't about—"

"Yes, it is! This whole friggin' thing was your idea! You wanted us to take this big-assed trip to drink the Toe and see the longest day. Just us. You and me. Together. Now you're wussing out. Oh, you know, just fuck it. It's not the first time you bailed on me. Probably not the last."

"Goddammit, you have no fucking idea what this is about, do you?"

"No, I don't. Maybe you don't either. I probably won't know for a long time. But I know we're not done. Jeezus, you're always talking shit about going to the end of the road. It's up there, dude"—he points to his truest north—"it ain't here. This isn't where the story ends."

He asked no question and I had no answer. Maybe later, sometime on the road to here or to there, I'll know what to say. Or maybe this is the time to forget some things completely. Maybe this is just us, although I hope not. Hope against hope. This isn't how it was supposed to turn out.

In a futile effort to make everything fit together just so, I retrace our steps to find the wrong turn, but I am distracted by the memory of a little boy who praised handles and professed his love—or what passes for love—beneath a tree full of girls and the sound of his laughter in the hallway and other subtle moments of remembered joy illuminated by this strange light. These are things I never want to forget.

My ears pulse like a funeral parade of passing bass drums, but we are alone, nothing to say under a blithe sky. The campground is almost empty and we must choose our road. I touch the reflected light in the van's grimy window and with my forefinger, I scrawl in the dust: *Malibu.*

———•—•———

Barely twenty miles into it, I can tell the Dempster Highway is a beautiful bitch of a road.

Only one road leads where we are going, to spend the summer solstice—the longest day of the year—in a magical place where the sun will never set. Just a father, a son, and a day without darkness. For us, that could only happen above the Arctic Circle. And in all of Canada, only two roads cross the Arctic Circle, and the Dempster is the only public one.

Since we came here seeking something, anything, to reassure us that our hearts, brains, and courage were undamaged, I begin to wonder: Exactly how long was the Yellow Brick Road again? Will there be flying monkeys and angry trees? When is far enough too far? And when did my son first see me as flawed?

Before we start we already know this: Running 456 miles from Dawson City to the village of Inuvik, the Dempster will beckon you to the top of the world . . . and then kick your ass for trying. It's a hellish washboard-and-gravel path through Heaven's back forty, a tire-shredding, windshield-busting, fender-furrowing trail too mean for asphalt. And we're both hungover. A Sunday drive in Afghanistan is less nerve-wracking.

The Dempster crisscrosses the Continental Divide three times, and your car must be ferried across two great rivers. Even in midsummer, when the sun shines nearly twenty-four hours a day, the road can be closed by snowstorms (although the native Inuit call summer "the season of inferior sledding"). You traverse two untamed mountain ranges, two time zones, a few remnant glaciers, and five rivers on the way to Inuvik, one of only three loosely organized communities along the whole sixteen-hour route.

In Inuvik, where natives sleep an average of eleven hours a night in the dark winter, and are proud to have the northernmost traffic light in North America, they will call you an "end-of-the-roader" because (a) you're a little bit insane; and (b) to go beyond where the Dempster will take you in summer, you must wait until winter freezes a solid path—an ice road—across the rivers, bays, and tundra. In other words, you're not going farther.

So as we cross a wooden bridge over the Klondike River and enter this netherworld, a sign warns NEXT SERVICES 370 KILOMETERS (for the metrically challenged, that's 229 miles). I check the bars on my cell phone in case my heart, my brains, or my courage failed somewhere on this ungodly journey. Nothing. We are on our own.

Except for mosquitoes the size of hummingbirds, wolves, the stone men known as *inukshuks,* arctic hares, hoary marmots, gyrfalcons, butterflies, grizzlies, caribou, foxes, and a smattering of windblown, pagophilous[4] humans huddled in a handful of roadside stops, you are alone here. Cell phones won't work—not above the Arctic Circle or below it. No Internet either, unless you've got a direct satellite feed to God. The radio is electric fuzz. The Dempster sneers at humans' pitiful yearning for community.

Mile by mile, more is revealed to us. This corrugated highway once known as the "Road to Nowhere" is an otherworldly path

4. Any species that prefers environments of ice.

through a Tolkienesque world. Built in dribs and drabs between 1959 and 1979 to help Canada tap the vast oil and gas reserves in its inhospitable and largely unexplored Great Empty, it was the brainchild of engineers from a different world—ours. In their insufferably civilized minds, a road was a great civilizer, because nothing could domesticate a place like motor traffic. But as one thoughtful road-builder said, the Dempster was "developed by a society elsewhere, made for vehicles designed and constructed for social conditions typical of other climates and places."

Indeed. Where else would a highway double as an airstrip for bush pilots—in six different places?

It was named after William John Duncan Dempster, a survivor of the Klondike Gold Rush of 1898, and a legendary Royal Canadian Mountie who patrolled between the rough-and-tumble Dawson City and the rougher-and-tumbler Fort McPherson, 342 miles away in the Northwest Territories. On a dogsled.

Dempster rose to mythic status in 1911 when he was dispatched in perversely frigid weather to find and rescue a lost patrol of four fellow Mounties. After a month of hunting for them in unrelenting subzero weather, he found their frozen corpses and brought them home. Under orders to make the trail safer for future patrols, Dempster spent a winter caching food along the treacherous path, building small shelter cabins, and carving trees into trail markers. When he retired from the RCMP in 1934, he was more than a hero, more than Wyatt Earp in mukluks. He was a god whose name would eventually be borne by a road that was even tougher than he was.

But the Dempster Highway's history goes back thousands of years beyond its namesake.

The northern Yukon is one of the few northern regions untouched by the last ice age. While the rest of Canada was being carved by immense continental glaciers, this landscape remained unglaciated. Of course, that made it easy for the first humans to literally walk on a land bridge across the Bering Strait and populate North America.

But it didn't make twentieth-century road-building easy. Instead of gravel worn smooth and tough by receding glaciers—perfect for roadbeds—construction crews had only native black shale, razor-sharp when dry and slurpy-slick when wet. Imagine driving on crushed arrowheads. Thus, a spare tire is more important than food on the Dempster, world-famous for obliterating tires and windshields.

Our morning slips into afternoon. The sun moves around the corners of the sky, but the light doesn't change. After a few hours, we are lulled into a false sense of invulnerability, always bad and always awakened rudely.

More than 250 miles into our journey, our asses still thrumming with the constant burr of the freakishly fluted road, we stop for gas at Eagle Plains Lodge, a tiny hotel / service station / diner that is the only sign of humanity for almost 350 miles. With only eight permanent residents, it's an outpost straight out of *Ice Station Zebra*.

While I pump, Matt hunts down a hissing sound. The news isn't good. Our left rear tire is slowly going flat. The dastardly blade of sharp shale is still lodged between the grooves.

Luckily, the attendant—a timeworn Gwich'in named Johnny—squeezes us in just ahead of an eighteen-wheeler hauling cars that had also popped a tire.

"How many tires have you fixed today?" I ask Johnny.

"Twelve," he says. It is only mid-afternoon.

"Does anyone get through this road without a flat?"

"Sure."

"What's the trick?" I ask.

He doesn't skip a beat.

"Miss the sharp ones."

———

The Dempster's treachery goes deeper than its surface.

It was built entirely in winter so that an insulating barrier up to eight feet thick could be laid across the permafrost underneath. Without the protective berm, the permafrost would melt and the road would sink into the tundra, which it does from time to time anyway.

The Dempster doesn't just eat tires. It chews glass, too. Miles back, our windshield was chipped badly by a passing truck spewing road rock like a ten-ton corn popper. Then again an hour later by a passing pickup.

Ah, but the view through a cracked windshield. Yes, we'd been warned about the Dempster's hazards, but not its unearthly beauty. The distances are so vast you think you are peeking over the far edge of the Earth, which, in a way, you are.

This gravel passage to the brink of the Arctic Ocean snakes through tundra and the boreal forest biome known as the *taiga*, which grows dark to absorb as much warmth from the sun as possible.

Alpine lakes reflect big, brooding skies where pillars of sunlight illuminate distant mountains with weighty names like Tombstone and Anvil, and beyond them, mountains never named.

In summer, like now, the spongy tundra is alive with purple saxifrage, cotton grass, wild crocus, arctic poppies and azaleas, buttercups, cinquefoil and lupine. Higher up in the *taiga*, the evergreen woodlands are dotted with dwarf willow and the occasional birch or tamarack. The flora might seem fragile but it isn't: Plants grow small and closely knit in the thin millennial dust called *loess,* as if to protect each other from arctic winds and cold. Oddly, they also insulate the permafrost below from warming.

Around Eagle Plains, a stunted black spruce forest claws desperately for purchase. The unstable permafrost beneath the trees' roots skews them into out-of-plumb poses, but they survive because that's the price paid for living a life on ice.

And the ice skews people, too. In Inuvik, the local paper offers a prize to the kid who kills the first mosquito every spring.

———•———

Someone is watching us.

Where our road crested on a rocky hill overlooking an endless tundra basin, we stopped to take pictures. On our way back to the van, we noticed a gaggle of strange little men, foot-high stone figures made with roadside rocks, and a half-dozen more that had tumbled down in disarticulated little heaps. Amateurs, probably Americans, had been here.

For more than 4,000 years, these "stone men" have stood in for humans in the Arctic. They point the way to a nearby village, warn of thin ice or deep snow, fool stupid caribou into killing grounds every season, hide a food cache, mark where Eskimo women were swept out to sea, or simply help tell time or measure the long, dark winter by pointing to the always-constant North Star.

Technically, they are called *inunnguat*—cairns of stacked stones built in the shape of a man with outstretched arms. But they are more widely (and erroneously) known in non-Inuit Canada as *inukshuks,* which loosely means "substitute people." The hair-thin semantic difference seems to be that the *inunnguat* (in the plural) are structures which actually resemble human figures, and *inukshuks* (pronounced *in-OOK-shooks*) are simpler cairns that generally only perform certain functions on behalf of real people. Think of one (*inukshuk*) as a traffic light, and the other (*inunnguaq,* in the singular) as a traffic cop.

It's a niggling difference widely disregarded among most Canadians, who love funny-sounding words as much as the next guy, and call all these arctic stone men *inukshuks*. So I will, too.

Although *inukshuks* sometimes resemble a Christian cross from a distance and occasionally mark hallowed ground, they have no apparent religious significance. They are merely way markers, beacons to anyone looking for safe passage in a dangerous, desolate landscape. *You are not alone. Someone was here before you.*

Inukshuks—some standing silently for a thousand years—speak subtle messages to knowing travelers. For example, an *inukshuk* on land with two arms and two legs means there is a valley ahead, and at the end of the valley, you can choose to go either way safely. If he has no arms but both legs, you can travel only one way.

Some have built-in "windows," or spyglass gaps through which a traveler can see the path he must follow, or important landmarks ahead.

They appear in some poignant places, too.

In 2002, Canadian soldiers in Kandahar, Afghanistan, built an *inukshuk* from Afghan stone as a memorial to four comrades killed when a U.S. warplane dropped a five-hundred-pound laser-guided bomb on them during a night-firing exercise. The Kandahar *inukshuk* points toward home.

And an *inukshuk* was placed at Juno Beach in Normandy, where Canadian soldiers landed on D-Day in 1944.

But *inukshuks* have now been expropriated by profit-minded outlanders who have slapped the ancient icon on beer cans, websites, real estate signs, banks, rock albums, environmental initiatives, kayaks, hotels, and dog food. They appear on two Canadian flags, a coin, and Canada's 47-cent postage stamp. Even a polar bear at the Toronto Zoo is named Inukshuk. Some traditionalists grumble the *inukshuk* is stealthily displacing the maple leaf as Canada's most potent symbol.

And in case it didn't appear on the front page of your local newspaper, a brief semiotic thumb-wrestle ensued when a happy-faced cartoon stone man was chosen as the logo for the 2010 Winter Olympics in Vancouver. Most folks called it an *inukshuk,* although it was, in fact, an *inunnguaq,* but only the normally bashful Eskimo street and a few precise ethnographers seemed to care. The artist who created it said, "[The] logo had to fit as much [on] a Visa Card as it did in a stadium or in the middle of an ice rink."

So *inukshuks,* patient pinch hitters who have waited for millennia on the lonely tundra until someone passes, continue to do man's bidding by waiting on a beer label, billboard, store shelf, or website until someone passes . . . with money to spend.

Beside the road, Matt and I gathered exactly ten stones and cobbled together our own *inukshuk.* He pointed us—or we pointed his long arm—due north, deeper into the Arctic and one never-ending day. We built him together, maybe on a whim, or maybe as evidence of our passing, of our pausing. *We were here.*

Back in the van, I turned the key and the obviously jealous Sydney piped up. Calling on her array of satellites, trilateration, microchips, and mathematics, she advised us more specifically (and snippily): "Continue north."

Inukshuks are literal metaphors. They are more than ancient GPS devices. These artfully balanced piles of rock represent shared risk and acknowledge lessons learned, sometimes painfully. How would the builder know if the ice ahead was dangerously thin if someone or something hadn't fallen through it?

Maybe a landscape without any evidence of man's presence is a landscape without memory, expectation, or mythology.

The Arctic shapes men infinitely more than men shape the Arctic. In fact, man isn't even a necessary part of this place. If he weren't here, the tundra and the taiga wouldn't notice. So maybe these stone men are religious symbols after all. Maybe each is a prayer for relevance. Nobody wants to be irrelevant. Everyone wants to matter.

And unless you've actually built one, you cannot understand the delicate equilibrium it requires. Each one is like a house of cards, only much heavier. Each stone rests upon every stone below it, without mortar or any other connective tissue. Every one is no more and no less important than any other. Somewhere deep in the Inuit heart there must be a similar formula for building teenage boys—and men.

But *inukshuks* are not men. They are only *like* men, made by men to fulfill certain limited functions men cannot or will not do. They are simple and primitive machines. They don't love. They don't cry. They don't screw up. They don't die; they just fall over and wait for the next Eskimo to come along and rearrange their remains into a new *inukshuk*. Real men aren't so easily resurrected.

Forgive me. Being recently dead, maybe I worry too much about this resurrection stuff.

———

Another hour on, we finally come upon our quixotic threshold, the roadside way marker where the Dempster crosses the Arctic Circle.

Nothing monumental. Just a gravel turnout with a carved wooden sign and an infinite horizon. A chilling wind slices across the tundra as we get out of the van, and an angry storm is gathering to the east, so I grab my khaki field jacket. But Matt, true to his odd fashion, is wearing only a black T-shirt, shorts, and a skully.

On one day of every year since the Earth entered its orbit around the sun, the light shines constantly here for one complete rotation. Truth be told, it shines constantly for most of six months at the North Pole, but according to the circles mortals have drawn around the globe, it shines for one full day unobstructed by the horizon at the Arctic Circle. It's an entirely natural occurrence caused by the Earth's tilt, but we mortals want to give it meaning, like serendipity, sex, and reality TV.

This is a mostly ceremonial spot that marks latitude 66 degrees, 30 minutes North. Because the Earth slowly wobbles on its axis, the actual Arctic Circle roams up to twenty-five feet every year, and usually isn't in the same spot from day to day. Go figure: an imaginary line that moves. It's good to be invisible.

For many years, a retired road worker named Harry Waldron sat in a rocking chair on this spot all summer. The eccentric fellow wore a tuxedo and top hat, sipped champagne, recited Robert Service poems, spun wild tales, and posed for tourists' pictures. Eventually the Yukon's territorial government paid this self-described "Keeper of the Arctic Circle" a stipend so he would continue being crazy.

And now us. Except maybe we were crazy before we started. Despite the biting wind, we take a few photos of ourselves, an outwardly sane act to prove we are insane. And that we came. Matt runs back to the van while I try to imagine.

Then an unlikely discovery which leads to another: a Canadian two-dollar coin, a "toonie," is lying on the ground. Someone must have dropped it, because a two-dollar wish seems extravagant. As I stoop to pick it up, I wonder how many wayward coins lie in the open ground, waiting to be found in this world. Would all the lost pennies on Earth matter at all? Would they make someone rich? If they were all found, would we hope less?

I unzip one of the twenty or so concealed pockets in my field jacket to keep this special toonie safe, but I find something else, from another time, another place, another life. I must have carried the note all over the Middle East, then home, where it hung safe and unremembered in closets for many years. Until now.

It is a handwritten note from a man I met in Cairo while reporting for the *Denver Post* there after the September 11 attacks.

His name was Shoukry, about my age, and he cooked in a pizza place on 26 July Corridore. When he discovered I was an American, he stood very close to me. "I am sorry for the happening in New York. Very sorry," he murmured in his heavy Egyptian accent. He begged me to come to his pizzeria that night, where he cooked a pie as good as any I ever tasted, and we talked like two old friends about our families as I ate. He, too, had a son.

When the time came to leave, Shoukry wouldn't let me pay for my meal. Instead, on the grimy sidewalk outside his tidy little shop, with tears in his eyes, he handed me a folded scrap of paper and hugged me as tightly as any man has ever hugged me.

I walked back to the American hotel that night through the dark streets of Cairo, past the open-air shops where whole lambs hung from the eaves, headless, foreleg-less, sinewy. Along the polluted banks of the Nile, where river rats skittered over the riverbank rubble, scavenging for fish guts and garbage drifting from the heart of Africa toward the Mediterranean. Past the grottoes and *maqhahs* where the hubbly-bubbly sheesha boys smoked rose and peach and vanilla tobaccos in the shadows. My protective driver Mahmoud, a Bedouin who keeps his peace with Allah by feeding the stray dogs who lurk outside the hotel, would never have allowed me to walk these streets after dark in these unstill days less than a month after the World Trade Center came tumbling down, but I had never felt more alive.

Later, sitting on my bed, I unfolded Shoukry's brief note, but he had written it in Arabic. I took it down to the front desk and asked a handsome young Egyptian clerk in a jacket and tie to translate the backward squiggles. He glanced at it and smiled.

"Live far," the young man interpreted, "God willing."

I considered the poetry of it, this wish for a traveler to exist happily at a distance with God's blessing.

"No, no, sorry, my English no good," the clerk apologized abruptly. "Uh, this mean to live long. Long, no far. Sorry."

And so, at this moment, in another latitude, a life's distance and duration are again all tangled as I refold Shoukry's note along its old creases and tuck it back into my hidden pocket with the serendipitous toonie.

It's a slight and silly notion, maybe, that a good life is not just long but goes somewhere.

And that, plus two dollars from Heaven, will buy you the rest of your days.

———•———

All day, we have slouched upcountry through the perpetual afternoon and a light rain. Without dusk, without evening, without sunset, without the sloping of the Earth into night, we cannot trust the sky to tell us when we've gone far enough and when it's time to make camp.

An hour beyond the Circle, the road rises and falls through boreal badlands as we cross the Richardsons, a frumpy range of mountains where sluggish raindrops harry the van, which is now caked with grimy arctic dust.

Matt peeks up through the slapping wipers and the silted windshield at the gray sky.

"Man, wouldn't it suck if it rained all day tomorrow?"

"Don't jinx it," I say. "Imagine sunlight."

"Yeah, but what if we came thousands of miles for twenty-four hours of sunshine and it rains the whole time?"

"Nah-nah-nah-nah . . . I'm not listening to you. Keep a good thought, goddammit."

The road, which now seems to have resigned itself to our passing, crests a hill and slumps into a hollow at the foot of a gray mountain, through a greenish-gray hallway of white spruce and balsam poplars. It is past nine—although the trickster sky swears it's only early afternoon—so we pitch our camp beside a shallow creek that runs among the trees, fifty yards off the road.

Outside the van, even in the rain, giant mosquitoes descend on us like the Wicked Witch's flying monkeys. So we build a smoky fire from damp deadfall and prop smoldering branches around the perimeter. The smudge is our only defense against these bloodsuckers, who actually seem to enjoy the aroma of DEET and the playful pawing of humans. And they'll eat better tonight than we do.

We had intended to restock our pantry in Dawson, but in all the excitement and hangover fog, we forgot. For most of the next two days, we had a hot-dog bun, four little Danish butter cookies, and an unexploded can of chili. And beer.

So dinner was two cookies and a beer each, but we were more tired than hungry. Dizzy with woodsmoke and wet with naked rain, we took shelter in the van to nap for a couple hours until midnight, when the longest day of our lives would begin.

———•———

My beeping watch wakes us at five to midnight. In a few minutes, it will be June 21, the summer solstice.

Groggy and damp, we stoke the fire with more wet wood and wish for coffee. Matt is sullen and brooding, not talking. The odd light of night shines between us.

It's chilly, so we wear sweatshirts saturated with old sweat, smoke, and bug spray. The rain has stopped and the clouds are breaking up. The midnight sun, running its crazy purlicue around the horizon, lights a watercolored sky that is neither blue nor gray, but something in between.

"No rain," I say. "It turned out to be a good morning."

"It's not morning," Matt carps in his grated morning voice. "It's the middle of the friggin' night."

"Well, technically it's morning from midnight to noon."

"Don't start."

"What?"

"The 'technically' crap. You know what I meant."

"Sorry. It just doesn't feel like night. The sun is out and our day has started. It feels like . . . morning."

"But it's night. We can't see the moon or the stars, but it's friggin' night. The bars wouldn't even be closed yet back home. We should be asleep."

I look up into the luminous night. If we could see the stars, we'd see Vega, the second most important star in the sky after our own sun. We'd see Andromeda in her chains. Or Aldebaran, the orange giant that's forty-four times bigger than our insane sun, and past which *Pioneer 10* will fly in, oh, two million years or so.

There would be Orion in the southwestern sky, his belt here in cold northern latitudes known as the Three Kings—and I would remember that they are the Three Marys in Panama. If we could see the stars, I'd point out Rigel to Matt, there at the foot of Orion, and, as if I were speaking poetry, I would tell him that in the Middle East, Rigel is known as the Toe Star, and that would seem mystical-cool to both of us.

There would be a half-moon, too, chasing the sun around the bowl of sky.

And maybe we'd see a shooting star and I could recite Jack London's credo once more, about ashes and dust and meteors, just to make Matt laugh at me.

But Matt is just staring at the fire, occasionally coughing up old smoke, his face dark. He's hard to be around when he's like this. So am I.

So I walk through the trees, still dripping with last night's rain, down to the creek. Its bank is a broad bar of shale, with odd bits of old driftwood. Walking on the sharp, angular stones is like strolling on a bed of nails—*miss the sharp ones*—but among them are flatter, smoother rocks, most no bigger than a pocket watch. Surrendering to a part of me that I haven't seen in a good while, I skip one across a glassy pool, then hunt for more. The frigid stream isn't wide, but I manage to skip one stone seven times by aiming downstream.

Satisfied that seven will stand as my record for eternity (only since nobody else was ever likely to skip river-washed stones on this particular stretch of arctic water), I begin to throw the flat stones as high into the air as I can so they'll knife the water with a zip and a bubble, barely disturbing the surface.

Then I take aim at an imaginary catcher—in reality, a broken stump at what passes for sixty feet—on the far bank, and for a moment in my head, I am young again, playing my first and only season of semipro ball in that twilight of dusty roads, night games in small towns, fresh-sprinkled grass and the young girls who waited after the game. But I'm old now; my right shoulder hurts most nights for no good reason, my throws are too wild to even imagine how it once was, and my sins are merely amusing. It's not a realization, because I've known I'm old since I began turning old. It's just more proof, and, funny, it makes me smile.

This would be a nice way to die, I think. Throwing rocks in a stream at two in the morning. Playing baseball in my tired heart. On a day without night when I finally stopped the sunset. But it isn't time. *This isn't where it ends.*

I wind up like a geezer and lob another rock at the stump. It misses.

"You suck."

I turn to see Matt leaning against a tree like a shadow.

"Yeah, I do."

"You used to tell me to step into it. Draw back until your arms are both straight out and throw past your ear."

"I remember. I didn't think you were listening."

"You're throwing like a girl."

"Let's see *your* stuff, Koufax."

"Who?"

"Never mind. Just throw."

Matt pulls off his sweatshirt and he's wearing a white T-shirt I made especially for our trip that says HEAD TO TOE on the breast pocket. I'm pleased, in a stupidly sentimental way.

Standing beside me now, he searches for a rock with the right heft and size, grippable and weighty enough, something comfortably between a golf ball and a shotput. He pushes back his gray Snoogans skully and draws his arm back in an elegant line, like the beautiful athlete he always was. In one smooth forty-mile-an-hour pitch, he hits the stump dead center.

"Whoa, I'm good," Matt says. "Want to see it again?"

"Sure," I say. "If you can hit it a second time, you can have that orphan hot-dog bun for lunch."

He finds another rock and, again, pitches a perfect strike.

"You never should have quit baseball when you were a kid," I say. "You were good. Still are."

In this moment of hidden stars, Matt says nothing. He tosses a few more rocks into the water, then wanders back to our camp. It was as if the clouds had parted and the warm sun had peeked out for one brief, shining moment, then was obscured again.

I wander downstream and cross on a natural bridge of fallen stones. The forest is nearly impenetrable here, but I find a narrow trail where the mountain sheep likely come down from their ledges above to drink. I follow the worn path a hundred yards into a profound wild. The woods grow darker and deeper, and I cannot see the sky through the tangled canopy. I sit on a boulder, where the only sounds I can hear are the distant creek, some birds, and my own breathing.

In some undreamed dream, I must have wanted Matt to be here with me. I didn't want to feel alone. Still. Again. I wanted to know, beyond any shadow, that we were still two halves of the same whole.

And I thought of my *Mi Padre,* who likely never had the same wish, except in my imagination. If every son has two fathers—a real one complete with flaws and an idealized one who exists only in dreams—then every father must also have two sons: the one he knows and the one he wishes. I love the one I know, and it would be unfair to him to wish for something else, even if I had such a thing in mind. And I want him to love me that way, too.

A contemplation of regret would naturally follow, except that I notice some bear traces around the boulder where I'm sitting. My mind drops into a lower gear, where survival is suddenly more important than Freudian poppycock. I am no longer Rodin's *Thinker* on my meditative monolith . . . I am bait on a plate.

I slide off my philosopher's stone and retrace my steps through the dense foliage back to the stream, to the broad, rocky strand where no Arctic grizzly could sneak up on me in the imaginary darkness. I duck into the trees and return to camp, where Matt is staring into the smoky fire.

"I saw bear sign in the forest across the stream," I tell him.

"Did the bear shit in the woods?" he joshes.

"If he did, I'm sure I stepped in it," I say. "But I only saw tracks."

He twirls a stick glumly in the fire, surrounded by swirls of smoke. He's adrift in it.

"You're quiet today. What's up?"

Matt shrugs.

"Tired. Hungry. Stuff."

"What . . . stuff?"

He says nothing for a long time. And neither do I while I stack flat stones in the shape of a little man, an *inukshuk*. It's harder than it looks, like threading a needle in twilight. The choice of stones is as integral to the precise balance as their placement. The little guy keeps falling over, and I keep cussing. I start fresh with a new combination of stones, seeking the proper alchemy to make a man out of rock.

"Today's just a bad day," Matt says at long last. "Exactly a year ago, I broke up with Kelly."

I scoot next to him and put my hand on his shoulder.

"Sorry. I know . . . believe me . . . I know how it feels. It takes time. Sometimes a year isn't long enough."

The muscles in his jaw flex, but he doesn't speak.

"It goes away," I say, trying to comfort him. "It'll get better. I promise."

"But I don't want it to go away completely," he says. "I don't want to forget how I felt about her."

"You won't forget. She'll always be in your heart somewhere. You'll feel love again. But the pain—well, that's the price we pay for remembering."

"I know. It just hurts."

"I hate to say it, especially right now, but the pain you're feeling now, you'll feel it again. Learn from it. Don't stop trying to love somebody."

"You did."

Funny how this role-model thing works.

"Maybe so. Yeah, I did. Learn from me. I've been there, and sometimes I wonder if I ever want to go back. I'm not sure I'll trust anyone with my fears and passions ever again. And that's really more about my flaws than anybody else's. I guess I'm . . . afraid. It hurts bad, you know? But I don't see how I could be a complete partner to someone. You? You can still be everything somebody needs. You're the hero of the story, man."

Matt retreats back into his silence.

"Hey, why don't you go get some sleep?" I tell him. "You'll feel better."

Matt tugs his cap lower. "I don't want to miss this day. I'm okay."

"One hour. It's, what, three a.m., so I'll get you up at four. It'll make the rest of the day much better. You're just tired."

Permission is all he needed, although he'd never seek it. He trudges to the van and slides the door shut behind him.

And I go back, briefly, to my little stone man and the enigma of equilibrium. Eventually, I decide he is more than the sum of his parts—that the delicate symmetry of his stone-bones is an unbroken code, that he is lacking some metaphysical element which will let him stand against the cruel tug of gravity. I'll never take connective tissue for granted again. One thing is clear: Once he is built, there will be no dismantling, no rethinking, no substitution of one rock for another without great risk.

I need glue.

—————

While Matt sleeps, I watch the subtly changing sky as the sun circles around to the north. The clouds are breaking up and patches of blue are oozing through. The day is warming. I smell spruce, woodsmoke, and musky earth. It is the first day of summer, yet it tastes and feels like spring here. It's the kind of morning that made Least Heat-Moon doubt the existence of death, and now I know what he meant.

I have strong visions of this place in empty times, before and after us. Its timelessness is daunting, relentless. It is not moved by our presence, nor changed in any significant way. It is as unchangeable as the past. Any wound we might inflict eventually heals without a trace. Even the rearrangement of its stones in our own image is ultimately temporary. As far as I can see beyond our camp, there is no evidence of human existence.

But I am here. My son is here. We came to this alien place for a reason that won't matter in a thousand years, but why can't it matter in twenty? Why can't this moment between a father and son last long enough, like a shadow that lingers, to change the future? I don't need a millennium, just a generation.

And a metal box.

My heart leaps. Rummaging through the van, I fetch a sheet of paper from my notebook, and under the midnight sun I begin to write a letter.

I address it to my unborn and unimagined grandson, whenever he may be.

> *On the day I write this, you don't yet exist. And maybe when you read this, I won't exist anymore. I hope truly, madly, deeply that we crossed paths.*

I tell him how I died once, how I have come with his father to this place to be reborn. I tell him about all the accidental bastards in his family tree, and how I wished he would never be one of them.

> *We came to share the longest day any father and son could possibly share, and I hope you and your father are doing the same now.*

I can't finish for the tears in my eyes, so I weight the half-written letter with a stone while I dig our empty cookie tin from the garbage and poke around for tiny treasures. Two pennies from my pocket . . . a picture of Matt and me from my wallet . . . the rusty link from Valhalla . . . a green sea-stone from Panama that went overlooked in my camera bag . . . and a black stone I've carried for luck since my first novel was published. They all go into the cookie tin.

Today, a day without darkness, I am happy. Honest to god,
I hope you feel this way at least once in your life. Full and
alive near the top of the world. If you are here today with your
father, embrace him. Hold him so tight that no ray of that
extraordinary sunlight can shine between you. And never let
go. Never let him let you go either.

There's so much to say, but too little time; just one brilliant day. I must trust that if he comes here one day with his own father—my son—the vital lifeline that connects two generations of fathers and sons will finally run unbroken. So I close:

Let this spot be a symbol of your love for and faith in your
father. Bring your son here someday. Along the way, tell him
all the stories you know . . . and promise me as if no greater
promise will ever be made: Never walk away.

———————

It is morning, in the customary sense, when Matt rises. He rolls out of the van slightly more rumpled than when he went in.

"Good morning, sunshine. Feeling better?"

"What time is it?"

"Seven-thirty."

"Dammit, you said an hour."

"Chill. You needed more than an hour, and so did I. You didn't miss a thing. Nothing happened while you were out."

He sits beside me and picks up my letter. He reads no further than the salutation.

"You don't have a grandson . . . do you?"

"Not yet."

"So what's this?"

"Go ahead and read it."

While he reads, I lay the last of our scavenged logs on the campfire. The morning is warming and the mosquitoes are mostly banished, but I need a fire for something else.

"You keep saying 'here.' So where's 'here'?"

I stretch out my arms. "Here."

"And how will this future kid know where 'here' is?"

"He'll come here. With you."

"Dude, you're trippin'."

"No, listen. You'll bring your son . . ."

"What if I have a daughter?"

". . . or your *daughter* here someday. It doesn't matter, okay? Because if you can do that, then I know you are close to your children. Maybe I'll still be alive, maybe I won't, but I never want you to feel distant from your kids. Trust me—it sucks."

"Do you feel distant from me?"

I do what bewildered fathers do when they don't have a good answer. Something else. Something that looks wise and deliberate, or what passes for wise and deliberate. In this case, precisely modify the position of logs on the fire, presumably for more-efficient burning but, in fact, for more time.

"Sometimes. When I'm less confident about a lot of things. Or when I am missing you. Or when you don't call. But most of the time, no. I just want, you know, to be sure we are okay, that's all."

Matt just shakes his head and smirk-snorts the way teenagers do several times a day with their goofy fathers.

"What?" I ask, slightly affronted by his reaction. "I go all warm and fuzzy and you snort at me?"

"You worry too much, dude. First, I smiled, I didn't snort. Second, we're okay. We've always been okay. And third, what the hell is this all about?"

"Well, we have to mail the letter."

"Dude, you been drinking already? You're going to mail a letter to the future?"

"Yep."

He smirk-snorts again. "Okay, now *that* was a snort. I just can't wait to hear how you're gonna mail a letter to the future."

I pick up the empty cookie tin. "In this," I say.

"Dude, you are freakin' me out here. Tell me you're on drugs."

"I'm gonna put the letter in this tin, with these other things, and I'm gonna ship it to your child, who you haven't even dreamed about yet. And I'm going to do it today. No, *we* are going to do it today. You and me. Together."

"Just drop it in the nearest post office box, huh?"

"Nope. We're gonna bury it."

"Bury it." He says it like a question, but without the question mark.

"Yep. Bury it. With the shovel I dreamed about. Wrapped in duct tape and candle wax. Under that stupid white rock. Somewhere out there"—I wipe my sooty hand across the horizon—"where nobody can find it. Except you and me and the stars. Like a treasure. Like pirates."

"Where exactly, Long John?" Matt asks.

"I don't know yet. Just . . . somewhere. Not just anywhere. I'll know it when I see it."

You'll recognize a place you've never seen before . . . in the Arctic? This is getting too weird, even for a retarded pirate."

"Not a place I haven't seen, but a place I might see again. Someday. Or a place you'll see again, I hope."

Pffft is how Matt starts his next thought. "And how will you know this place you haven't seen when you see it again, or after you've seen it today but want to see it again someday . . . or whatever the hell you're saying?"

"Sydney."

"The GPS?"

"Right. I'll just take a reading and we'll always know exactly where it is. When you come back, there it'll be."

Matt can't argue with science, so he tries a new tack.

"What if I never have a kid? What if there's nobody to receive your letter in the future? Then what?"

Even though I hadn't considered this possibility, I shrug.

"Then the game is over. We don't win, but we don't lose either. No more accidental bastards. No more fathers who leave. No more road trips. No more Panama. No more Valhalla. No more mummified human toes. No more . . . That's it, just no more. It won't matter for one goddamned second because we won't matter anymore. We'll be a dead branch in somebody else's family tree. That's the risk we take. And maybe some twenty-fifth-century archaeologist someday will come across an ancient cookie tin covered in wax and duct tape and wonder who the fuck buried it in such a godforsaken place. Prob'ly some fuckin' idiot pirate with a forgotten name."

"Cool."

"But just in case you decide you can be a better dad than I ever was, or my dad, or his dad, or his dad before him . . . well, it isn't what we know today that matters anyway. It's what we know tomorrow."

"Why, what are we doing tomorrow?"

"Not that tomorrow, goddammit," I huff. "The other tomorrow. Like, the future."

"Chill, dude," he says. "You weren't specific."

"The future."

"Got it," Matt insists. "But why are you so friggin' worried about the future? You covered a war, dude! You rode out a hurricane. You drank the Toe. You came here on that fucking badass road. You never worried about the day after. Seems like the only things you're afraid of are being a bad dad and being married."

I am without words. He's right, but confirming or denying it won't help. And he's not done anyway.

"That's pretty lame, dude. You take the big risks and avoid the little ones like they'll kill you or something. You don't care about dying, but you don't wanna hurt. You want to be invisible but you also want to be remembered. Sheesh."

"You wouldn't understand."

"Try me."

I stare off into a distance that, for once, is truly distant.

"Do you ever wonder what fire is made of?"

"I did once, and that was enough. Light and life and time and shit we don't understand."

"Exactly."

"Dude," Matt smiles, "you suck."

And so finally it happened like this:

On the longest day of the year, not far from the very top of the Earth, while a curious sun circled the sky over a lonely hill four thousand miles from home, my son stabbed a folding camp shovel into the rocky soil, probing for soft dirt where we could bury a piece of my heart in a cookie tin swathed with duct tape and coated completely in wax from a jar candle melted over the campfire.

I knew the spot when I saw it: on a taiga hill's far slope beneath a young balsam poplar, overlooking a vast arctic valley that unfurled like a bolt of dark green velvet to the east. This first day of summer had turned warm and windless, so the only sound for miles was the clang of Matt's metal spade against stone.

For a fleeting moment, I worried about the young poplar's roots entangling the tin, or thrusting it up to the surface as they grew. But in the end it didn't matter. This was the spot, and I couldn't change that.

We buried the letter and the coins and everything else, then placed the odd white rock above it. No other rock within our view gleamed so brightly.

With Sydney's technical expertise, we recorded the latitude and longitude of the treasure and hiked back to the van.

As we got in, Matt spoke first.

"Okay, that was way cooler than I thought it was going to be."

It made me smile.

"Didn't I promise we'd do some time-traveling?"

Back at camp, I took off my clothes and waded into the stream. It was more bath than baptism, and I emerged cold but cleansed, as if the mountains and the stars and the rain had soaked into my pores. A kingdom's worth of millennial dust washed away.

For supper, Matt and I shared the last can of chili, warmed to bubbling over the campfire. Afterward, we drank the rest of the Chilkoots and watched the fire dwindle to near-death, a signal to the kamikaze mosquitoes that the war was not yet lost.

But we surrendered. We retreated to the van. Sanctuary on an ordinary night at the end of the Earth.

That night—or rather, near midnight on that extraordinary nightless day—we watched a DVD of Tim Burton's movie, Big Fish, *about the repair between a father full of stories and a son who never understood. Between a dying man who has made up his life as he went along and a son who wants only to know one real thing.*

We both cried at the end, when everybody in the movie realized that we are our own stories and what hovers in the balance is memory. We are the myths we build. We are our own blessings.

Past midnight on the next day, the long day after the longest day, when the new sunset was but a moment long, we lay together in our bed, safe in the artificially cooled air, to sleep and maybe dream about the road home and all our roads forever after.

I reached over and touched my son's hand.

"You said you didn't know what this was about. You really don't?"

Matt put his hand on mine. It was warm and strong. A man's hand.

"It doesn't matter what I know today," he said. "It only matters what I know tomorrow."

AFTER WORDS

Roads don't always go where you'd like them to go. Our journeys represent love, progress, escape, family outings, remedy, adventure, sex, wasted time, the gaining of wisdom, the loss of youth, growth, drift, exploration, desperation, disappearance, and memory . . . and all can be dead ends.

Ah, but all roads are connected. No road begins and ends without crossing another. And there's no road someone hasn't traveled before me. That's both a comfort and a disappointment.

On this road, I thought about Gyula Szecsi and that twilight in the desert. He was another story from a different life . . . or the same life in a different world . . . or the same story.

So I detoured down an unexpected road that day. At the junction between the road home and the road back to Dawson, we turned toward Dawson. Honestly, I didn't know which way I'd turn right up to the moment I turned.

In Dawson, we parked in front of Andrew Kuczynski's little jewelry shop.

"Wait here," I told Matt.

Another lover of roads, Larry McMurtry, once wrote that we face only two important questions in life. The first: *How shall we marry?* And the second: *Where does the road go?*

It is entirely possible, at least to me, that they are the same question.

You begin a thousand miles away and, if you choose the right roads, you travel closer to the one you will marry until you find her and the road between you is the shortest it will ever be.

As the road home unfolded before us, Mary and I decided that she should take the teaching job in San Antonio, so I returned home as she was preparing to go.

One day, near the end of her leaving, it was time for her to dig up her favorite rosebush, a Valentine's Day gift from me, so she could transplant it to our new home in San Antonio. Beneath it, she found a small wooden box containing a folded letter and a simple ring made of Yukon gold.

"I have dug in many mines, and in a few, I've struck gold. But I never struck gold like you. You are unique and strong and valuable. Especially to me," she read as she uncreased the note. "I would be a lucky man if you would spend the rest of my life with me. To care for me the way you have for the past five years. To complete me. To love and be loved . . . Will you marry me?"

She said yes.

——•——

Almost exactly a year after returning from the Arctic, Ron and Mary were married on July 5, 2008, in San Antonio, Texas.

Matt was his father's best man.

ACKNOWLEDGMENTS

Like our journey to the Arctic, this book traveled its own long road before it found its way to you. And like the ancient *inukshuks* we found there, many real people—and a few ghosts—pointed the way.

First, there's Thomas Edison, the dreamer who just two years after Custer was annihilated first imagined voices could be captured in a machine and played back later. Over the years, a few minor modifications to his tinfoil-cylinder phonograph allowed us to carry a small digital voice recorder not much bigger than a PEZ dispenser on our Yukon sojourn, capturing more than three hundred hours of road-hum, heavy-metal music, and father-son conversation that nobody else will ever listen to in its entirety. But I did.

This book also pays homage to the travelers who came before—Kerouac, Pirsig, Least Heat Moon, Steinbeck, and others—to whom I am connected by roads. They were all there in spirit.

I am grateful to my agent Gina Panettieri for sticking with this little book; to editors Erin Turner and Ellen Urban at Globe Pequot Press for their faith in it.

And this seems like the best place to express my deepest love for my stepfather, Joe Franscell. Dad, you played a bigger role in my life than this narrative could ever explain or than I ever acknowledged.

My most heartfelt gratitude goes to the one who waited at the end of the road: Mary. More than any other, she knew what this odyssey meant. Although I have given her plenty of reason to doubt, she has never stopped believing, never stopped waiting.

—Ron Franscell

ABOUT THE AUTHOR

Ron Franscell is the author of *The Crime Buff's Guide to the Outlaw Rockies* and *The Crime Buff's Guide to Outlaw Texas* (both Globe Pequot Press), as well as the bestselling *The Darkest Night,* which established him as one of the most provocative new voices in narrative nonfiction. He lives in San Antonio, Texas.

For more information about The Sourtoe Cocktail Club, visit www.ronfranscell.com/books/sourtoe.html.